MW00639160

SIGN OF CONTRADICTION:

CONTRACEPTION, FAMILY PLANNING,

AND CATHOLICISM

BY

ANTHONY J. DIGMANN

One More Soul
Dayton, Ohio

Imprimatur
Most Rev. Joseph R. Binzer
Vicar General and Auxiliary Bishop of Cincinnati
July 14, 2015

The *Imprimatur* ("Permission to Publish") is a declaration that a book or pamphlet is considered to be free of doctrinal or moral error. It is not implied that those who have granted the *Imprimatur* agree with the contents, opinions, or statements expressed.

Copyright © 2015 Anthony J. Digmann

All rights reserved

ISBN 978-0-9861591-0-7

A Publication of
One More Soul
1846 N Main St.
Dayton, OH 45405-3832

Cover images by iStock. Used with permission.

.

Cover design by Joanna D. Sacksteder

This book is dedicated to you, the reader;
it is entrusted to the Immaculate Heart of Mary.

CONTENTS

ACKNOWLEDGMENTS

Always first, I express my deepest appreciation to God—the Father, my Creator; the Son, Jesus Christ, my Savior and Lord of my life; and the Holy Spirit, my Sanctifier and help—to whom I owe everything. Thanks also to the Blessed Virgin Mary, my Mother, and all the Angels and Saints for their unceasing guidance and intercession. In addition, I am forever grateful to the Catholic Church for being my mother and teacher on my pilgrimage of faith and helping me live my Christian vocation.

Furthermore, I thank my family, colleagues, and friends, all of whom have formed me and shaped my life, faith, and values. Profound thanks to One More Soul and its supporters for bringing this manuscript to publication, especially the detailed redactions and guidance provided by Steve Koob, Vince Sacksteder, and Jason Adams. Special thanks as well to John Kippley for his expert suggestions on the manuscript. I would also like to express my appreciation to the Loras College theology faculty, especially Matthew Shadle, and my students and colleagues at Beckman Catholic High School who have sharpened me as a perpetual student of Christ, the Gospel, and the Church. Furthermore, I thank my children for proving to me what a gracious blessing children are and what a gift it is to be a father.

Finally, to my wife, Stephanie, I express unspeakable gratitude. Without her tireless encouragement and support, this work would not have been possible. Her efforts have not only facilitated its research and writing, through our life together she has taught and lived with me what it means to be bride and groom as a sign of God's love for humanity and Christ's love for the Church. She has shown me God's love, challenged me to holiness, and is truly bone of my bone and flesh of my flesh.

ABBREVIATIONS

CCC	*Catechism of the Catholic Church*
CCL	Couple to Couple League
CDF	Congregation for the Doctrine of the Faith
GS	*Gaudium et Spes*
HPV	Human Papilloma Virus
HV	*Humanae Vitae*
MHC	Major histocompatibility complex
NFP	Natural Family Planning
NSYR	National Study of Youth and Religion
OCP	Oral contraceptive pill
TOB	*Theology of the Body*
USCCB	United States Conference of Catholic Bishops
VS	*Veritatis Splendor*
WHO	World Health Organization

NOTE ON TERMINOLOGY

An effort to avoid the term "birth control" was employed throughout this work, because most means of preventing the procreation of children are not really "controlling births," *per se*, which is more obstetrical. Most means of family planning today focus on regulating *fertility*, by which they block or alter the fertility of one or both partners to avoid conception. For this reason, "contraception" (opposed or hostile to conception) is a more suitable term.

The term "family planning," a concept consistent with the responsibility of parents according to the Church, will be used to address all means by which couples may try to prevent, avoid, or delay conceiving a child. This will include means condemned by the Church (i.e. contraceptives) as well as means approved by the Church (i.e. the several variations of systematic Natural Family Planning—known as "NFP"—the calendar rhythm method, ecological breastfeeding, or any additional means utilizing periodic abstinence). When applicable, specific contraceptives or methods of NFP will be identified individually.

The term "Natural Family Planning" (NFP) used in this book will refer to what is also called "systematic Natural Family Planning." This includes various types such as the sympto-thermal method, Creighton Method, Marquette Method, etc. NFP in this sense refers to the variety of systems that monitor the signs of an individual woman's body to determine whether she is in a fertile or infertile phase of her cycle for the purposes of avoiding or achieving pregnancy, as well as monitoring health. Worthy of note is the Lactational Amenorrhea Method, also known as "Ecological Breastfeeding" thanks to Sheila Kippley's work on the subject in Catholic circles. While this is certainly a means of employing literally "natural family planning" in the broad sense, it is not the same as systematic NFP as will be discussed in the first chapter.

While the term contraception in its strict sense may only refer to means that prevent the meeting of sperm and egg, the use of the term in the medical community and popular culture is broader, involving methods that work in other ways. For instance some methods work primarily as an abortifacient, which functions not so much to prevent

xi

conception but to prevent nidation (implantation) of the embryo in the endometrial lining of the uterus. In such cases, a life is conceived but is greeted by a womb not properly suited to harbor it, so it is lost without notice. An example of this is the intra-uterine device (IUD), while oral contraceptive pills (OCPs, a.k.a. "the pill") are abortifacient as a secondary means of preventing conception. There are also other options to prevent conception from taking place through an act of intercourse, essentially foiling any typical union between sperm and egg, such as withdrawal (*coitus interruptus*) or sterilization. This work will likewise employ a broadened definition for contraception. For our purposes, it includes all actions or physiological manipulations intended to prevent conception (including withdrawal and sterilization), methods intended to prevent conception (contraceptives in the strict sense), and methods to prevent nidation or destroy a recently implanted embryo (abortifacients). Therefore, our definition for contraception is intended to correlate with all things condemned by HV §14 and reiterated in paragraph 2370 of the *Catechism of the Catholic Church* (CCC), which states: "'Every action which, whether in anticipation of the conjugal act, or in its accomplishment, or in the development of its natural consequences, proposes, whether as an end or as a means, to render procreation impossible' is intrinsically evil."[1]

---

[1] *Catechism of the Catholic Church: Modifications from the Editio Typica*, 2nd ed. (Washington, DC: United States Catholic Conference, Inc.—Libreria Editrice Vaticana, 1997), §2370.

Introduction

Most American Catholics who encounter an article or discussion on contraception would probably be disinterested, thinking, "What is the point in talking about contraception; hasn't that issue been settled?" It depends on what one means by "settled." The Magisterium considers it settled, especially following the publication of Pope Blessed Paul VI's encyclical *Humanae Vitae* (HV) in 1968. Most Catholic married couples would also probably consider it settled, at least in terms of their relationship and sexual practice, having decided that the use of contraception is the best option for them and does not violate their relationship with God, the Church, and their marriage vows. The problem in the Catholic Church regarding the issue of contraception is that the official Church teaching and the practice of most of the laity have "settled" on opposite sides of the fence. Recent sources and surveys indicate that four out of five Catholic couples do not agree with the Church's moral teaching on family planning and approve use of a contraceptive method condemned by the Church.[1] This significant chasm between official Church teaching and practice by the faithful has been the source of dissension and division among both hierarchy and laity and has persisted as a thorn in the side of the body of Christ for decades. The Catholic opponents of the teaching will be referred to as revisionists, because they wanted to revise the Church's teaching on family planning. The supporters of the Church's teaching will be called traditionalists.[2] The results of such longstanding disagreement include frustration on both sides of the issue, dissent from this and other issues of morality within the Church, and genuine scandal created by such division and dissension. It has truly become a sign of contradiction.

---

[1] Todd A. Salzman and Michael G. Lawler, *The Sexual Person: Toward a Renewed Catholic Anthropology* (Washington D.C.: Georgetown University Press, 2008), 176; Howard P. Kainz, "Contraception & Logical Consistency," *New Oxford Review* 76, no. 8 (September 2009): 39.

[2] Those supportive of Magisterial Church teaching may be identified by a number of labels, such as "orthodox"; however, this group has acquired the label of "traditionalist" in the years following *Humanae Vitae*. Its use here is intended to be consistent with other works on this subject, not to be pejorative.

Jesus set the example for how to be a sign of contradiction. At his presentation in the Temple, Simeon prophesied about him saying, "This child is destined for the fall and rise of many in Israel, and to be a sign that will be contradicted" (Lk 2:34). Jesus stood up for the kingdom of God, truth, and authentic love; he stood against the ideals of the world and culture around him, which did not conform to these heavenly values—values that reach to our deepest core and fulfill the longing in our hearts. As Christians we too are called to be signs of contradiction. However, we ought to be united in our stand for the values of Christ and against those of the world, should the two conflict. Fewer than two years before being elected Pope John Paul II, then Cardinal Karol Wojtyla led the annual Lenten retreat for Pope Paul VI titled *Sign of Contradiction* in which he noted:

> Nearly two thousand years have passed but the words then spoken have lost none of their validity or relevance. It is becoming more and more evident that those words sum up most felicitously the whole truth about Jesus Christ, his mission and his Church. "A sign of contradiction". … The times in which we are living provide particularly strong confirmation of the truth of what Simeon said: Jesus is both the light that shines for mankind and at the same time a sign of contradiction.[3]

On this issue Catholics have become much more a sign of self-contradiction in view of the world than a sign contradicting worldly values as Christ was and calls his followers to be.

Much must yet be done to correct this discontinuity and heal this long-festering wound, a wound that is largely ignored in the Church of this new millennium. Any reparation will be arduous, prolonged, involve a reopening of discussion with newfound interest and vigor, and necessitate open and honest critique and reconsideration. It must overcome the great confusion, frustration, apathy, and disinterest by many laity, theologians, and pastors. Some are entrenched in divergent camps, and others are regrettably ignorant about the Church's teaching. It will necessitate an opening of hearts and minds

---

[3] Wojtyla, Karol. *Sign of Contradiction.* (New York: Seabury, 1979), 197-198.

that only the grace of God can accomplish. With time, new generations may be able to overcome the current impasse, as may have already begun. Too often, theologians have been divided, clergy have sent conflicting messages to laity, and entire generations have been left without clarity. Perhaps by bringing this issue back to the fore, all may eventually work together toward a healthier communion in the body of Christ.

The Church's teaching on contraception seems to have been swept under the rug. Occasionally the topic comes up; consider for example the comments about contraceptives by Pope Benedict XVI during his 2009 trip to Africa, his 2010 interview in Light of the World, or the 2012-2014 conflict between the U.S. Bishops and the Obama Administration's Health and Human Services mandate in the Affordable Care Act. However, in each of these cases the moral quality of contraceptive activity and its effects on families, society, and the Church is obfuscated by the AIDS epidemic, anticipation of the Church *finally* changing its teaching, and *rights* to access contraceptives. We need to take a step back and address the fundamental morality of contraceptives.[4]

Since means of responsible procreation provoke contention within Catholicism, this work is primarily intended for Catholics. However, as many other Christians have already realized, what occurs within Catholicism has a major effect upon all other Christian denominations and the world. Constituting approximately one-half of Christians throughout the world, the Catholic Church is by far the most significant reflection of Christianity to the non-Christian world. Moreover, her influence within Christianity is significant not only because half of Christians are under her care, but also because what happens in Catholicism has an inevitable effect upon other Christians. Since the Catholic Church shepherds one-sixth of the world's population, this official position of the Church cannot be ignored by anyone with an eye for global issues, particularly those affecting other Christians, and especially Catholics. Consequently, while this work is by a Catholic and principally intended for Catholics, it is by no means exclusive. Christians, as well as all men and women of good will, will find herein a concern of significance—

---

[4] Regarding terminology such as "birth control", "contraception", and "family planning" use herein, please see the "Note on Terminology" in the preamble.

if not for their personal lives, for Christianity and the rest of the world.

What few Catholics and others in contemporary society have appreciated in past decades, though it is now being more clearly understood, is that the significance of the issue of family planning is of monumental importance both within and beyond the confines of the Catholic Church, and families have been at the center of it all. Contraceptives, the Church's teaching on family planning, and people's reactions to that teaching have dramatically impacted marriages, families, parishes, how Christianity is lived, and the entire Church—not to mention our society, laws, morality, health care, economics, quality of life, perception of the world, social justice, and even the environment. This topic has no less than shaped who we have become, and it will undoubtedly continue to form and affect us and our progeny as we continue throughout the twenty-first century and beyond. How we plan our families as well as appreciate and regulate our fertility are of utmost importance for reasons people rarely take the time to discover and consider. All of these issues are of great concern to the Catholic Church, because they are all intertwined. Society is not well if families are not well; families are not well if the spouses are not well; spouses cannot be well if their relationship is not well; and their relationship cannot be well if there is a severing of their very beings and the purposes of their sexual love. Archbishop Emeritus of Indianapolis, Daniel M. Buechlein, once commented:

> The Catholic Church's concern for the human person and the human family is holistic—that is, the Church holds the needs of body, mind and soul together. Both for the individual person and for society as a whole, the physical, psychological, moral and spiritual welfare are of a piece. The welfare of the human person and of human society is not served if the whole human person is not served. We believe that respect for the integrity of the ends of marriage is important for the welfare of the institution of marriage in society as well as for individual spouses. We believe that the psychological health of the

4

individual person is deeply affected by whether the ends of marriage are respected in their totality. So is the welfare of the family in society.[5]

These topics deserve much greater attention than most people have given them. As Michael Novak who stood against the Church's prohibition of contraceptive behaviors stated soon after HV, "Matters of life and death, of love and hate, are at stake; our lives are touched at the very center by this discussion."[6] In the decades since, Novak has seen the wisdom and truth of the Church's teaching on family planning and has changed his views, yet he was and is right about how significant this topic was and remains.

A special concern for the purpose of this work is to help younger generations understand the dynamics of how this situation has come to be at this time in history as well as providing recent evidence by which they will be empowered to arrive at their own educated conclusion on the topic, with the assistance of God and his Church. We are living at a time when Catholic couples of childbearing years were not a part of the discussion prior to and immediately following HV—they did not deal with the issues involved firsthand, nor were they forced to make the difficult decision about contraception that troubled many Catholic couples in the 1950s, 60s, and 70s. At the time of the composition of this work, the only people who would have been 18 years old or older in 1968 are those of retirement age. Consequently, Catholics who are of childbearing years today learned about contraception, and the Church's teaching on it, largely from within a milieu hostile to the Church's teaching and removed from the debate concerning it. We now have an additional generation removed from the encyclical crisis coming into childbearing years, the grandchildren of the first generation. They are even farther from the difficult times and decisions their grandparents experienced, and—generations removed

---

[5] Daniel M. Buechlein, "Integrating Faith and Science through Natural Family Planning," In *Integrating Faith and Science through Natural Family Planning,* ed. Richard J. Fehring and Theresa Notare (Milwaukee: Marquette UP, 2004), 24.

[6] Michael Novak, "*Frequent,* Even Daily, Communion," in *The Catholic Case for Contraception,* ed. Daniel Callahan (London: Macmillan, 1969), 93.

from Humanae Vitae—their understanding of this teaching is radically deficient.

A brief historical, causal explanation may be useful to explain the current climate for young Catholic couples. Prior to 1930 all Christians taught that contraceptives were immoral. From 1930-1960 the Catholic Church virtually stood alone in its condemnation while all other Christians allowed them, at least on some level. The practice of many Catholics around the Second Vatican Council (1962-65), yet before HV (1968), was to begin using contraceptives in anticipation of a change in official Church teaching. When HV was finally released, the encyclical affirmed that every morally licit sexual action by its very nature was to be both unitive (bond the couple) and procreative (open to life). Therefore it maintained that contraceptives are immoral and opposed to God's plan for marriage and sexuality; however, means of avoiding pregnancy by utilizing periodic abstinence were affirmed under conditions. When this occurred, few among those who had already begun using contraceptives gave them up, and even some more couples joined them in the years after the encyclical, disobeying the Church's moral teaching.

It is likely that Catholic parents who took a position contrary to official Church teaching taught their children to do the same, modeling such behavior. Such a lapse would have demonstrated that one could be a "good" Catholic while refusing to adhere to the Church's explicit moral teaching. Today the first and second generations are passing their lifestyle on to the youngest of Catholic couples. These young adults are inheriting their parents' and grandparents' attitudes. After all, what would motivate subsequent generations to reevaluate such a challenging and personal issue for themselves? Most American Catholics take it for granted that very few subscribe to Church teaching on family planning. Those who do are often perceived as merely functioning out of blind obedience without any further support for their position than saying, "The Church says so." Many may consider the Church's teaching ridiculous, archaic, unreasonable, imprudent, or even impossible. Add to this the perceived challenges of practicing systematic family planning as permitted by the Church, most notably the allegedly "prolonged" periods of abstinence, and few young Catholic couples today have an impetus to go any deeper than taking their parents' and grandparents' word and experience as their own.

The troubling problem with this situation is not necessarily that the decision of the first generation has continued through to subsequent generations—that is how the faith has been perpetuated for twenty centuries, after all. The problem is that this decision made decades ago by the first generation has, for all practical purposes, been inherited by a second and third generation for the most part *uncritically*. On such an important topic, with such inconsistency between official Church teaching and practice among the faithful, reconsideration is necessary in order to see if new information or the working of the Holy Spirit may lead us in another direction or confirm the received teaching. Few Catholics from older generations, though, have reconsidered the issue based upon updated information, nor have many from younger generations thoughtfully given the topic due consideration for themselves in their own social and ecclesial environment with fresh data. With negligible recent discernment by many people, the same position on contraception and Church-approved methods of family planning common among many Catholics *has remained largely based upon the information, milieu, and context of the 1960s*—a situation further fueled by the emergence of new contraceptive technologies.

As a number of young Catholics, among others, are noticing and articulating—this simply does not work anymore. We are part of a different ecclesiastical and social environment, and our experiences, needs, and problems are different from those of the 1960s. Furthermore, we have nearly half of a century of hindsight from which to evaluate the decisions made by earlier generations to arrive at our own conclusions. Considering how this topic has changed and impacted the familial, sexual, moral, ecclesial, and social landscape of American Catholics, it deserves considerable attention both by young couples and by older generations.

This book is an invitation to explore and investigate the topic of the Church's teaching on family planning anew. The hope of this work is to inspire and equip readers with twenty-first century data and a historical context for the topic of family planning—both to help them joyfully and responsibly embrace their unitive and procreative sexual power, as well as to

empower them to proficiently share the Church's teaching with others. Perhaps it will help us better understand such a pertinent topic in the Church and our world so that our future will be blessed through our willingness and courage to continue exploring this teaching and seeking God's will in our lives and vocations

This work is divided into two parts. Part I considers the twenty-first century status of contraception and family planning. It explores a multitude of changes and current information related to the issue that have developed over the course of the decades since HV and the divergence that followed it, such as new information about both contraceptives and contemporary Church-approved methods of NFP. Moreover, it looks at the changes that have occurred in the Church and society over the last several decades in order to draw upon the experiences, data, and hindsight necessary for twenty-first century couples to give the issue the consideration, or reconsideration, it is due.

Part II provides historical background on the topics of contraception and family planning in the Church. For those born in the last few decades, such background is essential to provide the context out of which the current situation has sprung and the positions that have shaped it. Its purpose is to provide sufficient background history and information for the reader to appreciate the development of the Church's understanding of this issue that led to the crisis within the Church this past half-century. It begins with an overall consideration of the Church's historical position, how that position came to be increasingly challenged, and the Church's response to such challenges through HV in 1968, including its immediate aftermath. Thereafter, Part II identifies and explores the positions taken and arguments used by opponents and proponents of HV's teaching on family planning.

PART I
TWENTY-FIRST
CENTURY

Chapter 1
Natural Family Planning

Amid the public controversy over the morality of contraception in the last several decades, our understanding of the biological and spiritual realities of fertility expanded to produce and approve the art and science of Natural Family Planning (NFP). NFP in its modern form alleviates much of the frustration users experienced with the calendar rhythm, which was a significant factor in driving support for contraception in the latter half of the twentieth century. As the calendar rhythm method was superseded by contemporary systems of NFP, many of the objections to Church-approved methods melted away and were largely replaced by overwhelming advantages. NFP has been mischaracterized by those who misunderstand or fear it. The truth about NFP is that its challenges are minimal, and its advantages are considerable. When spouses have a legitimate need to temporarily or indefinitely limit their family size, NFP is a moral option for the couple to employ.

Considering Church Teaching

As faithful members of the Church, all Catholics ought to begin their discernment about family planning by first considering the Church's teaching carefully, sincerely, and open-mindedly. This is something even those opposed to the Church's teaching throughout the decades have admitted. For example, even the strongly revisionist work of Kosnik et al. in 1977, which suggested Catholic couples ought to be able to morally utilize contraceptives, stated, "Natural family planning deserves serious consideration among the alternatives for exercising responsible parenthood."[1] However, many young couples today are not likely to have given it serious consideration. Instead, for the most part they are likely to adopt popular attitudes about contraceptives, which are largely in opposition to Church teaching, without always knowing why. Some do not even know what NFP is, so a definition may be helpful. **NFP may be understood as a variety of systems that monitor the signs of an individual**

---

[1] Anthony Kosnik et al., *Human Sexuality: New Directions in American Catholic Thought* (New York: Paulist, 1977), 128.

woman's body to determine whether she is in a fertile or infertile phase of her cycle for the purposes of avoiding or achieving pregnancy, as well as monitoring health. In secular practice, NFP is often called "fertility awareness methods" or "fertility awareness-based methods," and some may refer to it simply as "periodic abstinence." There are different methods of NFP, and some—depending upon the method effectiveness, or the effectiveness of the way they are taught—may be more successful than others. NFP ought not to be confused with the calendar rhythm method, which is a common misconception. Historian Leslie Tentler recognizes how attitudes and methods have changed in NFP when she notes the "small population of young Catholics who in recent years have unexpectedly embraced *Humanae Vitae* and the various methods of Natural Family Planning."[2]

Another point to keep in mind is that the contemporary widespread use of contraception is not even what revisionists (those opposed to the Church's re-affirmed teaching in the 1960s and thereafter) had in mind. Author Daniel Callahan, who advocated contraception, wrote shortly after the release of *Humanae Vitae* (HV):

> Indeed, there is an argument to be made that the Catholic case for contraception should never receive monolithic support in the Church. There are many things not yet known about the long-range effects of a widespread use of contraceptives. It is conceivable that many of these effects will turn out to be harmful. But as yet we do not know what the effects will be and there is no special reason to fear the worst. We must work with what we now know and form our conscience from the information, experience, and insights at hand. It will do the Church no harm, and may someday do it some good, that some remain resolutely opposed to contraception.[3]

---

[2] Leslie Woodcock Tentler, "Catholics and Contraception: An American History" (Ithaca: Cornell UP, 2004), 279.

[3] Daniel Callahan, introduction to *The Catholic Case for Contraception*, ed. Daniel Callahan (London: Macmillan, 1969), xi.

Even though this same source was promoting dissent, he was also honest about the possibility that history could prove him wrong. Indeed, some noted revisionists have changed their minds as Tentler reports, "Some once ardent proponents of change would eventually conclude that its costs outweighed the benefits. Hence Michael Novak's eventual rebirth as a religious and political conservative."[4]

As time has continued to unveil the negative effects of contraceptives, it has also revealed remarkable successes in the development of the methods of NFP that have not yet been popularly appreciated. Consequently, one of the strongest arguments of revisionists—that the Church's alternatives to contraceptives were inadequate—has fallen through, and revisionists have been forced to abandon it as a viable argument. Writing in 1993, revisionist Richard McCormick stated, "At this point it would be helpful to emphasize what is not the issue. ... Natural family planning is highly method-effective for highly motivated couples. ... Its desirability is not in question. The basic issue is the moral wrongfulness of some other methods."[5] The narrowing of the argument seems to be linked to the improved reputation of contemporary NFP.

McCormick correctly observes that NFP's effectiveness is no longer part of the *theological* debate. Even though statistics and experience have demolished concerns revisionists held previously, and problems with contraceptives have largely turned the tables, this is hardly common knowledge among *lay people*. For example, how many lay Catholics are familiar with the fact that a 1987 World Health Organization (WHO) study throughout New Zealand, Ireland, Philippines, India, and El Salvador resulted in men reporting a 97% satisfaction rate, and women a 98% satisfaction rate, with NFP?[6] This same study indicated, "83% of women and 53% of men reported no difficulty with abstinence."[7] Unfortunately, NFP has been undervalued and has unjustly carried a negative stigma since it

---

[4] Tentler, 231.

[5] Richard A. McCormick, "'Humanae Vitae' 25 Years Later," *America* (July 17, 1993), http://www. americamagazine.org/content/article.cfm? article_id=10960 (accessed October 14, 2009): 4 of 7.

[6] Leona VandeVusse et al., "Couples' Views of the Effects of Natural Family Planning on Marital Dynamics," *Journal of Nursing Scholarship* 35, no. 2 (2nd Quarter 2003): 172.

[7] Ibid.

was first developed, perhaps as a result of people's negative experiences with the calendar rhythm method, bias against Catholicism, or the perception of Catholic authorities as impinging upon couples' sexual freedom. NFP deserves reconsideration by couples whose positions have been "settled" based upon inadequate or obsolete information, as well as those couples who have never given serious consideration to the Church's teaching or the methods she promotes. Ask some clergy and religious who have wrestled with their vocation—sometimes the gift of a lifetime may come in the package one desperately attempts to avoid opening.

Moral Use of NFP

Before considering NFP more deeply, it is important to understand that NFP cannot morally be used any way a person likes—one must not assume that recourse to infertile periods, as is accomplished effectively through modern NFP, is always permissible. It is possible to use NFP immorally. In HV Pope Bl. Paul VI stated that the use of NFP or similar methods *may* be permissible at the judgment of the couple only when "there are well-grounded reasons for spacing births, arising from the physical or psychological condition of husband or wife, or from external circumstances."[8] The teaching of the Church is that marriage is oriented to the procreation and education of offspring. While this essential good of marriage may not be thwarted under any circumstances, it does not mandate that conception must be pursued under any circumstances. The terms used by HV to describe the reasons are "serious," "just," "worthy and weighty," and "defensible."[9] The Church is intentionally vague on what may constitute sufficient reasons, but the basic issue is discerning what would impose "undue burden."[10] Citing Pope Pius XII, Janet Smith notes,

---

[8] Pope Paul VI, *Humanae Vitae*,
   http://www.vatican.va/holy_father/paul_vi/encyclicals/documents/hf_p-vi_enc_25071968_humanae-vitae_en.html (accessed July 14, 2009),§16.
[9] HV, §10, 16; Janet E. Smith, *Humanae Vitae: A Generation Later* (Washington D.C.: Catholic University of America Press, 1991), 119-120.
[10] Janet E. Smith, "The Moral Use of Natural Family Planning," in *Why Humanae Vitae Was Right: A Reader*, ed. Janet E. Smith (San Francisco: Ignatius Press, 1993), 460.

He counsels that couples with known genetic defects or a woman whose life may be threatened by a pregnancy could enter a marriage intending to practice periodic abstinence for the whole of a marriage as long as the spouses would accept lovingly any children they may happen to conceive," so the positive moral prescription for married couples to procreate is not absolute.[11] Smith further notes five types of reasons posited by HV 10 and 16 that may constitute a "serious reason" such as: "physical, economic, psychological, … social conditions, … or may be based on external factors.[12]

Overall, the Church intends to leave discernment of "serious reasons" to the consciences of the couples. It simply provides some direction with the general meaning that no "trivial reasons" are sufficient, and that "reasons less than life-threatening conditions" may suffice.[13] Couples must weigh their duties to "God, to each other, to the family they already have, and to all their commitments," and they must avoid selfishness in their use of family planning.[14] A question worthy at the outset is whether God wills for a particular couple to use any method of NFP at all. Scripture and the Tradition of the Church demonstrate that God values fecundity—it is consistently considered a blessing, not the curse the secular world sees it as. Considered in this context, couples are called to be generous in their gift of life to their own family, society, and with God. The default orientation of spouses should be to participate with God's creative power and be fruitful.

Development and Effectiveness of NFP

The development of contraceptive and NFP methods occurred under very different circumstances. Contraceptives had the support of medical and pharmaceutical companies with a vested interest in their success. Granted, contraceptives had walls to break down—

---

[11] Ibid.
[12] Janet E. Smith, "The Moral Use," 461; *HV*, §10, 16.
[13] Janet E. Smith, "The Moral Use," 461.
[14] Ibid., 462.

religiously, socially, and ethically—but they were a welcome development of control over human reproduction by many, while their negative effects were not yet evident.[15] Polish physician Elzbieta Wojcik explains many additional factors why contraception use boomed: they were believed to be easy and convenient; some had a "new" appeal; pharmaceutical companies had much to gain financially from some methods, so they promoted their products heavily; and contraceptives allowed for control over nature and assertiveness, which were strongly valued by American society.[16]

Methods approved by the church were also further developing. NFP methods, however, lacked the hype and financial interests of contraceptives. They were perceived to be more challenging and less effective, and the idea of conforming to nature rather than mastering and dominating it was only popular among a few.[17] Unfortunately, the 1950s and 1960s saw these methods lagging behind slightly in their development and considerably in their appeal at the time when the Church was really considering what should be allowable methods of family planning. Nonetheless, through the 1960s and 1970s significant progress was made, and studies began to suggest that their effectiveness was capable of outstanding results. Doubt about the effectiveness of NFP, however, persists in medical circles and popular opinion. Since the calendar rhythm method had a negative connotation, it led to a poor name for Church-approved family planning methods involving periodic abstinence. NFP, therefore, would have major walls of its own to raze, a situation that continues into the twenty-first century.

In 1982, Dr. Hanna Klaus published an article in *Obstetrical & Gynecological Survey* that discussed the development of NFP methods and the remarkable success rates they produced compared to the old rhythm method. Klaus explains that the rhythm method was developed in the early 1900s and was based upon statistical averages of when women were likely to be in the infertile part of their cycle

---

[15] Ronald Lawler, Joseph Boyle Jr., and William E. May, *Catholic Sexual Ethics: A Summary, Explanation, & Defense*, 2nd ed. (Huntington, Indiana: Our Sunday Visitor, 1998), 145.

[16] Elzbieta Wojcik, "Natural Regulation of Conception and Contraception," in *Why Humanae Vitae Was Right: A Reader*, ed. Janet E. Smith (San Francisco: Ignatius Press, 1993), 423-424.

[17] Ibid., 424.

with a failure rate of at least 20%.[18] Fertility rates for such studies are figured on the likelihood of pregnancy under the tested method after one year of use. For the rhythm method, women counted days from their menstrual period to determine where they were in their cycle based upon numerical averages of a sample of women. For a method to accurately determine when a woman is fertile, though, it is necessary to be able to identify when an *individual* woman is ovulating and in the fertile part of her cycle, rather than assuming her cycle fits a *statistical average*. The development of NFP methods capable of individual observation has led to much greater effectiveness, fewer days needed for abstinence, and greater satisfaction by users than methods that are based solely upon women's monthly averages— though rhythm eventually began including such observations.

Throughout the twentieth century, physicians began to discover ways in which the woman's body indicates where she is in her fertility cycle. One of the earliest of these indicators or "biological markers," discovered in the early 1900s, was the rise in basal body temperature, which indicates that ovulation has taken place and the transition to the infertile period of the cycle is commencing.[19] This temperature is typically collected after a woman has had a few hours of sleep, promptly upon waking, and prior to substantial activity. Klaus notes that in the 1930s and 1940s physicians further developed their ability to determine that ovulation had taken place through thermal shifts in basal body temperature, and by 1946 doctors included the changes in cervical mucus as an indicator of the onset and fading of fertility in each cycle and correlated this biological marker with basal body temperature.[20]

Things continued to improve throughout later decades as scientists and doctors continued to learn more about the indicators of women's fertility cycles. In 1967 Dr. Doering's studies in Germany, which included temperature observation, were over 98% effective after 19 years of study.[21] Thus, even before HV was published, evidence based on nearly two decades of success began to surface

---

[18] Hanna Klaus, "Natural Family Planning: A Review," *Obstetrical & Gynecological Survey* 37, no. 2 (1982): 132.

[19] Ibid.

[20] Ibid., 132-133.

[21] Ibid., 133, 142-143.

that methods of pre-modern NFP were emerging that were very effective.[22] This "calendar-thermal" method led to the "sympto-thermal" method, which combines observations of multiple biological markers such as basal body temperature, cervical mucus, and other observations about changes in the body like the position, firmness, and openness of the cervix.[23] All of these signs are recorded daily on a chart by which a couple is able to see the changes in a woman's body taking place and determine on a day-to-day-basis how likely she is to conceive if she has intercourse.

One of the most prominent organizations to offer this method in the United States is the Couple to Couple League (CCL), based in Cincinnati. This organization was founded in 1971 by John and Sheila Kippley, who wrote the manual on the method for the organization with the help of Dr. Konald A. Prem. The CCL approach to teaching NFP involves trained couples teaching the method to other couples, usually in a group format. Set over the course of a few classes (or through a home study course) a couple is able to learn the method with considerable effectiveness. In 2004 the Kippleys left CCL, which underwent some revision and updating in the following years, and a new textbook and revised program were released in 2007.[24] The Kippleys' work has continued with the founding of a new NFP organization: Natural Family Planning International, Inc., also in Cincinnati.[25] According to Klaus's 1982 report, success rates for a combination use of the indicators of the sympto-thermal method exceeded 98.5%.[26]

Another method that grew in popularity and effectiveness was a cervical mucus method that has become known as the ovulation

---

[22] John F. Kippley, "The Sexual Revolution: How to Counter It," *Catholic Social Science Review* 13 (2008), 376.

[23] Klaus, 133-134; John F. Kippley and Sheila K, *The Art of Natural Family Planning*, 4th ed. (Cincinnati: Couple to Couple League International Inc., 1996), 172-173.

[24] Couple to Couple League, *The Art of Natural Family Planning: Student Guide* (Cincinnati: The Couple to Couple League International, Inc., 2007), vii, ix.

[25] John F. Kippley and Sheila K. Kippley, *Natural Family Planning: The Complete Approach*, (Cincinnati: NFP International, 2009), http://www.nfpandmore.org/nfphowto.shtml (accessed January 15, 2010), 8, 14-16, 122-124.

[26] Klaus, 142-143.

method, as developed in the 1960s by the Australian Drs. John and Evelyn Billings.[27] This method is primarily focused on monitoring the cervical mucus generated by the woman at various points in her cycle—similar to monitoring nasal mucus to assist in diagnosing a cold. Through observation of the color, clarity, consistency, and stretch of mucus discharge throughout the day, taking only seconds to complete at each restroom visit, a woman is able to determine her level of fertility or infertility on any given day with considerable accuracy.[28] The data is recorded daily on a chart so that couples can determine where they are in the woman's cycle, and the chart serves as a record of the woman's fertility cycle to assist in monitoring fertility and for evaluation in case of gynecological or fertility problems.

One of the most prominent practitioners of this method in the United States is Dr. Thomas W. Hilgers, who in 1976 started "an independent evaluation" and was "able to independently verify" the value and effectiveness of the method.[29] Under the direction of Dr. Hilgers over several decades, the "Creighton Model" of NFP has developed with a number of specialties.[30] Working with "St. Louis University and Creighton University Schools of Medicine," Hilgers has created a highly systematic teaching program for other doctors, nurses, and instructors of the method that has spread internationally.[31] He has also founded the *Pope Paul VI Institute for the Study of Human Reproduction* in Omaha, which goes beyond the teaching of this NFP method to establish a "new women's health science."[32] They have proven their success in solving women's reproductive health and fertility issues in a manner consistent with Catholic moral teaching, while identifying and treating the *underlying causes* of problems rather than circumventing or merely masking them.[33] The Creighton Method of NFP can be taught over several

---

[27] Ibid., 134; Thomas W. Hilgers, *Creighton Model FertilityCare System: An Authentic Language of a Woman's Health and Fertility*, 5th ed. (Omaha: Pope Paul VI Institute Press, 2003), ix.

[28] Hilgers, *Creighton Model*, ix, 16.

[29] Ibid., ix.

[30] Ibid., iii.

[31] Ibid.

[32] Ibid.

[33] Ibid.

sessions in which a couple meets with an instructor that is trained by Hilgers's program and is part of his network. Studies of the ovulation method have shown outstanding success rates. In 1980 Hilgers and others in the United States demonstrated a success rate for postponing pregnancy of 99.6%, and a year later a study of almost 1,800 participants in India resulted in a success rate of 99.87%.[34]

Hilgers and CCL agree on what the Kipplers make clear: "Systematic natural family planning is not 'Catholic Birth Control.'"[35] Consistent with the Catholic ethic, Hilgers further notes, "This is not a method of contraception. It is not, even, a natural method of contraception. It is a system that takes into account the wholeness of the human person. Furthermore, it considers fertility as a part of health and not a disease."[36] Rather than "either suppressing or destroying the procreative capability," methods of NFP are interested in helping a couple come to appreciate, respect, and understand their fertility as they utilize the method to avoid or achieve pregnancy.[37]

Despite the effectiveness results recognized by Klaus and available to the international medical community, NFP was not widely embraced, and it suffered under a shroud of misunderstanding and misinformation. In 1993 Dr. R. E. J. Ryder published an article in the *British Medical Journal* that worked to show NFP's true effectiveness, without any confusion with the calendar rhythm method. Ryder explained that world overpopulation was a significant issue on the table at the 1992 "earth summit" in Rio de Janeiro.[38] At that conference the Catholic Church's position on family planning was seen as "a particular threat," and NFP was perceived as "unreliable, unacceptable, and ineffective."[39] In light of this situation, Ryder published an alternative picture of NFP by emphasizing its effectiveness in identifying the times of fertility as cross-checked by ultrasound observation, at rates comparable with highly effective contraceptive methods.[40] Ryder cited a WHO study that stated almost

---

[34] Klaus, 142-143.
[35] Kippley and Kippley, *The Complete Approach*, 6.
[36] Hilgers, *Creighton Model*, 5.
[37] Ibid.
[38] R. E. J. Ryder, "'Natural Family Planning': Effective Birth Control Supported by the Catholic Church," *British Medical Journal* 307 (September 1993): 723.
[39] Ibid.
[40] Ibid.

all women are capable of reading their fertility signs to identify when they are fertile, and she further defended NFP methods as safe, inexpensive, and well-suited to use in impoverished countries.[41] Ryder recognized motivation as a significant factor for the success rates of NFP; however, motivation greatly affects the success rates of contraceptives as well. For example, according to Ryder, failure rate differences between well motivated and less motivated condom users go from 3.6% to 22%, diaphragm rates go from 1.9% to 23%, and at least among "developing countries" OCP rates jump from as low as 0.18% to as high as 28%.[42] Therefore, motivation has a significant effect upon failure rates no matter the method of family planning employed.

Furthermore, NFP has been recognized by other reputable organizations and studies as being highly effective. A 1983 WHO study reported the likelihood of pregnancy resulting from couples following the cervical mucus method and refraining from intercourse within the fertile period was only 0.4%, a success rate of 99.6%.[43] One of the largest studies (almost 20,000 women) to demonstrate NFP's effectiveness was conducted amongst "predominantly poor women" in Calcutta, India and published in 1982.[44] Catholics can probably guess who was involved with this endeavor. In Mother Teresa's 1979 Nobel Peace Prize speech, she explained that her sisters were teaching NFP to thousands of poor and uneducated women and couples in Calcutta at very high effectiveness rates and with considerable success.[45] Ryder reports that the high motivation for these impoverished users helped produce a 99.8% success rate.[46] When the effectiveness is combined with other advantages such as price, self-knowledge, lack of side effects, and the ability to be learned by the illiterate, Ryder argues that NFP is extremely well suited to developing countries.[47] Consequently, the medical

---

[41] Ibid.
[42] Ibid., 724.
[43] Ibid., 725.
[44] Ibid.
[45] Mother Teresa of Calcutta, "Nobel Lecture," http://nobelprize.org/ nobel_prizes/peace/laureates/1979/teresa-lecture.html (accessed December 15, 2009).
[46] Ryder, 725.
[47] Ibid.

community, general populace, and especially Catholics need to be more familiar with the fact that NFP is comparable in effectiveness with the most highly effective contraceptives. Ryder concludes, "It is therefore important that the misconception that Catholicism is synonymous with ineffective birth control is laid to rest."[48]

Finally, there have been advancements in the area of technology improving its ability to detect fertility phases. For example, the *OvaCue Fertility Monitor* is touted as "clinically proven to be 98.3% accurate in monitoring ovulation" with a two decade history helping couples trying to conceive, simply by testing electrolyte concentration in women's saliva.[49] A small-scale study indicated that OvaCue "correctly processed 46 of 48 cycles (96%)" and compared similarly to the sympto-thermal method of NFP, outperforming it in determining the onset of ovulation.[50] Researchers call for additional and larger-scale studies and conclude that OvaCue "has potential to be used as an adjunctive device in the learning and use of NFP methods."[51] Such technological assistance is likely to be much more accepted in societies that value such means over less "scientific," evaluations of fertility. For such reasons, one medical professional respondent to the study indicates that OvaCue may help increase the credibility for longstanding methods of NFP.[52]

Utilizing such new technology, a new method of NFP has been introduced by Marquette University health professionals known as the Marquette Method. The monitor used with this method is the ClearBlue Easy Fertility Monitor. The objective observations of this device are coupled with biological observation (especially cervical

---

[48] Ibid.

[49] "OvaCue Fertility Monitor: Ovulation Prediction Made Easy," Home Page http://www.ovacue.com (accessed December 30, 2011).

[50] Jennine Regas and Philip Regas, "Preliminary Comparison of Algorithm-Interpreted Fertility Monitor Readings with Established Natural Family Planning Methods," In Integrating Faith and Science Through Natural Family Planning, ed. Richard J. Fehring and Theresa Notare (Milwaukee: Marquette UP, 2004), 175-176.

[51] Ibid., 176.

[52] Barbara Savinetti-Rose, "Response to 'Preliminary Comparison of Algorithm—Interpreted Fertility Monitor Readings with Established NFP Methods," In *Integrating Faith and Science Through Natural Family Planning*, ed. Richard J. Fehring and Theresa Notare (Milwaukee: Marquette UP, 2004), 182.

mucus) to determine the onset and expiration of peak fertility. Its effectiveness is similar to other methods of NFP, but the cost of the monitor adds an additional, ongoing expense.

Effectiveness Considerations

A few additional notes on effectiveness are necessary. First, a difference exists between the rate of effectiveness for the method itself and the effectiveness common among users, which is also true for contraceptives like OCPs. The Creighton Model ovulation method boasts a *"method effectiveness"* of "98.7-99.9 percent" based upon "five major effectiveness studies."[53] These statistics, with a remarkable failure rate of no more than 1.3 pregnancies per 100 women per year, are based upon the method only—they do not consider errors in terms of teaching, learning, and using the method. These other issues are considered by the *"use effectiveness* (as a means to avoid pregnancy) [that] ranged from 94.6 to 97.9 percent."[54] According to Dr. Hilgers, "Both of these effectiveness ratings are equal to or better than birth control pills or other drugs and devices."[55] The best NFP methods are second in effectiveness only to methods that eliminate or significantly decrease user effectiveness such as sterilization, hormonal implants, and the IUD—its effectiveness is reliably high.

The sympto-thermal method as taught by CCL and the Kippleys claims comparable effectiveness rates in recent studies. Several studies have shown a "perfect-use" failure rating of less than 1%, and CCL claims its users can expect 98-99% effectiveness when the method is used "correctly and consistently."[56] The Kippley's new textbook and the CCL's new textbook both cite a 2007 study on the sympto-thermal method in Germany demonstrating a 99.6% rate of method effectiveness.[57] The high rate of effectiveness stated above may be achieved by using the method conservatively, and following the method correctly. User effectiveness rates for the sympto-thermal method in studies range from 92.5% to 99.2%, also not significantly

---

[53] Hilgers, *Creighton Model*, 53.
[54] Ibid.
[55] Ibid.
[56] Kippley and Kippley, *The Art*, 146-151; CCL, *Student Guide*, 151.
[57] Kippley and Kippley, *The Complete Approach*, 2; CCL, *Student Guide*, 151.

different than user effectiveness rates for many contraceptive methods.[58]

Second, some hostile sources will indicate that rates for NFP are not nearly as effective as has been indicated above. There is a considerable deficiency in such information, because the wide range of different NFP methods are often lumped together in studies that determine effectiveness, so very effective methods have their success rates reduced by less effective methods. This is why some medical statistics will claim NFP, or fertility awareness methods, have failure rates much higher than those earlier mentioned. Furthermore, many types of NFP are in use throughout the world, and in some cases people use less-effective methods or may not be sufficiently educated in the use of a method. Several researchers have indicated that while up to 20% of women worldwide may use some form of NFP, "Many of these women lack correct knowledge of when during their menstrual cycle they are most likely to become pregnant. They simply avoid unprotected intercourse on certain days of the cycle, without accurate information about how to determine when they are fertile."[59] Consequently, this leads to higher failure rates when these matters are not considered.

Therefore, medical sources that give NFP methods a failure rate higher than two or three percent are taking the best and worst of such "methods" into consideration, as if it were possible to combine all sorts of contraceptives into one effectiveness category. For instance, if contraceptives were treated the same way in evaluating effectiveness, sterilization (<1% failure rate) and spermicides (approximately 30% failure rate) would average out to about 15%—a rate that degrades the effectiveness of sterilization considerably and unfairly.[60] Different NFP methods, like the sympto-thermal or ovulation methods, must have their effectiveness ratings recognized individually so as not to be unjustly worsened by other methods of "periodic abstinence." Failure to do so leads sources like Planned

---

[58] CCL, *Student Guide*, 151.

[59] Irit Sinai et al., "Fertility Awareness-Based Methods of Family Planning: Predictors of Correct Use," *International Family Planning Perspectives* 32, no. 2 (June 2006): 94.

[60] Planned Parenthood, "Comparing Effectiveness of Birth Control Methods" Chart, http://www.plannedparenthood.org/health-topics/birth-control /birth-control-effectiveness-chart-22710.htm (accessed December 21, 2009).

Parenthood to suggest "Fertility-Awareness Based Methods" are only 75-85% effective, meaning 15-25 "pregnancies per 100 women each year."[61] Conversely, though, this source is more careful to distinguish the effectiveness of a variety of forms of contraceptives in comparison to NFP. Thus, even contraceptive methods that are similar enough to work as barriers, like condoms and diaphragms, are listed separately. This is as it should be; however, equal treatment and distinction for "fertility-awareness based methods" would also be appropriate, more accurate, and more helpful. Planned Parenthood, among others, is failing to truly empower women to make family planning choices based upon accurate information. To some fertility centers and medical professionals, any method of periodic abstinence is the same as any other; they neglect important differences.

Third, those who cite rates of effectiveness for NFP methods may state that the method has a high failure rate, except when used correctly *all the time*. For example, The "Adult Health Advisor" from Clinical Reference Systems, states, "If it is not practiced carefully, the failure rate can be 20 to 30%."[62] This is around ten times the failure rate of the method when used correctly, but the source does not even reveal the correct use effectiveness ratings. Such a high rate of ineffectiveness when not used correctly all the time is obvious, as any contraceptive used incorrectly will also have significantly reduced rates of effectiveness. However, such sources will then cite rates of effectiveness for other means of family planning—like hormonal contraceptives or barriers—based upon their maximum method effectiveness, regardless of whether they are used correctly all the time. While Planned Parenthood mentions that, "Like all birth control methods, fertility awareness-based methods are more effective when you use them correctly," they persist in citing a failure rate as high as 12-25% for those who do not use the methods correctly *all the time*.[63] Simply noting that, "Always practicing these methods correctly will make them more effective," gives no indication of how effective such NFP methods actually are *when used*

[61] Ibid.

[62] "Natural Family Planning," *CRS—Adult Health Advisor* (January 1, 2009).

[63] Planned Parenthood. "Fertility Awareness-Based Methods (FAMs)," http://www.plannedparenthood. org/heath-topics/birth-control/fertility-awareness-4217.htm (accessed December 21, 2009).

correctly.[64] All the contraceptives they show are listed independently and at a rate of effectiveness when used correctly, but methods of periodic abstinence are lumped together and given an effectiveness based upon using them incorrectly. The double standard is conspicuous.

Finally, some sources suggest that NFP is not for everyone. They claim women may have unpredictable cycles that vary in length, irregular mucus patterns, and the like, which makes NFP methods impossible. This was also a common complaint by couples in the 1960s and 1970s.[65] While this is certainly true for methods like calendar rhythm, where its effectiveness is dependent on past cycles, it is entirely inaccurate when it comes to methods that track an individual woman's fertility as it progresses through each cycle, as is done with the sympto-thermal and ovulation methods. Contemporary methods of NFP are based on observation of current symptoms of fertility, not on past fertility cycles, so as to determine an *individual* woman's current fertility in an *individual* cycle, *independent* of past cycles or other women's cycles. One study indicated, "There was no clear profile of clients for whom these family planning methods would be inappropriate"; however, the study did find that shared responsibility by couples was important, as is even recognized by Planned Parenthood.[66]

For women with irregular cycles and other abnormalities, the methods generate data to indicate what underlying problems or health issues may be causing these conditions in ways contraceptives certainly cannot. For example, women experiencing problems with cycle irregularity may find nutritional and hormonal causes that are easily remedied. A clinical review in the *Journal of the American Board of Family Medicine* indicates: "The lowest pregnancy rates associated with [NFP] are achieved by women who choose to use these methods and have been properly instructed in how to do so."[67] NFP methods and

---

[64] Ibid.
[65] Andre E. Hellegers, "A Scientist's Analysis," In *Contraception: Authority and Dissent,* ed. Charles E. Curran (New York: Herder and Herder, 1969), 224-225.
[66] Sinai et al., 94.
[67] Stephen R. Pallone and George R. Bergus, "Fertility Awareness-Based Methods: Another Option for Family Planning," *Journal of the American Board of Family Medicine* 22 (2009): 149.

their providers can help to overcome most cycle challenges and assist practitioners in achieving greater reproductive and overall health.

Challenges

While NFP has some inherent disadvantages, like the time necessary to educate couples to practice the method effectively and an inability to protect against STDs, the greatest challenge of the method seems to be that it includes periodic abstinence from sexual intercourse during the fertile time when avoiding pregnancy. The concern of many couples has been their inability to use the method correctly due to struggling with periodic abstinence. Janet Smith notes, "One senses…that what [couples] don't trust is not the method, but themselves and the strength of their marriage."[68] Studies on this type of concern have been influential on the topic for decades. For example, the Crowleys' study of drawbacks of the rhythm method among Catholic couples in the mid-1960s had a significant impact on the outcome of the papal birth control commission's reports in 1966 (explored in Part II). More recently, an article in the *Journal of Nursing Scholarship* from 2003, by Dr. Leona VandeVusse et al., discusses the results of a new survey that seeks to determine if anything has changed among the satisfaction of NFP users (ovulation method only, i.e. the Billings/Creighton method). The results of the survey showed that positive comments significantly outweighed negative comments (74% vs. 26%).[69] This in itself is a dramatic improvement since the Crowleys' study. Critics may suggest, however, that the improvement could be due simply to the possibility that those using NFP continue to do so because it works for them, while the Crowleys' respondents (using calendar rhythm) may have felt morally obliged to continue the method. Additional studies are necessary to take factors such as these into further consideration. Nonetheless, it demonstrates that those practicing NFP today have a much more positive experience and perception of the method than those practicing the rhythm method fifty or more years ago.

Even with better responses to NFP, some concerns still remain. Among these concerns, thirteen percent involved "strained sexual

---

[68] Janet E. Smith, "Paul VI as Prophet," in *Why Humanae Vitae Was Right: A Reader*, ed. Janet E. Smith (San Francisco: Ignatius Press, 1993), 530.

[69] VandeVusse et al., 173.

interactions" like "difficulties with abstinence" (5%), "decreased frequency & spontaneity" (5%), and "unbalanced drives between partners" (3%).[70] Six percent of comments complained of "worsened relationships" due to things like "anger and frustrations" (3%) or "misunderstandings" resulting from using the method (3%).[71] Finally, seven percent of comments involved "method problems" like "fear of pregnancy" (3%), "method failed" (2%), and "other problems" (2%).[72] Overall, negative comments were quite low, and "Rarely a participant expressed only strong negative reactions to NFP," according to the survey.[73] Thanks to newer, more effective methods, couples using NFP today—versus calendar rhythm method in the Crowleys' study from the 1960s—have much higher satisfaction, less anxiety from fear of pregnancy, fewer days of required abstinence, and they also recount numerous positive effects in much greater quantity than negative comments.[74] This dramatic reversal in attitudes about the method by users over the course of almost fifty years led the study to conclude the use of NFP "warrants further consideration."[75] While the results of this study and its conclusions are positive for proponents of official Catholic Church teaching, the persistent concerns—albeit much more limited today than past decades—are worthy of discussion.

Frustration with periodic abstinence should not be an unmanageable obstacle to the practice of NFP. Many forms of NFP offer means and strategies for couples to address periodic abstinence. Frequently, these ideas involve an attitude adjustment. For instance, the 4th edition of the CCL textbook suggests, "We need to see 'making love' in a much broader context. There are all sorts of marital 'love making' or love building activities that have nothing to do with coitus."[76] These could include back rubs, holding hands, love letters, date nights, or any other sort of healthy activity practiced by courting couples prior to marriage by which they foster their relationship in preparation for a deeper and more intimate marital

---

[70] Ibid.
[71] Ibid.
[72] Ibid.
[73] Ibid., 175.
[74] Ibid., 171-172, 173, 175-176.
[75] Ibid., 171.
[76] Kippley and Kippley, *The Art*, 256.

and sexual relationship at a later time. Too often American couples reduce love to sex. In reality, sex is not always the epitome of the passionate marital bonding between spouses. Ironically, by seeing sex as one among many ways of "making love," many NFP couples have been able to build a stronger foundation in their relationship—not exclusively or primarily founded on sex—which serves to enhance the relational bonding, intimacy, and satisfaction of their sexual experiences later on, even if the number of such experiences may be slightly fewer on average. In this way, NFP couples continue to rebuild and reinforce the foundation of love and affection, which makes for authentic "love making," solid relationships, and satisfying sex.

Dr. Hilgers's Creighton Model of NFP encourages a similar approach to adjusting to the demands of periodic abstinence through SPICE. He explains, "The Creighton Model System challenges married couples to look at sexuality from a broad multidimensional perspective. It challenges couples to be sexually whole and to view their sexuality from the spiritual, physical, intellectual, creative/communicative and emotional/psychological perspectives (SPICE)."[77] A healthy relationship must be built strongly upon each of these foundations, and an imbalance among them will detract even from the good of any one which is upheld at the expense of others. For instance, if the physical element is overemphasized at the expense of the other dimensions, even that physical element will be depleted from being the best it could be if all were in balance. Sex in a relationship without the depth of intellectual, emotional, communicative, and spiritual connections is shallow and far from what God planned for sex or marriage. Through this balanced approach, Hilgers is clear that "sexual contact is never to be avoided," yet couples need to learn the difference between "arousal touch and affirming touch."[78] Couples who are abstaining from intercourse during the fertile phase of a woman's cycle endanger their relationship by avoiding touching one another—or avoiding each other as a whole—during this time, out of fear of leading to sex and possible pregnancy. The psychological problems of avoiding one another altogether have been highlighted by many revisionists like

---

[77] Hilgers, *Creighton Model*, 6.
[78] Ibid., 35-36.

Bernard Haring and Michael Novak in critiques of rhythm.[79] Such an approach is not healthy and quite the opposite is now promoted by NFP programs.

Despite these helpful relationship building approaches, the challenge of abstinence may still persist to some extent. Under these circumstances couples have an additional help. They are not called to repress any sexual desires, for such repression is neither healthy nor fruitful. On the contrary, couples (or individual spouses struggling with sexual desire and abstinence in NFP) are called to strive for and experience the redemption of their desires in Christ. Jesus calls us beyond the Old Laws into something better, and he provides the means for us to do it. For example, in the Sermon on the Mount in Matthew 5, Jesus tells us not only to avoid adultery but to go deeper, to the root of such a problem, and avoid lust. While the Israelites could not fully meet the requirements of the Old Law, Christians have the assistance of the Holy Spirit, grace, and the Church with her sacraments to help us live as God calls us to live. This is why Pope Saint John Paul II wrote in VS, "God does not command the impossible, but in commanding he admonishes you to do what you can and to pray for what you cannot, and he gives his aid to enable you."[80] In our weaknesses, we must rely on God's grace to help us live as he has called us, as his children. This is not a condemnation, but a sign of great hope, as St. John Paul II explains, "Christ has redeemed us! This means that he has given us the possibility of realizing the entire truth of our being; he has set our freedom free from the domination of concupiscence. And if redeemed man still sins, this is not due to an imperfection of Christ's redemptive act, but to man's will not to avail himself of the grace which flows from that act."[81] When living as a Christian is tough—and it will be, as it must be—we must rely on God.

---

[79] Bernard Haring, "The Inseparability of the Unitive-Procreative Functions of the Marital Act," in *Readings in Moral Theology No. 8: Dialogue about Catholic Sexual Teaching*, ed. Charles E. Curran and Richard A. McCormick (New York: Paulist Press, 1993), 165; Michael Novak, "Frequent, Even Daily, Communion," in *The Catholic Case for Contraception*, ed. Daniel Callahan (London: Macmillan, 1969), 96-97.

[80] Pope John Paul II, *Veritatis Splendor* (1993), Vatican Translation (Boston: Pauline), §102.

[81] Ibid., §103.

We can also *count on* the fact that living as a Christian will be tough, and it will make certain demands on our lives. Living as a Christian means to do things God's way, even when they conflict with *my* way. With grace and sanctification, one's will conforms to God's will, and one happily and easily lives an integrated Christian life. St. John Paul II notes, "[Man's] history of sin begins when he no longer acknowledges the Lord as his Creator and himself wishes to be the one who determines with complete independence, what is good and what is evil."[82] Ratzinger echoes St. John Paul II in the following: "Today's discussion of morality is making great strides toward liberating man from guilt by precluding the occurrence of the conditions that make it possible. ... In their heart of hearts, those who have been liberated in this fashion know perfectly well that the whole experience is untrue."[83] Denial such as this is a thriving ideology today, but living as children of God and disciples of Christ is not easy, nor was it meant to be, and this stands in sharp contrast with the ways of the world. Lawler, Boyle, and May comment, "There will be difficulties in the practice of NFP, just as the Lord has promised us that there would be difficulties of discipleship in other areas of life, for he spoke about carrying the cross daily."[84] Similarly, G. E. M. Anscombe has argued that to be a Christian has always meant being held to a higher standard of morality than the rest of the world. Christians in the Roman world were expected not to commit infanticide, worship other gods, get divorced, allow concubines, commit fornication, or use contraception.[85] She explains that it must "cost" and "threaten" to be a true Christian, and "One should be glad if it does, rather than complain! If we will not let it cost anything..., then our religion is indistinguishable from pure worldliness."[86] In addition, the sacrifice required also brings with it a sense of joy not only at the end but in the process, as parents feels the joy of knowing they are making the appropriate sacrifices to do

---

[82] Ibid., §102.

[83] Joseph Ratzinger, *Called to Communion: Understanding the Church Today*, trans. Adrian Walker (San Francisco: Ignatius Press, 1996), 150.

[84] Lawler, Boyle, and May, 161.

[85] G. E. M. Anscombe, "Contraception and Chastity," in *Why Humanae Vitae Was Right: A Reader*, ed. Janet E. Smith (San Francisco: Ignatius Press, 1993), 122-123.

[86] Ibid., 145.

what is best for their children and families. Following the truth involves both sacrifice and satisfaction.

People often assume that conforming their will to that of God will mean they will be miserable and unable to do what they want. On the contrary, Matthew Kelly states, "The will of God is that you become the-best-version-of-yourself. God doesn't want to control you, or manipulate you, or stifle you, or force you to do things you don't want to do. … God wants you to become all you can be, and in the process he wants you to experience the greatest mystery of them all—love."[87] Master of the spiritual life, St. Francis de Sales, explains that living the Christian life is not equivalent to drudgery, but rather is profoundly joyous. In his *Introduction to the Devout Life*, de Sales provides tutelage by which the reader may grow in his or her spiritual and devotional life. Within these pages he notes, "I have said to you many things which will seem hard as you read them, but if you practice them, they will be sweet to you as sugar and honey."[88]

Moreover, as Christians we must be willing to be a sign of contradiction as Jesus was. The more we live in conformity with God's will, the easier it is to continue as we grow in virtue. This is likely why studies have shown those who have fostered chastity before marriage are less likely to struggle with abstinence when practicing NFP, because they have developed the virtue of chastity, a virtue that is largely counter-cultural.[89] Couples with the virtue of chastity are freed from their lusts and liberated to the possibility of truly loving their spouse in ways beyond sexually, not using their spouse for their own pleasure. To help in this process, it is the Church's job to call us to this greater way of life, as she has been commanded to do by Christ. She makes clear that the proper ordering of sexuality is a key to marital happiness. Anscombe suggests that teaching "against the grain of the world, against the current of our time" is, after all, "what the Church as teacher is for."[90] As chief shepherd of the Church, Pope Bl. Paul VI

---

[87] Matthew Kelly, *Rediscovering Catholicism: Journeying Toward Our Spiritual North Star* (Cincinnati: Beacon, 2002), 125

[88] St. Francis de Sales, *Philothea, or An Introduction to the Devout Life* (Rockford: TAN, 1994), 132 (Part III, Chapter VI).

[89] Janet E. Smith, *Humanae Vitae: A Generation Later* (Washington D.C.: Catholic University of America Press, 1991), 128.

[90] Anscombe, 146.

encouraged, "Do not be afraid, when necessary, to go against the tide of thought and opinion of a world ruled by paganized standards of behavior. ... And do not be discouraged in moments of weakness. Our God is a Father full of tenderness and goodness...and the Church is a mother who desires to help you live to the fullest this ideal of Christian marriage."[91] The challenges of NFP, in developing personal and marital virtue, are sources of ongoing happiness in our lives. The striving, itself, is a joy because it is a conscious cooperation with goodness. We experience the rewards of virtue in the process of developing it.

Finally, couples practicing NFP may not be missing out on all that much. Studies do indicate that couples practicing NFP have lower rates of intercourse, but not by much. The *Journal of the American Board of Family Medicine* reports that, while "coital frequency varies greatly by country, ranging from 2.6 to 8.9 acts per month," users of NFP average 5.1 acts of intercourse versus the 5.5 acts per month average internationally.[92] NFP couples seem to be making up for lost time, if you will, and report coital interactions only slightly lower than others. They just may not be able to be as spontaneous during the fertile phase. Yet even this challenge offers its own package of benefits and has a way of enhancing the sexual relationship.

Enhanced Relationships

Fifty years ago the disadvantages of the rhythm method seemed to overwhelm any advantages, while the possibilities of contraceptives, like the pill, seemed boundless. Over a decade into the twenty-first century this situation has nearly entirely inverted. Now the problems with contraceptives, especially OCPs, are becoming more and more prevalent (as will be discussed in the following chapter) while the benefits of the modern methods of NFP have proved stronger and stronger. Certainly, NFP has its unique challenges; however, even the challenge of periodic abstinence in

---

[91] Pope Paul VI, "To the Teams of Our Lady," in *Why Humanae Vitae Was Right: A Reader*, ed. Janet E. Smith (San Francisco: Ignatius Press, 1993), 98.

[92] Stephen R. Pallone and George R. Bergus, "Fertility Awareness-Based Methods: Another Option for Family Planning," *Journal of the American Board of Family Medicine* 22 (2009): 151..

NFP comes with a whole host of benefits. NFP enhances marriage in many ways, even as a result of periodic abstinence. In fact, the survey of Dr. VandeVusse et al. showed that many respondents identified NFP as having enhanced marital relationships in some way.[93]

NFP is well attested by couples to improve communication. One couple explains, "Practicing NFP has enhanced our marriage in practical ways. It has strengthened our communication tenfold. Discussing the inner workings of my body has made every other subject easy. We plan our family together consciously. If we didn't practice NFP, it would be all too easy to shelf those big-picture discussions for another day."[94] Catholic marriage counselor, Dr. Gregory Popcak, has explained that NFP improves communication because "[Couples] are forced to nurture their friendship more because they can't just 'throw sex' at their problems."[95] The improvement of a marriage due to increased communication affected by NFP is ironic, because increased communication was an argument used by early revisionists as a reason why couples need to be able to have intercourse at any time.[96]

The shared responsibility of NFP is also highly beneficial to the relationship. Joseph Boyle explains, "The efforts of self-control must be mutual; thus couples living by NFP are united in a common effort of will. This chaste union obviates the temptation for couples to treat one another as mere instruments for sexual gratification and allows their sexual expression to be an expression of human communication."[97] When a woman handles the brunt of the responsibility and side-effects on her own, as has become increasingly common with users of contraception in recent decades (further elaborated upon in the following chapter), the act of intercourse fails to be all it was meant to be and can lead to abuse. NFP helps counter and prevent this; the couple works more as a team.

---

[93] VandeVusse et al., 173.

[94] Ann Green, "Not Your Mother's Rhythm Method," *U.S. Catholic* 74, no. 5 (May 2009): 24.

[95] Sam Torode and Bethany Torode, *Open Embrace: A Protestant Couple Rethinks Contraception* (Grand Rapids: Wm. B. Eerdmans Publishing Co., 2002), 50.

[96] Novak, 101.

[97] Joseph M. Boyle, "Contraception and Natural Family Planning," in *Why Humanae Vitae Was Right: A Reader*, ed. Janet E. Smith (San Francisco: Ignatius Press, 1993), 417.

Not surprisingly, NFP couples report a heightened mutual respect. One wife reports, "It wasn't 'my responsibility' (as wife) or the sacrifice I had to make ... to 'keep my husband happy.' He is equally involved (he charts). He understands and respects my body more and I respect him more because he is supportive and not selfish."[98] A former contraceptive user, Ruth Lasseter, addresses the issue of respect in the following: "We women have always held the sexual standards of society... Now, we have the knowledge of our own fertility. Is it unreasonable to ask our husbands to respect this, to center relations around *female* sexuality instead of the male sexual drive?"[99] In this way, NFP couples tend to experience increased mutual respect.

Fourth, thanks to the challenge of periodic abstinence, sexual integration becomes a virtue NFP couples are called to master. According to the VandeVusse et al. survey, many respondents "expressed pride in the self-control they had developed by using NFP."[100] Couples well disciplined by self-control have obvious benefits for families and society. Janet Smith explains, "Control over one's sexual desires makes one a more thoughtful and attentive lover, for one will be having sexual intercourse in the context of what is good for the marriage, not as the result of uncontrollable sexual desires."[101] This prevents lust and objectification between spouses, especially of the female by the male. One man using NFP also discovered how his example of self-control had a positive effect on young men with whom he worked as he explained, "If he could sleep in the same bed with the woman he loved and control his sexual desire, they could control their sexual desire for the women they were dating."[102] Frequently, our attitudes and practices regarding our sexuality have a significant effect upon those for whom we care and with whom we interact, sometimes in ways we do not even perceive. The positive example of self-control can be a gift to all those around us, especially our spouses and children.

---

[98] VandeVusse et al., 173.
[99] Ruth D. Lasseter, "Sensible Sex," in *Why Humanae Vitae Was Right: A Reader*, ed. Janet E. Smith (San Francisco: Ignatius Press, 1993), 494.
[100] VandeVusse et al., 174.
[101] Lasseter, 471.
[102] Janet E. Smith, "Paul VI as Prophet," 530.

Fifth, as a likely result of these and a host of other benefits, NFP couples enjoy remarkably low divorce rates. Information reported by the Kippleys indicates that divorce rates among NFP couples may be around 1-2%, and at most 5%.[103] This indicates a divorce rate 10-25 times less than that of the general public. The *Journal of the American Board of Family Medicine* confirms that divorce rates are lower for users of NFP (as low as 0.2%), noting that Catholics are the primary users of it, though Catholics who do not use NFP have divorce rates similar to the general population, "suggesting that religion alone does not account for this difference."[104] How is this possible? The Kippleys suggest, "There is nothing automatically marriage building about taking your temperatures and observing your mucus, but the practice of NFP with self-discipline and generosity helps to build the attitudes, communication and respect that are needed for healthy and happy marriages."[105] While not all causes for divorce can be cured by practicing NFP, it is reasonable to believe that the lifestyle necessary to effectively practice NFP is conducive for happy, healthy marriages. Critics may argue that people who use NFP are the type of people less likely to get divorced anyway; however, the selection of NFP by those couples may just as easily be considered an endorsement from those who know something about a successful marriage.

Finally, the periodic abstinence of NFP has a tendency to create what some refer to as the "honeymoon effect." As a result of the time couples abstain, they must treat each other as if they were merely courting or dating. When the couple returns to a time of sexual activity, it is as if they have relived their pre-marriage experience and are able to anticipate and enjoy a mini-honeymoon again as their emotional, spiritual, and communicative relationship is once more expressed through physical intercourse. One man explains, "NFP gives us a courtship phase in which we abstain. ... I have to court Ellen once a cycle, and that is a good thing for our marriage. I have to talk to her. We have to be physically close but not maritally intimate. This has drawn us...closer together. ... Self-

---

[103] Kippley and Kippley, *The Art*, 245.
[104] Stephen R. Pallone and George R. Bergus, "Fertility Awareness-Based Methods: Another Option for Family Planning," *Journal of the American Board of Family Medicine* 22 (2009): 149-151.
[105] Kippley and Kippley, *The Complete Approach*, 23.

control is essential."[106] He continues, "It is a courtship phase, and we know that the courtship phase will always end and is always followed by a honeymoon phase. It is no surprise to me, therefore, that NFP couples have about a one percent divorce rate."[107]

This honeymoon effect has also been known to help alleviate the challenge of abstinence and improve sexual experiences. While periods of abstinence are not more than a few days, not being able to have something for even a short time makes it all the more desirable. Consider the phrase, "we want what we cannot have," for example. According to the study of NFP couples by VandeVusse et al., "Abstinence enhanced [couples'] anticipation of sexual intercourse during infertile times, thus lessening the frustrations associated with abstinence while increasing their appreciation of their sexuality. They also reported that the sexual intercourse and other intimate activities including foreplay had improved."[108] The study quotes one spouse saying, "Our sexual relationship is incredible. I have no complaints and truly believe the periodic abstinence [of] NFP caused us never to get in a rut sexually."[109] Another couple testifies, "NFP and a chaste attitude toward sex in marriage opened up a new world for us. It bonded my husband and me in a way that is so deep, so strong, that it's hard to describe. Sometimes it's difficult, but that makes us even closer. We revere each other. And when we do come together, we're like honeymooners."[110]

The benefits of NFP, *including* and often *as a result of* periodic abstinence, are overwhelming. When given a chance, NFP has been found by couples to be a remarkable blessing in their marriages and families. Another testimony is given by a woman who was trained with her husband in the sympto-thermal method of NFP by CCL in which she is grateful for having her marriage "instilled [with] the CCL

---

[106] R. Patrick Homan, "Marital Chastity: A Blessing for Marriage, Family and Spiritual Life," in *Trust the Truth: A symposium on the Twentieth Anniversary of the Encyclical Humanae Vitae*, ed. Russell E. Smith (Braintree, MA: The Pope John XXIII Medical-Moral Research and Education Center, 1991), 140.

[107] Homan, 140.

[108] VandeVusse et al., 173.

[109] Ibid.

[110] Janet E. Smith, *A Generation Later*, 127.

values of loving, selflessness, respect and communication."[111] Dr. John Grabowski offers some additional useful thoughts:

> [NFP] produces in spouses a certain reverence for the person of the other. The study and use of the method cannot but foster in the couple a certain wonder at the intricacy of human (especially female) fertility. This wonder, coupled with the interior freedom affected by periodic continence, engenders an awareness of the other as a person—a mysterious unity of body, emotions, subjectivity, and freedom (though this is not to say that couples who do not use NFP cannot experience this wonder and reverence for the other—only that the various methods themselves foster it in specific ways).[112]

Achieving Pregnancy

One of the great advantages of NFP methods is that they are not only easily reversible, they also help to achieve pregnancy. Since NFP methods work by identifying when a woman is most likely to conceive, they not only provide invaluable information about when to abstain from intercourse if avoiding pregnancy, but also when to engage in intercourse with the greatest likelihood of achieving pregnancy.[113] For the 20% of couples without peak fertility, NFP methods can alleviate the time, frustration, and fear related to infertility or decreased fertility, a problem that is becoming more common in America.[114]

The Creighton Method offers comprehensive assistance to couples trying to conceive. Hilgers reports 76% of couples using his method achieved pregnancy the first month when having intercourse

---

[111] Homan, 142.

[112] John S. Grabowski, "Natural Family Planning and Marital Spirituality," In *Integrating Faith and Science Through Natural Family Planning*, ed. Richard J. Fehring and Theresa Notare (Milwaukee: Marquette UP, 2004), 35.

[113] Michael J. Zinaman, "Using Cervical Mucus and Other Easily Observed Biomarkers to Identify Ovulation in Prospective Pregnancy Trials," *Paediatric & Perinatal Epidemiology* 20 supplement (November 2006): 28.

[114] Kippley and Kippley, *The Complete Approach*, 3.

during the fertile time.[115] For those struggling with infertility, Hilgers notes, "The overall pregnancy rate runs approximately 20 to 40 percent during the first six months in which the time of fertility is consistently used," because couples are able to calculate when best to try for pregnancy.[116] For those who do not conceive, Hilgers has developed NaProTECHNOLOGY, with "medical assessment and treatment" to help even more couples discover and correct the underlying health issues affecting their mutual fertility.[117] According to Hilgers, this approach "has now been shown to be 1.4 to 2.8 times more successful than the current artificial reproductive technologies [at overcoming infertility]. In addition, the underlying diseases are not ignored; they are treated."[118] Also, his means are consistent with Catholic moral theology and teaching. NFP methods are thus offering people a holistic approach to fertility and reproductive health.

Health Benefits

Methods of NFP are unmatched by other means of family planning in that they have no negative health side-effects, no physical barriers or things that interrupt the act of intercourse itself, and are even capable of working toward enhancing health. For example, since only about 5% of semen consists of sperm and the other 95% consists of multiple "mood enhancers" such as cortisol, estrone, prolactin, oxytocin, thyrotropin-releasing hormone, melatonin, and serotonin—a natural cocktail of bonding, antidepressant, mood elevating, and sleep-inducing hormones—women whose husbands do not use condoms are much less prone to depression, anxiety, and suicide.[119] Furthermore, one woman explains her experience, "In addition to church approval, Mike and I appreciate the health aspects of NFP. More people hold their food up to close scrutiny. Is it organic or natural? In the same spirit women who practice NFP do not ingest artificial hormones containing possibly toxic ingredients

---

[115] Hilgers, *Creighton Model*, 53.

[116] Ibid.

[117] Ibid.

[118] Thomas W. Hilgers, "Infertility," in *In Their Own Words: Women Healed*, ed. Jean Blair Packard (Omaha: Pope Paul VI Institute Press, 2004), 59-60.

[119] Gregory K. Popcak, "A Natural Argument for NFP," *Family Foundations* vol. 38 no. 2 (September/October 2011), 30.

manufactured in an unknown pharmaceutical plant."[120] Moreover, an article in the *Vegetarian Times* explains that while many methods of birth control are easy and convenient, they come with a high price of side-effects and health problems, so "many women are going *au natural*, opting, instead, for something that has no chemicals, no side effects and a surprisingly low risk of pregnancy. Something, ironically, that the Catholic Church has been pushing for years— natural family planning."[121] Is it really so "ironic" to the rest of the world that the Catholic Church might be on to something, as if the Church does not have wisdom and supernatural guidance beyond what mere unaided human reason can achieve? Likely so, yet a more significant irony is the fact that most of those who are *supposed* to believe these things taught by the Church—namely Catholics—are often just as surprised to learn about the overwhelming benefits of NFP as the secular world.

In addition, NFP promotes better health through self-awareness. One physician explains, "Any woman who knows her fertility patterns will detect an abnormality quickly and seek treatment."[122] There is a level of self-awareness involving fertility cycles and gynecological health inherently achieved through NFP methods that are unique over any other form of family planning. Dr. Thomas Hilgers explains that the Creighton Method "can be used not only to achieve or avoid pregnancy but also to further the evaluation of infertility, repetitive miscarriage, abnormal bleeding, recurrent ovarian cysts, pelvic pain, premenstrual syndrome," as well as ectopic pregnancy, assisting in hormone replacement therapy as truly needed, and identifying the true date of conception (as opposed to a calculated date after the last period used by most doctors, which ironically resembles a mentality similar to that of the calendar rhythm method—that all women are the same based upon statistical averages).[123] Hilgers's Pope Paul VI Institute has garnered a striking reputation for assisting couples dealing with these circumstances and more, such as pre-term births and post-partum depression. Marilyn

---

[120] Ann Green, 24.
[121] Norine Dworkin, "What You May Not Know About Natural Birth Control," *Vegetarian Times* no. 251 (July 1998): 82.
[122] Klaus, 139.
[123] Hilgers, *Creighton Model*, ix.

M. Shannon's book *Fertility, Cycles & Nutrition*, published by CCL, explores how diet and nutrition are tied to all kinds of problems like infertility, cycle irregularities, thyroid dysfunction, heavy periods, and PMS in order to help NFP couples handle some of these challenges, improve fertility when trying to conceive, and encourage overall health.[124] Finally, Gregory Popcak affirms, "I cannot tell you the number of stories I have collected over the years of NFP couples catching some problem so early that doctors were amazed but thrilled to have the opportunity to treat the disorder…with a much greater rate of success than they would have otherwise had. NFP is not just open to life. It saves lives."[125] NFP methods and their providers have the abilities and experience to assist couples in ways no other methods can.

Inexpensive and Easy to Learn

NFP methods are relatively easy to learn and quite inexpensive. According to one instructional organization, NFP methods can be effectively taught in two to three cycles.[126] Furthermore, "a large multinational study" has shown that "93% of women were able to learn to identify" key indicators of fertility "in their first cycle of instruction."[127] Most effective methods of NFP involve a training process that includes three or more cycles with instruction from a trained teacher. Therefore, vital elements of NFP can be learned quickly and easily for nearly all women.

Cost is also very low for methods of NFP. After paying a relatively nominal fee for instruction, perhaps a book, and any necessary instruments—like charts, thermometer, etc.—costs are virtually absent. The expense of the fertility monitor used in the Marquette Method is an exception here. The Kippleys explain, "Whatever you contribute for NFP instruction, it is very low compared to the costs of unnatural forms of birth control—costs that include not only the initial expense but regular medical checkups

124 Marilyn M. Shannon, *Fertility, Cycles & Nutrition*, 4th ed. (Cincinnati: Couple to Couple League, 2009).
125 Popcak, 31.
126 Kippley and Kippley, *The Art*, 4.
127 Zinaman, 28.

in the case of the Pill and other pharmaceutical products."[128] This may be one significant reason why NFP methods have not become incredibly popular in America—there is little money to be made from them, so they receive less publicity and are not advertised.

Implications for Third World Use

As a result of the ease of learning, inexpensiveness, and other advantages listed above, NFP may be the best option for couples in the Third World. Following HV, revisionists were severely critical of the Church's position, because it was not believed to be possible in impoverished countries. For example, in 1969 Bernard Haring commented:

> Women whose periods are regular, who can use all the necessary means, including the possibility of an undisturbed temperature reading and, if necessary, seven doctors at their disposal, can live in accordance with the teaching of the Church. What about the poor, the uneducated, when their periods are irregular, or when, because of their level of culture, they are simply incapable of understanding these methods?[129]

From the data previously considered, we have already countered some of Haring's concerns here. NFP certainly works for regular cycles, but it can also help women with irregular cycles determine what may be causing the irregularity, and work to heal the problem at its root without compromising effectiveness. Furthermore, modern NFP does not require "seven doctors," or even one doctor, to help a properly trained woman effectively determine her individual time of fertility each month. Finally, the ease of use, inexpensiveness, and other benefits make NFP especially attractive for Third World countries. Considering all that the sexual revolution and contraceptives have brought to America over the past several decades, why would we force such monumental problems on another

---

[128] Kippley and Kippley, *The Complete Approach*, 10-11.
[129] Bernard Haring, "The Encyclical Crisis," in *The Catholic Case for Contraception*, ed. Daniel Callahan (London: Macmillan, 1969), 87.

nation we are trying to help, rather than learn from our own mistakes and give them—not to mention ourselves and our children—something better for the future?

Due to the high method effectiveness of the best NFP methods, we have no reason to believe they could not work for poorer countries with less-educated, and even illiterate, populations. As a matter of fact, we possess significant data to show that NFP actually does work effectively for poorer countries, perhaps even better than for Americans. While the most challenging thing about NFP for couples in the U.S. may likely be the periodic abstinence, other countries, especially impoverished ones, may not see it as such a challenge. For instance, Klaus's research has shown, "When the couple had good reason to avoid pregnancy, they adhered to the rules of the method," and this was accomplished especially well among the poor.[130] Moreover, Ryder points to the 99.8% effectiveness rate found among the nearly 20,000 (mostly illiterate and uneducated) women studied in Calcutta as evidence of NFP working well in the Third World.[131] Mother Teresa explained that her sisters were "teaching our beggars, our leprosy patients, our slum dwellers, our people of the street, natural family planning," and spouses reported to her, "Our family is healthy, our family is united, and we can have a baby whenever we want."[132] Obviously, NFP works in Calcutta with the poorest of the poor and illiterate. Commenting on the outstanding qualities of NFP, Ryder concludes, "It might be argued that natural family planning being cheap, effective, without side effects, and potentially particularly effective and acceptable in areas of poverty may be the family planning method of choice for the Third World."[133]

Deficiencies Promoting NFP

The report on NFP is not entirely glowing, however. Efforts by the Church and others have been devastatingly poor in terms of allowing NFP to emerge in the twenty-first century as the blessing it truly is. In Pope St. John Paul II's 1981 Apostolic Exhortation,

---

[130] Klaus, 144.
[131] Ryder, 725.
[132] Mother Teresa of Calcutta, "Nobel Lecture."
[133] Ryder, 725.

Familiaris Consortio, he encouraged, "Every effort must be made to render such knowledge [of NFP] accessible to all married people and also to young adults before marriage, through clear, timely and serious instruction and education given by married couples, doctors, and experts."[134] Unfortunately, the ball has been dropped. In 1988 Auxiliary Bishop Austin B. Vaughan of Orange County, New York stated, "I think the encyclical [HV] is basically not accepted on any level in Church life. There is, relatively speaking, no clear teaching on birth control or purity in Catholic schools or colleges... To my knowledge, there is no insistence on uniform direction in the confessional in any diocese in our own country."[135] Vaughan continues, "I am as guilty as anybody; I have not pushed hard on it. Right up to the present, it is not an issue that we are prepared to push. Yet, if it is true, and if it is central...then we are not being true to the Faith if we do not push it."[136]

Many signs of our times point to this continued problem. John Kippley explains that in 1989 the USCCB's "Committee on Pastoral Research and Practices published a small book on marriage preparation, *Faithful to Each Other Forever*, in which they urged that every engaged couple should be required to attend a full course on NFP as a normal part of preparation for marriage"; however, as of 2007 only seven dioceses in the United States made plans to adhere to it, and these "are contingent upon the availability of NFP teachers."[137] The lack of teachers is an additional issue. A strong advocate of NFP programs, Mormon physician Dr. Joseph B. Stanford, recognizes, "Currently the number of NFP teachers in the U.S. is pitifully small and distributed such that many people in the

---

[134] Pope John Paul II, *Familiaris Consortio* (1981),
    http://www.vatican.va/holy_father/john_paul_ii/apost_exhortations/
    documents/hf_jp-ii_exh_19811122_familiaris-consortio_en.html (accessed
    July 14, 2009), §32.
[135] Austin B. Vaughan, "*Humanae Vitae* and Respect for the Dignity of the Human Person," in *Trust the Truth: A symposium on the Twentieth Anniversary of the Encyclical Humanae Vitae*, ed. Russell E. Smith (Braintree, MA: The Pope John XXIII Medical-Moral Research and Education Center, 1991), 20.
[136] Ibid., 22.
[137] Kippley, "The Sexual Revolution," 377.

population do not have access to quality instruction in NFP."[138] Some instructional groups are harnessing technology to make NFP education more widely available through online courses though, such as CCL.

Even where programs are in place, they can be easily undermined. Often couples report attending pre-marriage retreats where the Church's teaching and NFP are addressed in a manner mournfully deficient. For example, one Engaged Encounter retreat was led by three couples of various ages who gave energetic talks about their marriages and the way faith has played a part in them. While this retreat primarily involved talks and testimony from the three host couples, when it came to the point of discussing Church teaching on family planning and NFP, an outdated video was shown to the retreat couples. No personal testimony from the host couples was given. Little beyond what was in the video was introduced on the topic of NFP. The feeling in the room essentially communicated, "We do not really agree with this, but we have to show it to you, and if any of you are interested in NFP, good for you and here's a pamphlet, but if not, thanks for watching and listening." It was the only part of the retreat where the leaders did not present something themselves, yet after the video they encouraged retreat couples to "seriously consider" the Church's teaching and NFP. The effect upon the group was perfectly predictable.

This appears to be a widespread problem. Kippley notes, "In some dioceses, a mandatory pre-Cana lecture on sexuality has been hijacked by those who have no respect for Catholic morality."[139] In some cases, teachers of NFP may be invited to come speak at such pre-marriage retreats. While this is an improvement, such instruction must be supplemented by couples personally supportive of NFP for it to have a positive effect. If married couples leading such a retreat talk personally about things like communication, selflessness, and finances but someone else is brought in only to talk about NFP, there is a substantial disconnect, and it suggests the couple leaders are not

---

[138] Joseph Stanford, "My Personal and Professional Journey with Regard to Moral Issues in Human Procreation," in *Physicians Healed: Personal, Inspiring, and Compelling Stories of Fifteen Courageous Physicians Who Do Not Prescribe Contraception*, ed. Cleta Hartman (Dayton: One More Soul, 1998), 123.

[139] Kippley, "The Sexual Revolution," 378.

supporters of NFP themselves. Those attending the retreat are to find the couple leaders to be good role models, but on this issue the lack of testimony on the part of the couple leaders implicitly communicates that NFP content is a mandatory hoop the leaders have to jump through, and means little to them personally.

Lack of funding has handicapped NFP instruction as well. A 1993 article in the *National Catholic Reporter* by Fr. Robert Cannon, "vicar for marriage matters in the Venice, Fla., Diocese and a consultant to the bishops' Diocesan Development Program for Natural Family Planning," reveals two startling facts from a U.S. Bishop's diocesan survey: "NFP instruction is discussed less than 30 minutes in most marriage preparation programs," and, "On the average, less than $5,000 is spent on NFP programs by dioceses [annually]."[140] Little seems to have improved today. Long-time Catholic supporters of NFP Marie-Louise Ternier-Gommers and her husband Jim Ternier stated, "When it comes to transmitting Catholic teaching on sexual matters and promoting the use of NFP, the church has failed and continues to fail miserably."[141] Fr. Cannon legitimately questions the Church's commitment to NFP promotion, "Are we making it more difficult (because we are not making it easier) for couples to live marriage in all its sacramental fullness? Are we being truly faithful to *Humanae Vitae*?"[142]

NFP couples have not been silent about these problems. A critical 1995 article in *America* by Janet Claussen, M.R.E. demonstrates how difficult it can be for people, even dedicated Catholics, to find the support and resources necessary to effectively live this teaching.[143] Through a process of great struggle, lack of support, and self-education, she began to awaken to some of the benefits of NFP, yet at about that same time she became pregnant unexpectedly. She describes her frustration: "If someone as educated and motivated as I, with as willing and loving a spouse as I have,

---

[140] Robert R. Cannon, "Except in Theory, Dioceses Offer Little Support for Natural Family Planning," *National Catholic Reporter* 29, no. 39 (September 10, 1993): 24.

[141] Jim Ternier and Marie-Louise Ternier-Gommers, "Speaking up for Natural Family Planning," *National Catholic Reporter* 40, no. 15 (February 13, 2004): 19.

[142] Cannon, 24.

[143] Janet Claussen, "My Argument with Natural Family Planning," *America* 172, no. 4 (Feb 1995): 20-22.

could not make [NFP] work, how can it be sold as a means of family planning?"[144] She writes of anger about doctors who could not help her make a method work that she was convinced could work, drug companies who can do so well at producing drugs and means to prevent pregnancy but do nothing to provide a way to identify ovulation, and the Church, which did not offer the support or a network necessary to help her find the resources she needed.[145]

Claussen's grievances are relevant. Both the medical community and the Church have failed to help her effectively employ a method she knows can be successful. How can it work so well for thousands of poor and uneducated in India but not for her? Perhaps it has something to do with a lack of adequate training due to self-teaching, insufficient support from teachers and organizations specializing in NFP, and the absence of competent medical assistance. Maybe she just experienced one of the few in a thousand pregnancies per year that are naturally a part of the failure rate of any means of family planning. In any case, Claussen is correct that it may be difficult to find experienced educators in a couple's local area, though groups like CCL offer programs and support via internet and telephone. Even couples practicing NFP who are largely satisfied with its results have complained about a lack of support in the method. One survey of NFP respondents revealed:

> [Respondents] wished that NFP was better respected by the medical community, the general public, and the clergy. Some felt ridiculed by those inside and outside the church, including family members, for following "outdated" church teachings. Others said they were afraid to admit their NFP use, even to heath care providers, because it seemed that NFP was not considered a "real" form of [family planning].[146]

A 2009 article from the *Journal of the American Board of Family Medicine* concurs with the value of NFP as an option for family

---

[144] Ibid., 22.
[145] Ibid.
[146] VandeVusse et al., 175.

planning as well as the ignorance among medical professionals and suggests that the 1-3% of American women using such methods may increase significantly with greater support and education, especially considering that internationally "as many as 20% of married women in other countries use one of these methods."[147] Drs. Pallone and Bergus report:

> Although these methods have not gained wide use, modern FABMs [fertility awareness-based methods, a.k.a. NFP] can be mastered by most motivated couples. Physicians' and other medical personnel's limited knowledge of and experience with the methods inhibit broader use. Physicians should offer FABMs as a reasonable choice for family planning because there are no absolute contraindications. A woman's informed decision to use such methods should be supported with accurate information and referral to a certified provider.[148]

Any solution to the current predicament must be comprehensive to be successful. However, it will involve one mind at a time—one mind being open to the issue, honestly exploring it, and considering or reconsidering the Church's challenging but efficacious and fruitful teaching on marriage, family, and sexuality. In the meantime, testimonies like the following will continue to encourage those at work promoting the Church's teaching, and will elicit interest from those yet to discover it. One wife and mother shares her story:

> I learned...that my fertility is a sign of health. I learned that by simply observing and charting my fertility signals—a process that takes just [minutes] each day—I could tell whether or not I was in a fertile phase of my cycle. My husband and I could identify the fertile phase and time our marital relations

---

[147] Stephen R. Pallone and George R. Bergus, "Fertility Awareness-Based Methods: Another Option for Family Planning," *Journal of the American Board of Family Medicine* 22 (2009): 147-149.

[148] Ibid., 154.

accordingly. I could be free of possibly-unsafe artificial hormones, including their unwanted side effects like weight gain and irritability. I could enjoy our sex life free of unaesthetic and inconvenient barrier methods. And I could grow to appreciate my body the way God made it—with the blessing of fertility, not the "curse."

Most importantly, I learned that marriage is actually a sacrament, and that children are a blessing of marriage. … Through the practice of NFP, I have become more comfortable with my own body and have grown to appreciate its healthy processes. We have been able to grow in our ability to communicate with each other about fertility and sexuality and have been able to overcome shame and embarrassment related to these subjects that had troubled me earlier on. Natural family planning has enhanced our health, our marriage, our family and our faith.[149]

The woman quoted here was not a Catholic but more of an agnostic at the time of the quote. After several years of NFP experience, she entered the Catholic Church, and her husband followed her four years later—the right kind of NFP can be an agent of evangelization. Even though the NFP movement has become strong in a small circle within the Church and American society, it is going to take much more for it to overflow its current banks and flood our Church and world with its benefits to provide something better for our families, culture, and Church.

Differences between NFP and Contraception

Before closing our discussion of NFP and moving on to consider contraceptives, we must explore a vital point. Astute observers will likely ask: if couples using contraceptives are trying to prevent pregnancy, and couples using NFP are trying to avoid pregnancy, are they not essentially doing the same thing and thus morally equal? The answer lies in the difference between trying to *prevent* and trying to *avoid*. The same result can be sought, but this

---

[149] Kippley and Kippley, *The Complete Approach*, 126.

does not imply all means of obtaining that end are all morally equal. Lawler, Boyle, and May suggest the difference is as simple as a hungry person obtaining food by working for it or by stealing it.[150] Yet opponents persist, and the responses to this question go deeper, as there are many approaches taken by traditionalists to bring the differences to light.

One answer to this issue stems from the New Natural Law Theory (NNLT) perspective.[151] Theologians such as John Finnis and Joseph Boyle maintain that by using contraception, a couple chooses something contrary to a good of marriage—that of procreation—which is morally evil.[152] NFP is different, maintains Boyle, because, "This policy involves no intention to prevent an act of intercourse from being procreative. Refraining from intercourse is not contraceptive intercourse, it is not intercourse at all."[153] The essential difference for NNLT is that contraception is *violating* one of the essential elements of the sexual act (i.e. procreation), while the NFP couple respects all elements of the sexual act by choosing not to violate anything through periodic abstinence.

NNLT traditionalists also draw the distinction between contraception and NFP based on an anti-life intent. Grisez, Boyle, Finnis, and May explain that using contraceptives inherently involves making a choice not to have an additional child by choosing to act *against* the possibility of procreation. It is a choice to *prevent* a pregnancy, and this involves anti-life intent, which they consider immoral.[154] Non-contraceptive NFP also involves a choice not to have an additional child, but it accomplishes this by making an

---

[150] Ronald Lawler, Joseph Boyle Jr., and William E. May, *Catholic Sexual Ethics: A Summary, Explanation, & Defense*, 2nd ed. (Huntington, Indiana: Our Sunday Visitor, 1998), 160.

[151] See Chapter 6 for more information on New Natural Law Theory and its context.

[152] John M. Finnis, "Personal Integrity, Sexual Morality and Responsible Parenthood," in *Why Humanae Vitae Was Right: A Reader*, ed. Janet E. Smith (San Francisco: Ignatius Press, 1993), 181; Joseph M. Boyle, "Contraception and Natural Family Planning," in *Why Humanae Vitae Was Right: A Reader*, ed. Janet E. Smith (San Francisco: Ignatius Press, 1993), 410.

[153] Boyle, 415.

[154] Germain Grisez et al., "NFP: Not Contralife," In *Readings in Moral Theology No. 8: Dialogue about Catholic Sexual Teaching*, ed. Charles E. Curran and Richard A. McCormick (New York: Paulist Press, 1993), 131.

entirely different choice in which the couple chooses *not to perform any action by which an additional child might come into existence.*[155] By choosing not to put processes in motion that could lead to a pregnancy, NFP couples do not have an anti-life intent. Elsewhere they state that contraception "is a choice *to do something*, with the intent that the baby not be, as a means to a further end," while NFP, "is a choice *not to do something*—namely, not to engage in possibly fertile sexual intercourse."[156] Joseph Boyle suggests that when a couple knows they are incapable of getting pregnant they cannot have a contra-life intent, so they can have intercourse in order to promote and foster other goods of marriage (like the unitive good) while dealing no violence to the procreative good.[157]

Philosopher Martin Rhonheimer affirms the difference between periodic abstinence and contraception in the following: "The contraceptive choice involves a volition to act in a way that *prevents* sexual intercourse from being fertile; it is a choice to *prevent* conception where it is foreseen to occur. The choice of periodic continence, on the other hand, does not involve the volition of preventing naturally fertile acts from being fertile; instead it *avoids* conception by *abstaining* from those acts that are foreseen to bring it about."[158]

A couple of analogies may be helpful in understanding the distinction drawn by advocates of the Church's teaching. Mary Rosera Joyce compares contraception and NFP to speaking truth. She explains:

> Just as there are times when the truth should not be spoken, there are times when children should not be conceived. But the act of refraining from speaking differs essentially from the act of internally separating speech from its power truthfully to express and generate judgments in the mind of another. Similarly,

---

[155] Ibid.
[156] Ibid., 128.
[157] Boyle, 416-417.
[158] Martin Rhonheimer, *Ethics of Procreation and the Defense of Human Life: Contraception, Artificial Fertilization, and Abortion*, ed. William F. Murphy Jr. (Washington D.C.: Catholic University of America Press, 2010), 51.

51

the act of refraining from coital activity differs essentially from the act of internally separating coital union from its generative power.[159]

Lawler, Boyle, and May illustrate the differences in an example where contraception is compared to euthanasia, directly taking an innocent life for the purposes of ending a painful situation, while NFP is compared to the "withholding of extraordinary treatments."[160] In other words, there is a serious moral difference between allowing a patient to die and putting her to death, one that parallels the difference between NFP and contraception.

The other strong branch of traditionalism that takes up this question is the personalist school. Dietrich von Hildebrand posits, "The sin consists in this alone: the sundering by man of what God has joined together—the *artificial, active* severing of the mystery of bodily union from the creative act to which it is bound at the time."[161] For von Hildebrand, the problem with contraception separating the unitive and procreative elements of intercourse is its offensiveness to God and his design of human fertility. By utilizing such an "artificial intervention," a couple employing contraceptives commit a "sin of presumptuously exceeding the creatural rights of man."[162] While arguing from a different viewpoint, von Hildebrand uses essentially the same example as Lawler, Boyle, and May, though he likely used it first. Yet in his analogy the appeal to God's role is emphasized as he explains:

> I may very well wish (and pray) that an incurably sick and extremely suffering man would die. I may abstain from artificially prolonging his life for a matter of hours or days. But I am not allowed to kill him! There is an abyss between desiring someone's

---

[159] Mary Rosera Joyce, "The Meaning of Contraception," in *Why Humanae Vitae Was Right: A Reader*, ed. Janet E. Smith (San Francisco: Ignatius Press, 1993), 110.

[160] Lawler, Boyle, and May, 154.

[161] Dietrich von Hildebrand, "The Encyclical *Humanae Vitae*: A Sign of Contradiction," in *Why Humanae Vitae Was Right: A Reader*, ed. Janet E. Smith (San Francisco: Ignatius Press, 1993), 81.

[162] Ibid.

death and euthanasia. In both cases the *intention* is the same: out of sympathy I desire that he be delivered from suffering. But in the one case I do nothing that might prolong his suffering, whereas in the other I actively intervene and arrogate to myself a right over life and death that belongs to God alone.[163]

Furthermore, we must address the issue of what is truly "open" to life. Supporters of contraception might argue that the NFP couple is no more open to life than a contracepting couple. Perhaps too it is possible for a contracepting couple to be open to life in the sense that if their contraceptives failed, they would welcome that newly conceived life without seeking an abortion. Janet Smith suggests that the use of the term "open" here is too narrow: "'Open' does not mean wanting a child *now*; it means having done nothing to *close out* the possibility of having children."[164] Smith further explains that HV is not speaking about "openness" in the subjective sense, which people often read into the document, but rather in an objective sense—all marital intercourse must remain subjectively *and* objectively open to life, but using contraceptives is not objectively open.[165] Thus the contracepting couple who thinks they are open to life because they would not abort a baby accidentally conceived are only *subjectively* open to life, as all people by virtue of human dignity are called to be—direct abortion is intrinsically evil. However, such a couple is *objectively* closed to life by employing means that thwart their fertility from functioning.

We must also explore the use of the term "natural." Some may suggest that coitus interruptus (withdrawal) is at least equally natural to NFP, because it does not involve any artificial chemicals or devices. While the temperature and mucus checking combined with daily charting of the sympto-thermal NFP method may seem at least as unnatural as using a contraceptive, like OCPs, traditionalists

---

163 Ibid.

164 Janet E. Smith, "Pope John Paul II and *Humanae Vitae*," in *Why Humanae Vitae Was Right: A Reader*, ed. Janet E. Smith (San Francisco: Ignatius Press, 1993), 245.

165 Janet E. Smith, *Humanae Vitae: A Generation Later* (Washington D.C.: Catholic University of America Press, 1991), 79.

maintain that an equivocation on the term "natural" exists here.[166] Ashley, Deblois, and O'Rourke explain that "natural," in this sense, refers to whether or not the processes of nature are violated.[167] In this case, contraceptives work against "natural fertility," while NFP participates with and "perfects nature" in conformity with couples' "human intelligence and freedom."[168] Janet Smith provides examples like "eyeglasses and penicillin," which work with human nature to assist it in its natural function, while contraceptives inherently work against a healthy woman's natural fertility, and are thereby "unnatural," in the philosophical sense.[169] It is helpful to recognize in this instance that fertility is the normal and natural function of a woman's body. It is not the fertile woman whose body needs correction in terms of being natural; it is the infertile that are in need of correction for the body to function normally. In our culture this truth is frequently inverted.

Considering all of the approaches to this question of the differences between NFP and contraception, Janet Smith may provide the most concise explanation in the following:

> (a) There is nothing wrong with wanting, for good reasons, to limit one's family size and (b) there is nothing wrong with married couples either having sex or not having sex; thus, since it is not wrong to want to limit your family size and there is nothing wrong with not having sex, it follows quite smoothly that there is nothing wrong with not having sex because you want to limit your family size.[170]

Smith also offers an analogy to help clarify the issue. She suggests that the purpose of human digestive organs is to draw

---

[166] James Arraj, *Is there a Solution to the Catholic Debate on Contraception?* (Chiloquin, OR: Inner Growth Books, 1989), 34, 42, 65; Janet E. Smith, *A Generation Later*, 121; Benedict M. Ashley, Jean Deblois, and Kevin D. O'Rourke, *Health Care Ethics: A Catholic Theological Analysis*, 5th ed. (Washington D.C.: Georgetown University Press, 2006), 74.

[167] Ashley, Deblois, and O'Rourke, 74.

[168] Ibid.

[169] Janet E. Smith, *A Generation Later*, 121.

[170] Janet E. Smith, "Pope John Paul II," 244.

nutrition from food, while the activity of eating carries with it side-effects like the pleasure of eating and the bonding experienced by eating with others.[171] Now, there is a dramatic difference between a woman who is incapable of digesting food as efficiently as she ought and another woman who "deliberately tampers with her digestive system so that she might enjoy the sensation of eating without achieving the end of nutrition."[172]

This example might work even better if it were the natural case that humans processed food best in the morning and considerably less effectively in the evening. The difference is evident between one woman who determines with her intellect that this is not a good time to add calories to her diet, so she refrains from eating in the morning but enjoys dinner with some friends in the evening, and another woman who thwarts the natural processes of digestion by eating in the morning to bond with others and enjoy the pleasure of eating, yet subsequently induces vomiting. Our culture understands the latter to be an eating disorder—a disharmony with nature and unhealthy psychological condition—yet most people have not drawn the logical connection to contraception.

It may also help to consider some critiques of what we have been exploring. Gareth Moore offers a couple of situations worth considering from a position supportive of contraceptives. He suggests that NFP couples are not avoiding "doing anything" any more than a person who does not stand up as he is supposed to when an important dignitary enters the room is doing nothing—both are *doing something* even in their non-action.[173] The deficiency in this analogy is that one is *doing something* through non-action by not standing for the dignitary only if they have an *obligation* to do so. However, as both revisionists and traditionalists maintain, there may be times in which couples have serious reasons not to have children. Thus, couples may not have an obligation to "stand," as this analogy plays out.

Moore presents a second analogy to discredit the traditionalist position. He compares intercourse to going for a daily walk, yet

---

[171] Janet E. Smith, *A Generation Later*, 80-81.
[172] Ibid.
[173] Gareth Moore, *The Body in Context: Sex and Catholicism* (New York: Continuum, 1992), 165.

explains that he refrains from walking on a particular day of the week because he knows someone will ask him to make a donation to a charity.[174] He explains, "The charity is a good one, so I ought to give money to it if I can; but I don't want to. I also don't want to have to refuse the collector when she asks me, because it embarrasses me and makes me feel guilty. So I just stay in. ... Let us...assume...that my motives for not wanting to give are good ones."[175] Moore suggests that there would neither be anything wrong with going for a walk and refusing to donate (contraception), nor refraining from walking and staying home on a particular day (periodic abstinence), so both are morally equivalent.[176] The problem with this analogy is that giving to a charity is not inherently linked by virtue of the action itself to walking, which is entirely different from sexual intercourse being inherently linked to procreation. By going for a walk the man has no obligation to give a donation to this particular charity. Conversely, contraception involves preventing the possibility of an action from having the results inherently connected with conducting the action. Furthermore, the not giving to charity, which is supposed to relate to contraception, is a refusal to do something as opposed to the actually doing something involved with contraception. Moore's analogies are more applicable in a situation where a couple is utilizing NFP's effectiveness at preventing conception without serious or sufficient reasons—a topic that will be discussed subsequently.

For Moore's analogy to function accurately, adjustments must be made. For instance, the man would have to go up to the woman asking for a donation and feign a donation without really making any contribution for it to correlate to contraception. He could write out a check but have it cancelled by his bank before it is redeemed by the charity, or he could write out an old check from a closed account. In this way he could experience multiple benefits from the encounter with the woman (e.g. impress her or others, appear charitable, have an opportunity to meet her), while thwarting the inherently connected element of truly making a donation. He has done nothing by going on the walk to suggest that he is interested in making a donation, and he is under no obligation to do so. If we consider the

---

[174] Ibid., 177.
[175] Ibid.
[176] Ibid.

56

"language of the body," the difference is even more apparent. The "contracepting" man's action pretends a donation while intentionally preventing that action from being fruitful. The counterexample of Moore's analogy provided here further highlights the differences between NFP and contraception.

As recently as 2008, Lawrence Masek has written a defense of the consistency in the Church's teaching in terms of the difference between NFP and contraception that he believes is more accurately associated with the contraception versus NFP issue than other analogies previously published. He begins his contribution by explaining what must be present in a comparison analogy to function accurately and effectively: "(1) it must compare contraception to an action that is immoral because the agent acts against a certain good, and (2) it must compare periodic abstinence to a practice that is morally permissible even though the agent intends to avoid causing that same good."[177]

Masek's analogy involves a doctor at a prison hospital who regularly donates his rare O-negative blood to the prison hospital bank.[178] A prisoner at the hospital, also with O-negative blood, is receiving chemotherapy treatments for cancer and requires blood transfusions coming from the doctor—a process that costs the hospital so much that its ability to help other patients is diminished, yet must be continued by law.[179] However, if the prison hospital can no longer effectively provide care to the patient—should the chemotherapy or transfusions prove ineffective or impossible—it will be allowed to transfer him to another hospital, but this could have negative effects on the patient's health and successful treatment.[180]

Two options are available to the doctor. First, "The doctor decides to continue donating at the prison, but he injects a protein that inhibits chemotherapy into his blood after donating."[181] Second, "the doctor drives to another blood bank so that his blood will not

---

[177] Lawrence Masek, "Improving the Analogies in Contralife Arguments: The Consistency of Catholic Teachings about Regulating Births," *Heythrop Journal* 49, no. 3 (May 2008): 442.

[178] Ibid., 448.

[179] Ibid.

[180] Ibid.

[181] Ibid.

be used by the prisoner but will be used for other good purposes."[182] Masek then moves on to explain why the latter choice is morally permissible, while the former is not: "Doctors have an obligation to do no harm," yet, "the principle that doctors may not *act against* a patient's health does not mean that doctors have an obligation to do whatever they can *to promote* a patient's health."[183] Masek offers as an example the fact that there is nothing immoral with doctors taking time for rest, relaxation, and leisure when they could be working and researching to improve medicine and heal patients. [184] He notes, "Instead of *creating an obstacle* to the chemotherapy, the doctor *avoids providing assistance* to this chemotherapy."[185] In essence, the difference between contraception and methods of NFP, used appropriately, is that while periodic abstinence is "*non*procreative," contraceptives are "*anti*procreative" in the objective sense.[186]

Ecological Breastfeeding or the Lactational Amenorrhea Method

Before closing our discussion of NFP, a final topic deserves attention. Complementary to the systematic forms of NFP we have considered, and even more "natural," is the infertility which follows childbirth as maintained through breastfeeding. This is known in medical circles as the Lactational Amenorrhea Method, and was coined among Catholic NFP circles as Ecological Breastfeeding by Sheila Kippley. As a natural consequence of pre-modern infant nutrition the way mothers' bodies were built to do it, one might say it is baby spacing as God built it into our bodies. For millennia, it has been capable of spacing babies without mothers even being conscious of it. Bible scholars suggest it was typical to wean a child only after nursing for a few years, and 2 Maccabees 7:27 mentions that a mother nursed for three years. When utilized intentionally, it is natural family planning (note not capitalized) in its most fundamental and natural form.

---

182 Ibid.
183 Ibid., 448-449.
184 Ibid.
185 Ibid.
186 Howard P. Kainz, *Natural Law: An Introduction and Re-examination* (Chicago: Open Court, 2004), 121.

Breastfeeding delaying the return of fertility in a mother's body is brought about as a result of the "stress" of rearing the newborn. Even in a non-sexually active woman's cycle, stress brought on either emotionally or physically can postpone or inhibit ovulation. This is seen, for example, in athletes or during stressful times like when a college girl is experiencing the pressure of final exams. Following birth, continuous breastfeeding generates hormones in a mother's body which keep her fertility from resuming its cycles. Nursing a little baby on demand and exclusively communicates to her body that now is not the time for another baby.

Unfortunately, many health care professionals are ignorant of (or inaccurately deny) the ability of a woman's body to naturally space the births of children. It is sometimes even scoffed off as an "old wives' tale." Nonetheless, it is being better understood. Even Planned Parenthood recognizes that it is an "effective, safe, convenient, and free" method useful up to six months after birth.[187] In reality, it is useful for even longer, but it is during this period in which it has the highest level of effectiveness—up to 99%.[188] Sheila Kippley explains that this natural post-birth infertility (amenorrhea) typically lasts 12-24 months or more when properly utilized.[189] More specifically its effectiveness is 93-99% in the first 6 months postpartum, 56% at one year, and 33% at 18 months.[190]

Breastfeeding is only effective at postponing ovulation if done in the traditional, even Biblical, style rather than the Westernized breastfeeding common today. Kippley notes, "This norm of extended amenorrhea is so unusual in North America and most European cultures that I would like to repeat clearly: for a *nursing* mother to go one year, two years, three years, or even longer without any menstrual cycles is *normal*, even if not average."[191] To achieve this, Sheila Kippley organized "Seven Standards" to follow. She lists them as follows:

---

187 Planned Parenthood, "Breastfeeding as Birth Control," http://www.planned
   parenthood.org/health-info/birth-control/breastfeeding (accessed December
   15, 2014).
188 Ibid.
189 Sheila Kippley, *Breastfeeding and Catholic Motherhood: God's Plan for You & Your
   Baby* (Manchester, NH: Sophia Institute Press, 59.
190 Ibid., 63.
191 Ibid., 59.

1. Exclusively breastfeed for the first six months of life. 2. Pacify your baby at your breasts. 3. Don't use bottles and pacifiers. This includes not using pumps. 4. Sleep with your baby for night feedings. 5. Sleep with your baby for a daily-nap feeding. 6. Nurse frequently day and night, and avoid strict schedules. 7. Avoid any practice that restricts nursing or separates you from your baby.[192]

These standards are used for the first six months, at which time the first standard may be removed and food introduced.[193] Kippley sees this natural baby-spacing means as natural, safe, effective, health-promoting, spiritually enriching, enhances family bonding, encouraged by Catholic teaching, Biblical, and rooted in God's plan for motherhood.

---

[192] Ibid., 61.
[193] Ibid.

Chapter 2
Contraception

While the decades following HV have shown considerable advantages for methods of NFP, they have revealed major problems with contraceptives, especially hormonal contraceptives like OCPs. In order to reach a fuller appreciation for the effects of the Church's teaching beyond the confines of the Church and theology, it is necessary to consider the ramifications of contraception in our world:

> Contraception is the basis of several destabilizing developments in our culture over the past 40 years, including sex before marriage, general promiscuity, out-of-wedlock pregnancy, abortion, illegitimacy, adultery and divorce. The total separation of sex from children also leads to human manipulations, such as human cloning and embryonic stem cell research. "Give up" on this issue? Only if we are prepared to live with such de-stabilizing results, past present and future.[1]

Of primary concern are hormonal contraceptives such as OCPs, because "About 70 percent of women in their reproductive years use the Pill."[2] Secretary of the United States Department of Health and Human Services, Kathleen Sebelius, stated in 2012 that "birth control ... is the most commonly taken drug in America by young and middle-aged women."[3] The fallout from contraception, and the widespread blindness to its negative effects, is only further compounded by its ubiquity.

---

[1] Teresa Wagner, "Contraception, Natural Family Planning, and Women," In *Integrating Faith and Science Through Natural Family Planning*, ed. Richard J. Fehring and Theresa Notare (Milwaukee: Marquette UP, 2004), 49.

[2] Gregory K. Popcak, "A Natural Argument for NFP," *Family Foundations* vol. 38 no. 2 (September/October 2011), 30.

[3] Devin Dwyer, "Obama Rejects Contraception Exemption for Catholic Hospitals, Schools," *ABC News* (January 20, 2012), http://abcnews.go.com/blogs/politics/2012/01/obama-rejects-contraception-exemption-for-catholic-hospitals-schools/ (accessed April 5, 2012).

Health Concerns

Since HV in 1968, numerous health problems have been identified as associated with contraceptives, especially hormonal/chemical contraceptives like OCPs, Depo-Provera, and Norplant. In his critique of St. John Paul II's *Theology of the Body* (TOB), theologian Luke Timothy Johnson (typically resistant to the Church's teaching against contraceptives) states, "I will speak of 'artificial birth control' only in terms of using a condom, diaphragm, or other mechanical device, mainly because I have considerable unease concerning chemical interventions and their implications for women's long-term health."[4] He has good reason for concern. OCPs, for example, have a laundry list of side-effects and disadvantages as listed by Clinical Reference Systems' Pediatric Advisor:[5]

- Irregular menstrual bleeding or spotting for the first few months after you start birth control pills
- Dizziness
- Nausea and vomiting
- Swelling of your hands or ankles
- Pain, swelling, or tenderness in the abdomen
- Breast swelling or tenderness
- [Increased] appetite and weight gain
- Trouble sleeping, weakness, lack of energy, fatigue, or depression
- Headaches
- Vaginal infection (usually yeast)
- Allergic reaction, rash, itching
- Amenorrhea (absence of menstrual period)
- Less interest in sex
- Changes in hair growth patterns
- Vision or contact lens problems
- Acne

---

[4] Luke Timothy Johnson, "A Disembodied 'Theology of the Body'." *Commonweal* 128, no. 2 (Jan 2001): 7 of 9.

[5] "Birth Control Pills (Oral Contraceptives)," *CRS – Pediatric Advisor* (January 1, 2009).

- Yellowing of the skin or whites of the eyes (jaundice)
- Smoking increases the risk of serious side effects, such as heart attack, stroke, and blood clots
- Other risks of taking birth control pills include cataracts, gallstones, and non-cancerous liver tumors

A 2010 study indicated, "57 percent of women are unhappy with the Pill due to side effects that include depression and other mood changes, nausea, decreased libido, or in rare instances, blood clots or stroke," as well as typical use failure rates of 8.7%.[6] Interestingly, women may not even know they are experiencing side-effects, as some have only discovered problems after ceasing to take OCPs and felt improvements from what they previously thought was normal.[7] The knowledge of such risks was not as prevalent in the 60s and 70s, but by the 1980s such problems became well-documented.

Furthermore, hormonal/chemical contraceptives have been linked with multiple types of cancers. Dr. Chris Kahlenborn's *Breast Cancer: Its Link to Abortion and the Birth Control Pill* explains that while OCPs reduce the rates of both uterine and ovarian cancers, they increase the risk of cervical, liver, and most importantly breast cancer—the latter being more common than the other four combined for women in the U.S.[8] As early as 1972 OCPs were found to cause breast cancer in rhesus monkeys, which very rarely have been known to develop breast cancer, and later in beagles and rodents.[9] Studies in the 1990s have shown that women who take OCPs prior to their first full-term pregnancy are subject to a 40% greater risk (one study suggested risk up to 88% greater) of developing breast cancer, depending somewhat upon length of usage.[10]

Doctors and pharmaceutical companies have ignored the correlation between hormonal contraceptives and breast cancer.

---

[6] Popcak, 30.

[7] Sam Torode and Bethany Torode, *Open Embrace: A Protestant Couple Rethinks Contraception* (Grand Rapids: Wm. B. Eerdmans Publishing Co., 2002), 51-53.

[8] Chris Kahlenborn, *Breast Cancer: Its Link to Abortion and the Birth Control Pill* (New Hope, KY: One More Soul, 2000), 37-38.

[9] Ibid., 29.

[10] Ibid., 30-31, 33.

Doubters of the contraceptive-breast cancer link prefer studies that obscure the connection.[11] Kahlenborn discusses the methodological deficiencies in these studies, most notably the fact that they do not consider the differences between women who have and have not already had one child. He explains, "The breast undergoes a maturing process throughout a woman's first pregnancy," so this makes women who have not had their first full-term pregnancy especially at risk to OCPs causing breast cancer.[12] Considering this fact, it is not difficult to understand why the longer a woman is on OCPs, and the earlier she begins to use them, the greater her risk of developing breast cancer, as Kahlenborn shows.[13]

More recent studies have continued to bring the connection between OCPs and breast cancer to light. For example, a press release from the World Health Organization in 2005 recognized OCPs as carcinogenic and holds that they increase the likelihood of breast cancer, especially for "current and recent users."[14] The press release notes that OCPs have been known to be carcinogenic for some time; however, only recently have they been associated with greater risk of breast cancer, specifically.[15] Similarly, a 2006 article in *Mayo Clinic Proceedings* by Kahlenborn et al. explains that understanding of the connection between breast cancer and OCPs "has varied within the medical literature over time," yet "more recent studies have noted an increase in risk among [OCP] users, especially among women who took them before a first full-term pregnancy."[16] The article suggests women in recent decades are using OCPs younger in life, for longer periods of time, and prior to the first full-term pregnancy, so newer studies are picking up an increase in OCP-

---

[11] Ibid., 31.
[12] Ibid., 32.
[13] Ibid., 37.
[14] World Health Organization, "IARC Monographs Programme Finds Combined Estrogen-Progestogen Contraceptives and Menopausal Therapy are Carcinogenic to Humans," *International Agency for Research on Cancer* Press Release 167 (29 July 2005).
[15] Ibid.
[16] Chris Kahlenborn et al., "Oral Contraceptive Use as a Risk Factor for Premenopausal Breast Cancer: A Meta-analysis," *Mayo Clinic Proceedings* 81, no. 10 (October 2006): 1290.

related breast cancer cases.[17] These findings occur in the context of increased incidence of breast cancer in America: "2 in 15 American women are expected to develop breast cancer in their lifetime," and, "Breast cancer is the leading cause of cancer in women worldwide and the most common cause of cancer death in US women aged 20-59."[18]

Other hormonal contraceptives are dangerous as well. By 2000, "low dose" progestin options like the "minipill" and Depo-Provera showed increased risk of breast cancer. An Oxford study indicated a 19% increased risk for users who took the minipill for more than four years; however, this study did not distinguish ages of women, nor women who took it prior to their first full-term pregnancy, which is likely to be a much higher risk group.[19] Depo-Provera seems much worse. A WHO study of women taking the active ingredient in Depo-Provera shots for 24-36 months prior to age 25, "had a 310% *statistically significant risk* of getting breast cancer."[20]

OCPs are also linked to increased risk of cervical cancer and liver cancer. According to a WHO study, *short-term* use of OCPs did not seem to increase the risk of liver cancer; however, two other studies have suggested that *long-term* use of OCPs had negative results: a 290% increased risk for women on OCPs for at least 5 years and a 340% increased risk for women on OCPs for at least 8 years.[21] Several more studies have been done in regards to cervical cancer. Kahlenborn explains, "If one takes into account the *relative contribution* of each of these studies that examined the risk of OCP use in women under the age of 20 and the corresponding increased risk of cervical cancer, one would find an 80.01% increased risk."[22]

Opponents may suggest that infection by the Human Papilloma Virus (HPV) may be directly to blame for the increases in cervical cancer, while OCPs are indirectly related as they make promiscuity less reproductively "risky." If this were true, one could avoid the cervical cancer risk with the HPV vaccine, as was heavily promoted

---

[17] Ibid.
[18] Ibid.
[19] Kahlenborn, *Breast Cancer*, 39.
[20] Ibid., 38.
[21] Ibid., 219-220.
[22] Ibid., 216.

by the "One Less" media ad campaign when the vaccine was released. However, Kahlenborn explains that one large study of women with cervical cancer "noted that OCP use increased the risk for cervical cancer although the study controlled for the variable of HPV status," and a WHO study "believed that HPV and OCP use were not confounding variables because they found no evidence of confounding in those variables closely related to HPV such as anal or genital warts."[23] In addition, "One animal study and one human study have suggested that OCPs actually accelerate or enhance the process of cervical carcinogenesis in the woman who is already infected with HPV," thus increasing her chances of developing cervical cancer.[24]

Finally, the experience of couples over the decades has provided testimony of the health problems related to contraceptives. One Catholic wife and mother who was a user of a variety of contraceptives throughout the years and eventually discovered and embraced NFP explains:

> Yes, I was alive and fertile in 1968. I was 19 and *knew* the pill was a gift from God and *Humanae Vitae* was a real crock. The pill was going to eliminate teenage pregnancy, marital disharmony and world population problems, bring a new era, etc.
>
> By my five-year reunion (high school), those of us who had been so confident about contraception had gone from euphoria to anger. Nothing seemed to work. I'd been on the pill less than two years before I'd quit. The pill depressed us. Or scared us (especially those of us who were smokers) because of the "stroke" factor. I didn't want to keep taking it year after year, or on-again, off-again after I broke up with my college lover. So I decided to live a minimally healthy life-style and quit both smoking and oral contraceptives.
>
> The "safer" IUD (copper-T) gave me cramps and heavy periods. I was lucky. A friend of mine got such a ghastly infection from her IUD she lost her uterus,

---

[23] Ibid., 215.
[24] Ibid.

tubes, ovaries—the works. The woman was devastated. She felt like a gutted shell. Now they've taken them all off the market.

I tried the diaphragm. Hard to keep motivated on that one. … I felt wadded up with junk, inwardly disgusted. I wanted to be delectable, like a Haagen Dazs ice cream cone; instead, I was a spermicidal sump. …

By the 10th high school reunion, my friends were still fiddling with this method and that, they'd had abortions, and/or their marriages were falling apart. Mine almost did.[25]

Contraception and Abortion

Studies of contraceptives have confirmed a great concern of Catholic moralists in the 1960s—many versions of OCPs and other contraceptives act as abortifacients. The Majority Report from the papal commission (endorsing contraceptive use), early revisionists, and dissenters from HV did not approve of abortion or anything that could cause an early abortion. For example, in 1969 Sidney Callahan wrote, "With the demythologization of sex, tolerance of the effective mechanical and chemical contraceptives (which, of course, do not attack new life) can be integrated in a new synthesis which incorporates the best of the old values with the best of the new."[26] When the IUD was first believed to operate as an abortifacient, it was refused support by many Christians. The abortifacient function of OCPs, however, was not well known by many early revisionists, though the information was available by 1965, as reported in John T. Noonan's classic historical text, *Contraception*.[27] It is remarkable that so many proponents of changing Church teaching on OCPs failed to recognize OCPs' abortifacient potential. Why did members of the

---

[25] Janet E. Smith, *Humanae Vitae: A Generation Later* (Washington D.C.: Catholic University of America Press, 1991), 126.

[26] Sidney Callahan, "Procreation and Control," in *The Catholic Case for Contraception*, ed. Daniel Callahan (London: Macmillan, 1969), 61.

[27] John T. Noonan Jr., *Contraception: A History of Its Treatment by the Catholic Theologians and Canonists* (Cambridge: Harvard University Press, 1965), 461.

papal birth control commission or the early revisionists not recognize this point in a text as popular and significant as Noonan's? Had that information been well known in the 1950's and early 1960's, Catholics may have witnessed a very different set of events at Vatican II, and perhaps totally different circumstances for HV.

OCPs are not the only abortifacients. We may consider two categories of contraceptives, ones that are frequently or principally abortifacients and others that may also be abortifacients in some cases. The former category includes, "The intrauterine device (IUD), 'morning-after pills,' and 'emergency contraceptives,'" and in the latter Norplant, Depo-Provera, and OCPs (even more likely in the "minipill").[28] OCPs, for example, work by reducing the endometrial lining from the 5-13 mm necessary for the proper implantation of a fertilized embryo to about 1 mm.[29] Newly conceived babies are thus unable to implant, which causes them to pass out of the uterus to their death. While information is limited, some studies indicate ovulations by women correctly using OCPs may be as high as 1-5% of cycles.[30] In addition, women who do not take doses perfectly may be susceptible to higher frequency of ovulation, and OCPs with lower doses of hormones, thus reducing risks of side-effects, increase the risk of breakthrough ovulation and the attendant risk of abortion. With regard to the IUD, Wojcik notes, "Fertilization in cases of IUD use can occur normally, that is, usually in the Fallopian tube, practically every month," largely due to the fact that the IUD operates principally as an abortifacient by causing "continuous damage to the delicate endometrium."[31]

An objection that may be quickly raised is the debate over when life begins, as is found primarily in abortion legislation discussions. It is also clearly an important issue when considering contraceptives that work primarily or secondarily as an abortifacient. The official Church teaching in the CCC states, "Human life must be respected

---

[28] Torode and Torode, *Open Embrace*, 73, 75, 76.

[29] Ibid., 77.

[30] Agnieszka Tennant, "A Hard Pill to Swallow," *Christianity Today* 49, no. 11 (November 2005): 70-73.

[31] Elzbieta Wojcik, "Natural Regulation of Conception and Contraception," in *Why Humanae Vitae Was Right: A Reader*, ed. Janet E. Smith (San Francisco: Ignatius Press, 1993), 442.

and protected absolutely from the moment of conception."[32] Consequently, for a Catholic to withhold the necessary "respect and protection" due to any newly conceived human life also carries with it a rejection of Church teaching. In any case, scientific evidence has come to identify OCPs and other contraceptives as working abortifaciently, at least some of the time—a fact that cannot be ignored.

Contraceptives have also been inextricably linked with full-fledged, legalized abortion. Sociobiologist Lionel Tiger explains why he can state, "effective contraception *causes* abortion," in the following:

> It is impossible to overestimate the impact of the contraceptive pill on human arrangements. The most striking display of this is the baffling historical fact that *after* the pill became available in the mid-1960s, the pressure for liberal abortion intensified worldwide. This is remarkably, even profoundly, counterintuitive. It is also an implacable historical reality. Only *after* women could control their reproduction excellently did they need more and more safe abortions. The likely reason is crude but simple: If men were not certain the pregnancy was theirs because they couldn't know, then they abandoned the relationship and the unexpected pregnancy. It appears that women (and presumably their parents, friends, and some of their partners) then exerted political pressure to change the laws to make safe abortions available to them.[33]

Elsewhere Tiger notes, "Beginning in the 1970s, abortion was legalized in jurisdiction after jurisdiction. Even Italy, the home of its most powerful opponent, the Roman Catholic Church, legalized

---

[32] *Catechism of the Catholic Church: Modifications from the Editio Typica*, 2nd ed. (Washington, DC: United States Catholic Conference, Inc.—Libreria Editrice Vaticana, 1997), §2269.

[33] Lionel Tiger, *The Decline of Males: The First Look at an Unexpected New World for Men and Women*, (New York: St. Martin's Griffin, 1999), 27, 35-36.

abortion in 1978. This followed the fact that a large new class of otherwise responsible young women found themselves pregnant and unmarried."[34] As the subsequent section on social consequences will further discuss, all kinds of social problems erupted from the fact that effective contraceptives allowed men to take less and less responsibility for the consequences of their sexual endeavors than in decades past. Concomitant with this development is the increase in and demand for abortions.

This connection between abortion and contraceptives is even supported by the logic of the U.S. Supreme Court. D. Brian Scarnecchia points to a statement from the U.S. Supreme Court in their 1992 decision of *Planned Parenthood of Southeastern Pennsylvania v. Casey*, where *Roe v. Wade* was upheld:

> [F]or two decades of economic and social developments, people have organized intimate relationships and made choices that define their views of themselves and their places in society, in reliance on the availability of abortion in the event that contraception should fail. The ability of women to participate equally in the economic and social life of the Nation has been facilitated by their ability to control their reproductive lives.[35]

In essence, this statement suggests that we must continue to have abortion available, because people have come to count upon it as a *backup* to their contraceptive lifestyle. This is the result of separating the unitive and procreative dimensions of the marital act as HV warned; the consequences for the desire to engage in sex without procreation has fully come to fruition.

Provocatively, this situation is not as new to humankind as some in the twenty-first century might think. In an excavation of the ancient Philistine city of Ashkelon, as reported in a 2001 issue of National Geographic, archaeologists found "an oil-burning lamp

---

[34] Ibid., 53.
[35] D. Brian Scarnecchia, *Bioethics, Law, and Human Life Issues: A Catholic Perspective on Marriage, Family, Contraception, Abortion, Reproductive Technology, and Death and Dying* (Lanham: Scarecrow Press, 2010), 258.

70

embellished with an image of two bodies united in intercourse," as well as "other erotic artifacts" next to "a sewer filled with the skeletons of discarded infants, likely the progeny of temple prostitutes."[36] One couple concludes, "Then as now, a culture that worships sex without procreation will sacrifice its children."[37] Those opposed to abortion cannot continue to stand in a contradictory position of accepting contraception and opposing abortion. For other than the invincibly ignorant, this situation smacks of hypocrisy.

The key to the connection between contraception and abortion is simply the unlinking of the procreative and unitive meanings of the sexual act. Fr. Martin Rhonheimer suggests:

> The person who is in favor of contraception, at least in the presence of serious motives to avoid a pregnancy, *promotes* that mentality which leads to the spread of the practice of abortion (even if they themselves would never consider having an abortion. This mentality is based on the choice of wanting to carry out sexual acts no longer as procreatively responsible acts, and as such to be unwilling to modify one's sexual behavior so as to avoid procreative consequences. ... The basic problem is not that of the refusal to have children, but of wanting to have "sex" without children.[38]

Physicians' Perspectives

Albeit hardly newsworthy, shifting attitudes about methods of family planning have been found among doctors and medical professionals. Nonetheless, physicians fully supportive of Church teaching are still a considerable minority. A 2005 survey of physicians indicates 93% of all doctors, and 87.5% of self-identified Catholic doctors, are willing to "prescribe birth control to any adult patients

---

[36] Torode and Torode, *Open Embrace*, 65.

[37] Ibid.

[38] Martin Rhonheimer, *Ethics of Procreation and the Defense of Human Life: Contraception, Artificial Fertilization, and Abortion*, ed. William F. Murphy Jr. (Washington D.C.: Catholic University of America Press, 2010), 120, 122.

that request them and for whom they are medically appropriate," yet this number is believed to be slightly lower than past years.[39] That said, a shift in conformity with Church teaching is not something most doctors, even other Catholic doctors, easily approve. One Catholic doctor expressed his disapproval of other Catholic doctors not prescribing birth control while promoting NFP by stating, "They're spreading myth and they're misguiding patients."[40] Conferring with his *Physician's Desk Reference*, another Catholic doctor explains that the failure rate of OCPs is 1%, condom 14%, and periodic abstinence 25%, so he also does not approve of some Catholic doctors refusing to prescribe contraceptives.[41] As discussed in the previous chapter, the success rates quoted by the doctor from the *Physician's Desk Reference* are flawed. There are serious problems with the means used to determine effectiveness for "periodic abstinence" for such statistics that are not relevant or fair to particular methods of NFP, because they lump all types of "periodic abstinence" methods into one. Such methods spoil the statistics for modern NFP methods, many of which have individually been shown to be highly effective.

Despite resistance from multiple fronts, a shift among Catholic doctors is apparent. Many have come to decide they cannot in good conscience prescribe contraceptives, and they offer effective methods of NFP as an alternative. For some, their realization of the truth in the Catholic Church's perspective came through study of and experience with the dangers of contraceptives, whereas for others it came through the link between contraceptives and abortion, while still for others it came after recognizing the damage contraceptives wrought upon relationships and society. One such doctor shares:

> My use of contraceptive agents early in my practice reflected the training I had received in medical school and family practice residency. I was bothered some by prescribing these to unmarried, often teenage, females who were involved in

---

[39] Religion News Service, "Poll: Catholic Doctors Don't Always Follow Church Teaching," *National Catholic Reporter* 41, no. 27 (May 6, 2005), 11.
[40] Ibid.
[41] Ibid.

relationships that they eventually found to be hollow and self-destructive. During my years in the Air Force, I frequently saw sexually transmitted diseases in the large unmarried population, but I reasoned that through the use of contraceptives I was at least preventing pregnancies that they would likely abort. My prescribing practices certainly never positively influenced behavior.[42]

Another doctor notes, "In my residency we had a contraception clinic. Mothers would bring in their 14-year-old daughters and demand that they be put on the 'Pill.' How unfortunate for these girls that their mothers wouldn't dream of expecting chastity."[43] Still another doctor recalls an incident in which a mother brought in her barely 13-year-old daughter for an OCP prescription, because the girl had just begun dating; the situation made the doctor nauseous, and he had to excuse himself from the room.[44] Such experiences seem to be relatively common.

It will be efficacious to further consider the testimonies of individual doctors and hear from them the purposes and results of their change of convictions, so we will proceed by looking at a few examples. First, as a college student in the late 1960s and early 1970s, Dr. Mary Davenport shares that she was an atheist, had a live-in boyfriend, eventually subscribed to New Age beliefs, and wrote her application to medical school on her desire to "make contraception and abortion available to women."[45] Having performed a few

[42] Mark Povich, "Truth and Consequences," in *Physicians Healed: Personal, Inspiring, and Compelling Stories of Fifteen Courageous Physicians Who Do Not Prescribe Contraception*, ed. Cleta Hartman (Dayton: One More Soul, 1998), 103.

[43] Paddy "Jim" Baggot, "Mea Culpa, Mea Culpa, Mea Maxima Culpa," in *Physicians Healed: Personal, Inspiring, and Compelling Stories of Fifteen Courageous Physicians Who Do Not Prescribe Contraception*, ed. Cleta Hartman (Dayton: One More Soul, 1998), 13.

[44] George Jay, "Thank You, Jesus, for Healing Me," in *Physicians Healed: Personal, Inspiring, and Compelling Stories of Fifteen Courageous Physicians Who Do Not Prescribe Contraception*, ed. Cleta Hartman (Dayton: One More Soul, 1998), 56.

[45] Mary Davenport, "Never Too Late," in *Physicians Healed: Personal, Inspiring, and Compelling Stories of Fifteen Courageous Physicians Who Do Not Prescribe Contraception*, ed. Cleta Hartman (Dayton: One More Soul, 1998), 16-17, 19-20.

abortions herself and delivering aborted babies up to 33 weeks old, Davenport began to struggle with the ethics of abortion.[46] Into her thirties she stopped taking her OCP, which cleared up some long-term depression she had been experiencing, and also improved her energy and increased her desire to be a mother.[47] Having become a mother, and experiencing the benefits of being off of her OCP, Davenport also began to find herself disappointed with her worldview and increasingly attracted to Christianity. Eventually she learned about NFP, renounced contraceptives, and began promoting only NFP as a method of family planning. She relates, "The peace I have felt since becoming an NFP-only medical practitioner has been immeasurable. … I now am more sure that I am helping, not compromising, the women under my care."[48] Having been entirely on the other side of the issue, Davenport's testimony to what is truly life-giving, professionally and literally, is profound.

Second, Dr. John R. Hartman's experience with contraceptives and their effects on relationships and society strongly influenced his position and practice. Having been a Catholic since birth, including spending six years studying as a seminarian, Hartman nevertheless admits not having been one to support the Church's teaching on family planning in the years after HV.[49] While struggling with his stance on abortion and how to handle it as a medical student, Hartman also found himself wrestling with the issue of contraception—a struggle he managed to suspend for another several years. He noticed a certain inconsistency in the idea of contraception, as he reflects, "How could we as adults expect our teenagers to be chaste before marriage if right after marriage we were allowed to have no restrictions on our sexual activity? It seemed like the call to be chaste and in control of our passions was just being promoted to our younger members."[50] He further recalls experiencing several of his patient couples, ones he knew well and respected, threatening

---

[46] Ibid., 18-19.

[47] Ibid., 20-21.

[48] Ibid., 26.

[49] John Hartman, "The Stone Which the Builders Rejected," in *Physicians Healed: Personal, Inspiring, and Compelling Stories of Fifteen Courageous Physicians Who Do Not Prescribe Contraception*, ed. Cleta Hartman (Dayton: One More Soul, 1998), 41.

[50] Ibid., 49-50.

divorce.[51] Out of this experience he began to believe that a loss of respect early in the marriage was the cause of much greater turmoil later in the marriage, and he believed NFP, "with periodic abstinence and unity of spirit," fostered respect in marital relationships.[52] Over time, Hartman went from rejecting the Church's teaching, to gradually seeing its wisdom, to finally discovering its necessity. Hartman reflected on his conversion: "The Church's teaching on artificial birth control and on human sexuality was at one time the mark for me that the Church was out of touch with the modern world. Now it has become a profound source of wisdom not only for myself in my marriage relationship, but also foundational in my work as a doctor."[53]

Dr. Kathleen Raviele experienced a similar turnaround:

> As an obstetrician-gynecologist who has been on both sides of the fence in our culture of death, I can well appreciate the secular and economic pressures on Catholic physicians, today, to disregard the Church's teaching on legitimate means to space children. I, too, for 18 years thought there was no problem with performing sterilizations or prescribing contraception. After all, everyone around me did it, and patients expected it.
>
> When Pope Paul VI issued his encyclical *Humanae Vitae* in 1968, I had just graduated from high school and [had] already been accepted into a six-year BS/MD program. Listening to the feminist arguments and witnessing the examples around me which rejected the Church's teaching in this area, I also rejected it as being optional.[54]

---

[51] Ibid., 50.

[52] Ibid., 51.

[53] Ibid., 54.

[54] Kathleen Raviele, "A Gynecologist's Journey from Contraception to NFP," in *Physicians Healed: Personal, Inspiring, and Compelling Stories of Fifteen Courageous Physicians Who Do Not Prescribe Contraception*, ed. Cleta Hartman (Dayton: One More Soul, 1998), 105.

Over time, Raviele had experiences that could have made her question the prudence of this position, yet she held firm.[55] It was not until she had a religious experience that she really began the process of reevaluating the issue. Having given up her lucrative position amongst several fellow physicians, Dr. Raviele learned to teach NFP and has not looked back, as she relates, "What an incredible treasure the Church has in modern natural family planning. ... It is not a coincidence that since 1990, several OB/GYNs, like me, have had a change of heart."[56] In a medical community, not to mention a broader culture, that so strongly contests what is perceived to be antiquated and authoritarian papal nonsense, these physicians have gone from one side of the issue to the other, and they have found themselves and their patients all the better-off for accepting and living the Church's teaching.

Social Consequences

Since the 1960s, social evidence has continued to mount against the sexual revolution, contraceptives, and the moral theologies that developed to justify them. In 2010 Twomey has noted, "It is only within the last three decades or so that it has become obvious...the underlying issues at stake in *Humanae Vitae* were deeper than originally assumed. With the gift of hindsight, we can now see that the crisis in fundamental moral theology reflected (and deepened) that deeper crisis in Western civilization."[57] This would be little surprise to Pope Bl. Paul VI. In HV he claimed that contraceptive sexuality may "open wide the way for marital infidelity and a general lowing of moral standards."[58] In 1968 such an assertion was entirely contradictory to the "wisdom" of the times—people thought he was crazy. Nonetheless, history has shown that the arguments of moral theology used to justify contraception logically opened the door to a plethora of traditionally condemned sexual activities, and these

---

[55] Ibid., 106.
[56] Ibid., 108.
[57] D. Vincent Twomey, *Moral Theology after Humanae Vitae: Fundamental Issues in Moral Theory and Sexual Ethics* (Dublin: Four Courts Press, 2010), 67.
[58] Pope Paul VI, Humanae Vitae, http://www.vatican.va/holy_father/paul_vi/encyclicals/documents/hf_p-vi_enc_25071968_humanae-vitae_en.html (accessed July 14, 2009), §17.

became more and more widespread in society as well. Writing in 1988, Janet Smith contends:

> That there has been a widespread decline in morality, especially sexual morality, in the last 20 years is very difficult to deny. The increase in the number of divorces, abortions, out-of-wedlock pregnancies, and venereal diseases should convince any skeptic that sexual morality is not the strong suit of our age. It would be wrong to say that contraception is the single cause of this decline, but it would also be unthinkable not to count contraception among the contributing factors.[59]

A 2010 survey of Catholics indicates most of them believe we are experiencing a moral decline.[60] Sixty-seven percent of Americans think "moral values in this country are headed in the wrong direction;" the older the respondents, the more likely they are to agree with this statement.[61] Interestingly, while "the youngest American Catholic adults" (18-29) have the highest percentage of respondents to self-identify as "liberal," they are second only to the 65 and older generation to say that "commitment to marriage is not valued enough in this country."[62] Generation X (30-44) and Baby Boomers (45-64) agreed with both the oldest and youngest American generations on these points, but not as strongly.[63] The perception of moral decline is undoubtedly linked to sexual promiscuity, which by definition pursues sexual gratification without the risk of pregnancy. Those polled would certainly not have exempted sexual license from their list of moral factors, yet sexual license is difficult to attain without the active use of contraception.

---

[59] Janet E. Smith, "Paul VI as Prophet," in Why *Humanae Vitae Was Right: A Reader*, ed. Janet E. Smith (San Francisco: Ignatius Press, 1993), 521.

[60] Nancy Frazier O'Brien, "Catholics of All Ages See U.S. Moral Values on Decline, Survey Says." *Catholic News Service* (February 15, 2010). http://www.catholicnews.com/data/Stories/cns/1000653.htm (accessed February 22, 2010).

[61] Ibid.

[62] Ibid.

[63] Ibid.

Evidence in support of this perception of moral decline can be found beyond the confines of the Church. Mary Eberstadt observes that while Catholics are primarily the ones noticing the connection between moral decline and contraception, the evidence itself is coming from "honest social scientists willing to follow the data wherever it may lead," many of whom are "not political or social conservatives."[64] One such scientist is "Nobel Prize-winning economist George Akerlof," who explained "why the sexual revolution—contrary to common prediction, especially prediction by those in and out of the Church who wanted the teaching on birth control changed—has led to an increase in both illegitimacy and abortion."[65] Furthermore, Akerlof has "traced the empirical connections between the decrease in marriage and married fatherhood for men—both clear consequences of the contraceptive revolution—and the simultaneous increase in behaviors to which single men appear more prone: substance abuse, incarceration, and arrests."[66] The results of contraceptives, and the sexual revolution that has bolstered and upheld their use, have not been as positive as revisionists had hoped.

According to Eberstadt, other writers have "observed that private actions, notably post-revolution sexual habits, were having massive public consequences."[67] For example, public policy professor Francis Fukuyama believes what he calls a "Great Disruption" has occurred in the developed world in the last several decades. This era is characterized by "deteriorating social conditions," a rise in "crime and social disorder," decline in fertility rates, eruption of divorce rates, and a rise in single-parent situations (now involving one-third of U.S. children).[68] Occurring throughout "a wide range of similar countries" at about the same time, Fukuyama concludes that something common to each of these countries must be to blame.[69] He further notes that these problems seem to be in decline in recent

---

[64] Mary Eberstadt, "The Vindication of Humanae Vitae," *First Things*, no. 185 (Aug/Sep 2008): 36.

[65] Ibid.

[66] Ibid.

[67] Ibid., 37.

[68] Francis Fukuyama, *The Great Disruption: Human Nature and the Reconstitution of Social Order* (New York: Touchstone, 1999), 4-5.

[69] Ibid.

years, concomitant with a rise in "more conservative social norms."[70] Fukuyama makes clear that the "no limits" attitudes of past decades' liberation movements—like "the sexual revolution, the women's liberation and feminist movements, and the movements in favor of gay and lesbian rights"—are problematic.[71] He warns of the consequences of licentiousness:

> We want to break rules that are unjust, unfair, irrelevant or outdated, and we seek to maximize personal freedom. But we also constantly need new rules to permit new forms of cooperative endeavor and to enable us to feel connected with one another in communities. These new rules always entail the limitation of individual freedom. A society dedicated to the constant upending of norms and rules in the name of increasing individual freedom of choice will find itself increasingly disorganized, atomized, isolated, and incapable of carrying out common goals and tasks. The same society that wants "no limits" to its technological innovation also sees "no limits" to many forms of personal behavior, and the consequent growth of crime, broken families, parents failing to fulfill obligations to children, neighbors not looking out for each other, and citizens opting out of public life.[72]

After the upheavals that we have witnessed, could it be that we will see a post-liberationist reconstruction that will restore vital structures, norms, and rules?

Of special concern to Fukuyama are families whose changing situation has been "captured in statistics on fertility, marriage, divorce, and out-of-wedlock childbearing."[73] He identifies two primary causes: (1) the sexual revolution and contraceptives, especially OCPs, and (2) feminism and the rising number of working

---

[70] Ibid., 7-8.
[71] Ibid., 13.
[72] Ibid., 15.
[73] Ibid., 36, 38.

women.[74] In identifying these causes, Fukuyama does not direct the blame exclusively toward women. On the contrary, he sees as positive "the entry of women into the workplace, the steady closing of the earnings gap with men, and the greater ability of women to control fertility."[75] On the contrary, Fukuyama blames men. He explains, "Since the Pill and abortion permitted women for the first time to have sex without worrying about the consequences, men felt liberated from norms requiring them to look after the women whom they had gotten pregnant."[76] While "shotgun marriages" declined, "birth control use, abortions, and illegitimacy all went up."[77] Concomitantly, women joining the workforce increased the likelihood of divorce, because women are "better able to support themselves and to raise children without husbands," and they tend to have fewer children as well as increased income that resulted in less "joint capital."[78] These circumstances reinforce one another, which has resulted in the changing of men's behavior for the worse, all to families' and society's detriment.[79]

Similarly, sociobiologist Lionel Tiger believes contraceptives have had devastating effects on society. Tiger is far from being a believer in any type of religion, let alone being a Catholic faithful to the Church on this teaching, yet he brings an enlightening perspective to this issue, especially valuable since he has no religious motivations for supporting the Church's teaching. Clarifying his rejection of Catholicism, Mary Eberstadt notes that Tiger "describes religion as 'a toxic issue'—[yet] Tiger has repeatedly emphasized the centrality of the sexual revolution to today's unique problems."[80] While no single cause is responsible for increasing divorce rates, abortions, and single-parent situations, Tiger believes contraceptives, especially OCPs, are the most significant factor.[81] In support of this assertion, Janet Smith indicates, "One researcher attributes 50 percent of the

---

[74] Ibid., 102.
[75] Ibid., 120.
[76] Ibid., 102.
[77] Ibid.
[78] Ibid., 103.
[79] Ibid., 104.
[80] Eberstadt, 37.
[81] Ibid.; Tiger, 18.

rise in the divorce rate from the early sixties to the mid-seventies to the increased use of contraception."[82] Why?

Throughout history, Tiger explains, when men have engaged in sexual activity, they have known that their action has the possibility of resulting in a pregnancy, and men seemed to take responsibility for this action, because even until the 1950s up to 50% of marriages were begun under the impetus of an unplanned pregnancy.[83] With the advent of contraceptives, which were not outwardly obvious to the other sexual partner, things changed. Tiger explains, "After the pill, the situation was overturned. Men assumed women were contracepted unless they were told otherwise. If they were not contracepted, that was the woman's choice, and so were any consequences."[84] Therefore, men lost a sense of responsibility, and became less likely to agree to a marriage following pregnancy from fornication. Tiger notes, "Seventy percent of men interviewed in a study of Americans asserted that women alone were responsible for contraception, not men. They have evidently come to expect free, unencumbered sex, if only because that has largely been their experience."[85]

This has prompted other social maladies as well. Numbers of out-of-wedlock births have soared. Consider the differences in percentages of out-of-wedlock births in 1960 versus 1992 throughout various countries: "25 to 59 percent of the total in Iceland, 11 to 53 percent in France, 5 to 32 percent in Britain, 7 to 30 percent in the United States, [and] 5 to 29 percent in Canada."[86] Tiger believes the lack of concern of men for the consequences of their sexual activity also led to the rise in abortions as women were abandoned at the onset of pregnancy.[87] The reader will note that NFP is not so susceptible to these same problems. NFP-using husbands are often significantly involved with the process of determining when the wife is or is not fertile, and a man's sense of responsibility is thereby reinforced. NFP is not easily practiced out of marriage, and couples

---

[82] Janet E. Smith, *Humanae Vitae: A Generation Later* (Washington D.C.: Catholic University of America Press, 1991), 127.

[83] Tiger, 44, 33, 34.

[84] Ibid., 44.

[85] Ibid., 33.

[86] Ibid., 51.

[87] Ibid., 49-50.

that use it have very low divorce rates, so single-parent situations are practically non-existent.

The impact of contraceptives goes even deeper, as newer information from more recent decades continues to indicate. The chemical alterations of contraceptives like OCPs and Depo-Provera are believed to have additional unique effects, thus invalidating earlier assumptions "that contraceptive drugs are merely chemical equivalents of mechanical barriers."[88] Tiger explains, "The pill is effective because it mimics pregnancy. Chemically, the user is like a pregnant woman."[89] Consequently, all sorts of social, psychological, and physical behaviors may be altered due to this chemical paradox in hormonally contracepting women. For one, Tiger notes, "It has been brilliantly suggested that one reason for the possible decline in male sperm counts in industrial countries is that the pregnant status of large numbers of otherwise attractive and sexually vivacious women depresses sperm production. After all, different social states of female partners affect male sperm production."[90] While likely not the only contributor to decreasing levels of fertility among men, chemical contraceptives may be significantly related.

Furthermore, Lionel Tiger demonstrated significant social and sexual changes in male behavior in the presence of chemically contracepted females. He conducted a study on one group of stumptail macaque monkeys with a dominant male named Austin.[91] In this study, consisting of Austin and nine sexually available females, three months were allowed for Austin to pick his "three favorite females with whom he had regular sexual episodes."[92] Five of the nine females were randomly selected to receive a shot of Depo-Provera chemical contraceptive—which is effective for three months—two of which were from Austin's three preferences. Austin continued to approach these two former favorites yet without resulting in sexual intercourse. Instead, he reacted by retaining sexual relations with the one non-contracepted female he previously favored and selected two new cohorts from among the other three still

---

88 Ibid., 40.
89 Ibid., 36.
90 Ibid.
91 Ibid., 38-39.
92 Ibid., 38.

unaltered females. With the elapse of three months, the drug wore off of the initial five females and the other four were injected with a dosage lasting the next three months. This time Austin reacted by ceasing sexual activity with the current three, and resumed sexual activity with the two original favorites who had earlier been injected, while adding another non-contracepted partner. After these next three months, all nine of the females were injected with Depo-Provera. Tiger explains the male's reaction to the situation: "Austin began to attempt rape, masturbate, and behave in a turbulent and confused manner. He approached females [and sexually evaluated them]. But no matter what he did, there was never the usual episode of intercourse"—the chemical signs from the females indicated that they were pregnant and unavailable.[93] At the end of the final three months, the drug wore off, and Austin resumed sexual activity with his three original favorites. Tiger is led to conclude, "It is plausible, if not likely, that chemical pregnancy has an effect on males, too. There is commonsense evidence that this is so."[94]

How might these effects take place? Tiger points to "pheromones," which he describes as "hormones that affect social behavior between individuals, not within bodies as hormones usually do. These mysterious substances are rather like smells—subtle and difficult to capture and measure."[95] He goes on to explain, "For primate couples, sex and the perfumes of the body are inextricably linked. But chemical pregnancy decisively interrupted their flow among stumptail macaques who are otherwise vigorously sexual."[96] Therefore, "It is altogether plausible that even the limited condition produced by the pill has an effect not only on the behavior of individual women and men but also on their community at large."[97]

For some supporting evidence, Tiger points to a 1996 study that shows three things about women who are not on a chemical contraceptive and are ovulating normally: (1) "They are especially reluctant to choose sexual partners in whom they have no confidence and thus threaten sexual risks;" (2) when they participate in

---

[93] Ibid., 39.
[94] Ibid.
[95] Ibid., 40.
[96] Ibid.
[97] Ibid.

"consensual sex," it increases in the middle portion of their cycles when they are naturally more fertile; and (3) these non-chemically contracepted women were "less likely to be raped during the mid-portion of the menstrual cycle than at other times."[98] All three of these scenarios suggest that pheromones play a highly influential role on both these women and men with whom they may have either consensual or unwanted sexual encounters, especially considering the fact that women on OCPs did not experience any of these phenomena. Thus, when women's bodies are chemically pregnant, it changes their pheromones, which, in turn, significantly impacts their sexual interactions (whether consensual or forced) with males. Tiger suggests this evidence as yet "another indication of possible interference by the pill of vital biosocial processes at the core of reproductive life. ... There is some form of reduced attraction felt by men and perhaps reduced female interest even while there is an obvious increase in their sexual freedom."[99] What we are learning is that hormonal/chemical adjustments like these do not come without consequences.

If the pheromones of women on chemical contraceptives indicate they are pregnant, what additional effects might this have? One seemingly obvious natural reaction is that men find women less sexually attractive. Consider one testimony by a visibly pregnant woman, "I glance at men, they glance at me. Then I watch as their eyes slide down the exaggerated pear of my midsection. In that slide I become invisible. I am clearly, hugely pregnant, and so I have been desexualized."[100] If men generally find women less sexually poignant when they are visibly pregnant, might this be replicated if a man, albeit inaccurately, detects that a woman is pregnant as a result of the pheromones her body is producing under the effects of chemical contraception—perhaps much like Austin, the ape from Tiger's earlier mentioned experiment?

Tiger believes this is likely, and consequently women may feel the need to make up for this by showing their sexual availability in other ways. "If hormonal attraction is changed and diminished by the pill, perhaps chemically pregnant females have to employ more

---

[98] Ibid., 41.
[99] Ibid., 41, 42.
[100] Ibid., 39.

vigorous external signals than before to feel vivacious and sexy themselves, and to attract the attention of men if that is their interest," he suggests.[101] This explains why, "Before the pill, women appeared to accept norms of moderation in clothes and behavior," yet, "In the 1960s women were subject to new forms of fashion and demeanor. They escalated the sex game. Rather suddenly there emerged a stunning array of candidly erotic and voluptuous novelties."[102] As examples of such "novelties" Tiger lists, "the abandonment of bras, the shortening of skirts, [and] the popularity of tight jeans."[103] These changes led to even more: "Nudity appeared routinely in legitimate theater, and public sexuality burgeoned as a social fact and commercial opportunity. Rules of censorship were relaxed. Unprecedented candor defined public discussion of sex and its varieties."[104]

Surely, women have changed the way they use their bodies to incite attention from men—a lesson that is learned very early by young girls. For evidence, consider the fashions advertised to girls of early adolescence that have even gone so far as to include lingerie, sometimes with cartoon characters, sold in malls and department stores. Another recent example we might include among teens and young adults is the upswing in "sexting" as a means by which females may make their sexual availability known to males in the absence of effective pheromones that have been suppressed by their chemical contraceptives. Sexual activity and awareness is present at considerably young ages, and fashion and popular culture have come to accommodate ever more revealing and provocative attire and attitudes. The alteration of pheromones may have played a role in this.

The power of pheromones and their effects go even further. Tiger notes Martha McClintock's 1970 discovery that "women who live together in dormitories and other close settings find that their menstrual cycles become synchronized over time, for reasons that presumably are pheromonal."[105] This phenomenon is not present

---

[101] Ibid., 44.
[102] Ibid., 44-45.
[103] Ibid., 45.
[104] Ibid., 47.
[105] Ibid., 42.

among women who are taking chemical contraceptives, however. Tiger argues, "Women on contraceptive medication do not respond to other women the way non-contracepted women do. ... It follows that it also affects how they relate to men."[106] Combining this study with one by Claus Wedekind from 1995 reveals some disturbing realities. In Wedekind's study, women both on and off of OCPs smelled men's clothes and ranked how attracted they were to each man, simply based upon the subconsciously detected pheromones remaining on his garments. Women who were not on a chemical contraceptive were more attracted to the pheromonal scents of men generally identified as more "desirable potential mates" with "the buzz appeal."[107] Remarkably, "Women using oral contraceptives *reversed* their preferences and chose inappropriate partners," reports Tiger.[108]

A 2008 study, building upon and imitating Wedekind's, was conducted by evolutionary biologists at the University of Newcastle in England, led by Craig Roberts. By comparing 60 women who were not taking OCPs with 37 women who began a regimen of OCPs in the midst of the study, the researchers showed that women not on OCPs are attracted to pheromone scents of men with genetically dissimilar DNA, while women who began taking OCPs changed their preferences to those with genetically similar DNA.[109] The evolutionary advantages are evident: "'When women are pregnant there's no selection pressure, evolutionarily speaking, for having a preference for genetically dissimilar odors,' Roberts said. 'And if there is any pressure at all it would be towards relatives, who would be more genetically similar, because the relatives would help those individuals rear the baby.'"[110] According to Roberts, "The pill is in

---

[106] Ibid.

[107] Ibid.

[108] Ibid., 42-43.

[109] Cat O'Donovan, "Birth Control Pills Can Make You Pick the Wrong Lover," *Cosmos Magazine* (August 13, 2008), http://www.cosmosmagazine.com/news/2136/birth-control-pills-make-you-pick-wrong-lover (accessed October 15, 2008).

[110] Jeanna Bryner, "The Pill Makes Women Pick Bad Mates," *Live Science* (August 12, 2008), http://www.livescience.com/culture/080812-contraceptive-smell.html (accessed October 15, 2008).

effect mirroring a natural shift but at an inappropriate time."[111] One reason why having dissimilar DNA—also known as major histocompatibility complex (MHC) genes—is beneficial is that, "When individuals with different MHC genes mate, their offspring's immune systems can recognize a broader range of foreign cells, making them more fit."[112] Dissimilar DNA mates produce offspring with natural selection advantages.

If that advantage was not enough, the detriments of being attracted to a person of similar DNA are more telling. First, parents with similar MHC genes are known to have more trouble conceiving.[113] Second, "Children of genetically similar parents are more likely to have birth defects that cause them to be naturally aborted in the womb."[114] Third, Roberts noted such dissimilarity "could ultimately lead to the breakdown of relationships when women stop using the contraceptive pill, as odor perception plays a significant role in maintaining attraction to partners."[115] Imagine, for example, a woman being attracted to a man throughout the whole dating, engagement, and early marriage process, but as soon as she ceases taking her hormonal/chemical contraceptive in an effort to conceive, she is no longer attracted to him "pheromonically." Fourth, "Past studies have suggested couples with dissimilar MHC genes are more satisfied and more likely to be *faithful to a mate*. And the opposite is also true with matching-MHC couples showing less satisfaction and more wandering eyes."[116] Consequently, evidence suggests being on OCPs influences women to choose partners less suitable for them, which can have many detrimental effects on their fertility, offspring, and relationships.

Following the social data over the past several decades on how contraceptives have impacted people, relationships, and society, the evidence against certain forms of contraceptives must be considered and weighed. Lionel Tiger states:

---

[111] Ibid.
[112] Ibid.
[113] O'Donovan.
[114] Ibid.
[115] Bryner.
[116] Ibid.

The pill has had a remarkable, defining, and underestimated impact on the communities in which it was introduced in the 1960s. It was not just another drug to correct a temporary physical illness; instead it was a powerful preparation given to *healthy people on a daily basis*. It did not repair a disability but promoted a robust social life. It has affected sex between men and women, the core relationship that has guided human evolution and continues to preoccupy people more than half their lives.[117]

On multiple levels, including social and biological evidence, which has only come to light in the last few years, the wisdom of the Church continues to be vindicated. All of the above supports the following assertion made by Twomey: "The Church's resistance to the hedonism and individualism of the 'new morality' is not based on an irrational system of taboos but on a solid foundation of 'biological and sociological principles.'"[118] Only in recent years are we coming to more clearly see and appreciate this truth.

Feminism

One remarkable example of proving Pope Bl. Paul VI's point for him, while sometimes simultaneously rejecting his message as anti-woman, is feminism. In the 1960s and following decades, contraceptives were hailed for their ability to free women from the social bonds of earlier centuries and allow them to pursue education and careers without the baggage of children. Some feminists have condemned the Catholic Church for oppressing women and preventing their rise to equality, especially due to its stance on contraceptives.[119] Jennifer J. Popiel observes, "According to many, adherence to Catholic doctrine is inimically opposed to respect for women, to claims of equality."[120] In HV Bl. Paul VI suggested that

---

[117] Tiger, 37.

[118] Twomey, 26.

[119] Ruth D. Lasseter, "Sensible Sex," in *Why Humanae Vitae Was Right: A Reader*, ed. Janet E. Smith (San Francisco: Ignatius Press, 1993), 484; Janet E. Smith, "Paul VI as Prophet," 520.

[120] Jennifer J. Popiel, "Necessary Connections? Catholicism, Feminism and Contraception," *America* (November 27, 1999): 22.

men who grow "accustomed to the use of contraceptive methods may forget the reverence due to a woman, and, disregarding her physical and emotional equilibrium, [reduce] her to being a mere instrument for the satisfaction of his own desires."[121] This position was seen as offensive to women at the time, and just the opposite was believed to be true.[122] Only a few early feminists, such as Germaine Greer, took an early position against contraceptives due to health concerns and the imposition of contraceptives on women in impoverished countries.[123]

A woman's knowledge of herself and her body, especially including her fertility, is powerful and empowering information. When a family planning method requires a woman's partner to encounter this knowledge as well, his respect and admiration for her and her fertility are bound to increase. Unfortunately though, women who use a contraceptive are robbed of an opportunity to more deeply understand and embrace their femininity and fertility. Teresa Wagner, Esq. explains how NFP honors femininity:

> NFP is not only a form of fertility awareness, but fertility *appreciation* and specifically, appreciation of *female* fertility (ultimately, appreciation of the woman). While no person can be reduced to his or her physical attributes, fertility cycles are indisputably feminine. How we treat this cycle tells us something about our attitude toward women.
>
> Proponents of contraception, intent on being able to control and manipulate fertility, are oblivious to the sophisticated and delicate ecology of the human female. Thus the first obvious difference between contraception use and NFP is this: The former

---

[121] Pope Paul VI, *Humanae Vitae*,
   http://www.vatican.va/holy_father/paul_vi/encyclicals/documents/hf_p-vi_enc_25071968_humanae-vitae_en.html (accessed July 14, 2009), §17.

[122] Austin B. Vaughan, "*Humanae Vitae* and Respect for the Dignity of the Human Person," in *Trust the Truth: A symposium on the Twentieth Anniversary of the Encyclical Humanae Vitae*, ed. Russell E. Smith (Braintree, MA: The Pope John XXIII Medical-Moral Research and Education Center, 1991), 20.

[123] Janet E. Smith, "Paul VI as Prophet," 525.

manipulates the female body and therefore never learns to respect it or women generally; the latter requires understanding of the female fertility cycle, fosters respect for it and for women generally.[124]

As a poignant illustration, Dr. Cynthia Jones-Nosacek recounts, "I have patients who have had multiple cultures performed by gynecologists because of a recurrent 'infection' that occurs every month, ending about 2 weeks before her next menses."[125] She offers this story with no additional information, and for many women, nearly all men, and sadly at least the gynecologists by whom these women were being treated, they will not get the point. Even this male author, however, being trained in NFP, with an appreciation for feminine fertility, could explain not only to these women but also to their gynecologists that what they are experiencing is the increased quantity and changing quality of cervical mucus near ovulation.

From both inside and outside of the Church in recent decades, many have suggested that contraceptives actually are anti-woman as Bl. Paul VI suggested. A veteran defender of the Church's contraception teaching, Bishop Austin B. Vaughan notes:

> I can personally attest to the way in which contraception leads to the demeaning of women. I live in a poor neighborhood, a neighborhood that is generally considered a "slum" area. It is a neighborhood that has many, many single-parent women now, who live below the poverty line, who often live in degradation or on the verge of it, who are the leftovers of liaisons with men who have felt no responsibility for them at all, and no responsibility for their children. ... Russell Baker, the columnist with *The New York Times*, wrote an article...[saying] that people like to know who won the wars; he asked who won the sexual revolution, and answered that

---

[124] Wagner, 58.

[125] Cynthia Jones-Nosacek, "Response to Teresa Wagner, Esq.," In *Integrating Faith and Science Through Natural Family Planning*," ed. Richard J. Fehring and Theresa Notare (Milwaukee: Marquette UP, 2004), 64.

sometimes we do not know, but in this case there was no doubt: "the boys won it." He said that this was because the women got stuck with all of the undesirable consequences of the sexual revolution. Paul VI predicted this in 1968, and people laughed at him. Nobody would laugh at him now.[126]

More recently, theologian David McCarthy has stated, "The radical feminist should find an ally in Paul VI who would see both pornography and contraceptive practices as giving women over to the desires of men."[127] This perspective is shared by Archbishop Chaput:

> Chaput suggested that support for birth control from advocates for women is self-defeating. He wrote that "an exaggerated feminism has actively colluded in women's dehumanization," and that while "many feminists have attacked the Catholic church for her alleged disregard of women…the church in Humanae Vitae identified and rejected sexual exploitation of women years before that message entered the cultural mainstream."[128]

As ridiculous as his position may have looked in 1968, Pope Bl. Paul VI was right.

With similar conclusions from outside of the Church, Francis Fukuyama agrees that women and children have been the primary losers in the past few decades. The children have lost the attention of and interaction with their mothers, as well as the likelihood of stable family lives, which were common prior to such liberations.[129] Women typically took "low-end service sector jobs," and, "In return for the meager financial independence this brought, many women found themselves abandoned by husbands who moved on to younger wives

---

[126] Vaughan, 20.

[127] David M. McCarthy, "Procreation, the Development of Peoples, and the Final Destiny of Humanity," *Communio* 26 (Winter 1999): 708.

[128] "Paul VI Vindicated, Denver Bishops Says," *National Catholic Reporter* 34, no. 35 (July 31, 1998): 12-13.

[129] Fukuyama, 120-121.

or girlfriends."[130] On the contrary, men have "come out about even," says Fukuyama.[131] If all of this information about contraceptives (especially OCPs) contributing to situations that led to the demise of families and the well-being of countless women and children was not enough, Fukuyama goes on to confirm one of Bl. Paul VI's major predictions and concerns in HV:

> One of the greatest frauds perpetrated during the Great Disruption was the notion that the sexual revolution was gender neutral, benefiting women and men equally, and that it somehow had a kinship with the feminist revolution. In fact, the sexual revolution served the interests of men, and in the end it put up a sharp limit on the kinds of gains that women might otherwise have expected from their liberation from traditional roles.[132]

For many women contraception is considered an essential right and something necessary in order to assure their advancement and happiness in a world previously dominated by men—a major assertion of the sexual revolution. This point has been refuted by a growing number of people from various perspectives who see contraceptives doing more harm to women than good.

There is a remarkable irony here that has become more appreciated in recent years. McCarthy notes, "In modern conception, reproductive rights (to abortion as well as contraception) have been hailed as guarantors of women's equality, autonomy, and bodily integrity."[133] Instead he states, "Contraceptive practices...diminish the dignity of women and the integrity of their bodies," as Bl. Paul VI suggested.[134] The irony comes into play, as McCarthy explains: "To liberal feminist ears, Paul VI's notion of 'a woman's proper role' rings of a tradition where men dominate women. Such control over

---

[130] Ibid., 120.
[131] Ibid., 121.
[132] Ibid., 121-122.
[133] McCarthy, "Procreation," 706.
[134] Ibid.

women is, however, precisely Paul VI's fear."[135] Jennifer Popiel points to some of the problem:

> If women can refuse to conceive children or carry them to term once conceived, if women refuse to acknowledge the reproductive possibilities of their actions, why should men not do the same? A contraceptive mentality leads to further gender injustices, with women bearing the brunt of the financial and social impact of child-rearing.[136]

Adding to the irony, a cursory consideration of feminist themes of recent years provides more support for the Church's teaching. Commenting on this phenomenon, Mary Eberstadt writes:

> The signature metaphors of feminism say everything we need to know about how happy liberation has been making these women: the suburban home as a concentration camp, men as rapists, children as intolerable burdens, fetuses as parasites, and so on. These are the sounds of liberation? Even the vaunted right to abortion, both claimed and exercised at extraordinary rates, did not seem to mitigate the misery of millions of these women after the sexual revolution.[137]

Again Eberstadt points to the wisdom of Bl. Paul VI in HV as condemning a method that would lead to further misuse of women while simultaneously permitting one that promotes self-discipline, mutuality, and communication:

> Beneath all the pathos, the subtext remains the same: Woman's chief adversary is Unreliable Man, who does not understand her sexual and romantic needs and who walks off time and again at the first

---

[135] Ibid.
[136] Popiel, 24.
[137] Eberstadt, 39.

sashay of a younger thing. What are all these but the generic cries of a woman who thinks that men are "disregarding her physical and emotional equilibrium" and "no longer considering her as his partner whom he should surround with care and affection"?[138]

According to "Third Wave feminist" Naomi Wolf, writes Eberstadt, "The power and charge of sex are maintained when there is some sacredness to it, when it is not on tap all the time"—a statement Eberstadt believes "with just a little tweaking could easily have appeared in *Humanae Vitae* itself."[139] Similarly, D. Vincent Twomey points to feminist Liz Hodgkinson's 1986 book in which she says, "Sex is essentially about exploitation, not love," it causes "forms of mental disorder, such as selfishness, self-centeredness and conceit," and it has wrought havoc on young girls' emotional and psychological well-being.[140] Unbelievably, this feminist's proposed solution is a rejection of sexuality, what Twomey summarizes as "celibacy for health and happiness."[141] This result, Twomey believes, "is but the reaction of an abused generation who believed that sex was a need which had to be satisfied and paid the price in personal suffering, exploitation and degradation."[142] A study conducted in 2000 quantifies the feelings presented by women hostile to their male partners. It indicates that "for each contraceptive method a woman reported using..., her odds of ever having felt like an object rather than truly loved by her spouse increased by ... 40%," while for those with greater "spousal communication" and "spousal support" for NFP, the study indicates a *decrease* in feeling like an object, at similar rates.[143] The experiential evidence of contemporary feminism is thus supporting the Church's teaching.

---

[138] Ibid.

[139] Ibid.

[140] Twomey, 133.

[141] Ibid.

[142] Ibid., 137.

[143] Andrew C. Pollard and Mercedes Arzu-Wilson, "Correlates of Marital Satisfaction in a Sample of NFP Women," In *Integrating Faith and Science Through Natural Family Planning*," ed. Richard J. Fehring and Theresa Notare (Milwaukee: Marquette UP, 2004), 156.

In addition, experiential evidence from couples using NFP suggests that Church-approved methods are much more conducive to equality and the dignity of women than contraceptives. One Catholic couple, Jim Ternier and Marie-Louise Ternier-Gommers, reflect on nearly a quarter-century of NFP in which they recall of the early years,

> It even appealed to those feminists who wanted to be in charge of their own fertility without pills or devices that jeopardize their health physically and otherwise. NFP was the method of choice for those among us who were advocates of social justice, with those of us who didn't want to be controlled by the medical profession and their technological solutions and for Catholic couples who strove to live a fruitful and mature marriage in accordance with church teaching.[144]

Suggesting the alternative of periodic abstinence as "objectively valuable and strengthening," and "crucial for feminism," Jennifer Popiel argues, "Women who use N.F.P. are actually more free to make informed decisions about sexual activity and more able to communicate their desires for children or postponement of conception," largely due to the fact that, unlike contraceptives, NFP "requires that both partners understand the signs of fertility and work together."[145]

Popiel maintains that so long as women "continue to insist that the widespread use of contraception and abortion does not contribute to the degradation of women's status in society," they will continue to be affected by these practices' inevitable effects."[146] One female physician comments, "If we do not respect ourselves, how can we demand that respect from others? And how can we accept ourselves if something so basic to ourselves, our female fertility is

---

[144] Jim Ternier and Marie-Louise Ternier-Gommers, "Speaking up for Natural Family Planning," *National Catholic Reporter* 40, no. 15 (February 13, 2004): 19.
[145] Popiel, 25.
[146] Ibid.

considered disordered"?[147] As some feminists have always known, and more are beginning to realize after seeing the social effects involved, contraception is not serving an agenda of respect and equality for women. After years of suffering the physical, psychological, and relational effects of contraceptives, Ruth Lasseter speaks out:

> We women have submitted our female sexuality's cyclic nature to the constant male sex drive of our husbands. Are we *ashamed* to have made ourselves *always* available to our spouses, from the very beginning of marriage beyond our menopause? Ashamed to admit that we sophisticated and independent women have followed the Old Wive's Tale that a woman MUST be available for her man? Why do we not ask ourselves, if not other women, why we should feel ashamed and exploited in having done so? Are we afraid that the answer just *might* be another Old Wives Tale: that a man will leave her for another, more accommodating woman, if she doesn't "turn on the heat?"[148]

A convert to Catholicism, Lasseter has since become an advocate of NFP. From another perspective, Ternier and Ternier-Gommers strongly support the Church's position, even from a feminist viewpoint, in the following:

> By its approval of NFP, the church indirectly proclaims and affirms that a woman's fertility is nobody's medical problem to fix, but, rather, that every woman's sexuality includes her fertility and this truth deserves to be respected both by the woman and her spouse. NFP teaches a man that there is virtue in sexual discipline within a relationship of love. Every woman should also have the freedom to choose to live in harmony with the natural cycles of

---

[147] Jones-Nosacek, 64.
[148] Lasseter, 476-477.

her fertility and should not have to be sexually available at all times. A marriage and a culture that expect women to be sexually available all the time, without becoming pregnant, smacks of exploitation and blatant disrespect.[149]

From another approach, McCarthy suggests economics play a major role in how contraceptives are not helping women. He explains that American culture has become decidedly anti-child, insofar as its idea of production continues to exclude procreation. He observes the current mindset as, "Economic and social equality for women is achieved by avoiding children or at least the practical burdens of bearing them. ... The modern economy will not allow a place for children and child rearing."[150] Contraception has become so important, because "Controlling births is risk management. Bearing and raising children (and domestic life as a whole) is no longer considered a productive venture, but a practice of consumption that drains rather than accrues resources."[151] The sexual revolution has thus dramatically changed even the way our economy has developed. McCarthy continues, "A distinctive woman's role has no economic currency, even if we give a modest description of this role as nine months of pregnancy and several more of breast feeding. Our economy is set against it, and contraception sustains the false promises of this so-called economic freedom."[152] What if we have things backwards, McCarthy asks: "Is childbearing set against money-making because the system of money-making is itself set against human solidarity and true social development?"[153] Perhaps we have it all wrong, and the misery of so many women is a strong indicator of the problem. Major social issues are at stake here, as McCarthy suggests:

> Contraception buttresses social practices that are inhospitable to children, so that women are burdened

---

149 Ternier and Ternier-Gommers, 19.
150 McCarthy, "Procreation," 707-708.
151 Ibid.,," 704.
152 Ibid., 708.
153 Ibid., 705.

with child rearing but allowed to enter public and economic life only without their offspring. All the while, pornography, strip clubs, and other facets of the sex industry are an economic boon. Contraception has been indispensable in shaping liberation so that women continue to serve the sexual needs of men. In this way, sexual liberation has given a new meaning to "a woman's role."[154]

While seeking liberation through contraceptives, feminists have made one step forward and two steps backward. This is why women are beginning to identify contraceptives and a contraceptive mentality as anti-woman.

Time and again feminism has instigated the misogyny that the Church has predicted would result from widespread contraception. Mary Eberstadt suggests that the "fundamental issue" has been identified by Archbishop Chaput:

> "If Paul VI was right about so many of the consequences deriving form contraception, it is because he was right about contraception itself." This is exactly the connection few people in 2008 want to make, because contraceptive sex—as commentators from all over, religious or not, agree—is the fundamental social fact of our time. And the fierce and widespread desire to keep it so is responsible for a great many perverse outcomes. Despite an empirical record that is unmistakably on Paul VI's side by now, there is extraordinary resistance to crediting Catholic moral teaching with having been right about anything, no matter how detailed the record.[155]

Overpopulation

Apocalyptic threats of overpopulation have been an ever present scare tactic among contraception advocates since the late 18th century. According to Herbert F. Smith, over two centuries ago

---

[154] Ibid., 708.
[155] Eberstadt, 42.

Thomas Malthus famously threatened that human population would increase geometrically while food resources would only increase arithmetically.[156] Malthus was not the first to warn about overpopulation, since even Plato and Aristotle expressed concerns about a "population explosion."[157] At the time of *Humanae Vitae*'s promulgation, society had become fearful of population growth. Paul Ehrlich's 1968 text, *The Population Bomb*, fueled panic with grave warnings like, "In the 1970s and 1980s hundreds of millions will starve to death in spite of any crash programs embarked on now."[158]

The panic was unfounded. In fact, in some places the issue of overpopulation has entirely reversed itself. In 1987, Herbert Smith showed Malthus's predictions regarding food supply to be incorrect: "World population rose from 1.6 billion in 1900 to 2.51 billion in 1950 to 3.8 billion in 1970 to 4.6 billion in 1982. Yet the food supply has not only kept up with this near-geometrical increase; it has exceeded it."[159] In 2008, Howard P. Kainz confirmed, "The world's food supply has steadily increased in something like 'geometrical' proportion; and with the help of agricultural technology and human ingenuity, food supplies can continue to increase in tandem with population."[160] Herbert Smith reports, "According to the U.N. statistics, world food production is growing about one percent faster than population, and the production of animal protein increases at twice that rate."[161] Remarkably, within three years of Ehrlich's scare, Dr. Pawley of the U.N.'s World Food and Agricultural Organization denounced such ideas; as Herbert Smith explains, "Pawley declared it was time to desist from claiming that a supposed global inability to provide food was an argument for limiting population. Such claims, he concluded, were worse than erroneous."[162] Considering the possibilities of food production, Pawley stated that they "could easily

---

[156] Herbert F. Smith, "The Proliferation of Population Problems," in *Why Humanae Vitae Was Right: A Reader*, ed. Janet E. Smith (San Francisco: Ignatius Press, 1993), 387.

[157] Ibid., 386.

[158] Ibid., 388.

[159] Ibid., 387.

[160] Howard P. Kainz, "Sexual Mores, Ethical Theories, and the Overpopulation Myth." *Heythrop Journal* 49, no. 3 (May 2008): 367.

[161] Herbert F. Smith, 387.

[162] Ibid., 395

be increased to 50 times its present level, [which] would suffice to feed 36 billion people."[163] If food supply is not a concern as men like Malthus and Ehrlich stated, what about a general growth in world population itself?

It is true that overall the world population continues to climb; however, it is not an evenly spread growth—the situation is different everywhere. In the United States the "native born" population was experiencing a "shrink" rate of "6.3 percent per generation in a geometrical digression" as of the 1980s.[164] Populations in many other developing countries are also falling at such a rate that they are unable to reproduce themselves—thus causing major problems. According to Francis Fukuyama, "Western societies are failing to produce enough of them to sustain themselves," which would require a fertility rate of "a little over two" to accomplish.[165] He further notes, "Some countries, like Spain, Italy, and Japan, have fallen so far below replacement fertility that their total population in each successive generation will be more than 30 percent smaller than in the previous one."[166] Citing *Family Planning Perspectives* from 1981, Herbert Smith writes, "'Fertility rates in Belgium, Denmark, France, Great Britain, Norway and the United States have dropped below replacement level.' Some have dropped far below. Today in France, the government provides incentives to promote births."[167] Many other countries have attempted such programs as well. Fukuyama explains that France, Sweden, Spain, and Italy, among others, have attempted to implement "pronatalist policies" to encourage greater reproduction, largely in vain.[168] Many countries—like the U.S. and Russia—are only replacing their populations among some minority groups and through immigration; countries like Germany and France are shrinking dramatically; and countries like Russia, France, and Germany are seeing major shifts in their populations as young Muslims are having large families while much of the rest of the

---

163 Ibid., 395-396.
164 Ibid., 391.
165 Fukuyama, 38-39.
166 Ibid., 39.
167 Herbert F. Smith, 392.
168 Fukuyama, 40.

population is depleting.[169] Eberstadt notes the way the overpopulation issue has been turned on its head in the following:

> So discredited has the overpopulation science become that this year [2008] Columbia University historian Matthew Connelly could publish *Fatal Misconception: The Struggle to Control World Population* and garner a starred review in *Publishers Weekly*—all in service of what is probably the single best demolition of the population arguments that some hoped would undermine church teaching.[170]

The tragedy of this situation has even been recognized by one of the co-developers of the Pill (OCP) in 1951, Carl Djerassi. In 2009, Djerassi "expressed dismay at the severance of sexuality and reproduction made possible by widespread use of the pill, and has warned against the impending demographic disaster from plummeting birth rates."[171] Faced with tumbling population rates in his native Austria, Djerassi suggests that new immigration policies may be the only way to avoid a population "national suicide," as he calls it.[172] Djerassi wrote, "My contribution is to help [Austrian couples using contraception] to wake up."[173]

Despite the overwhelming evidence about a reversed population problem in developed countries, some continue to use overpopulation as an excuse to promote contraception.[174] Fukuyama elaborates:

> The generation that came of age in America and Europe in the 1960s and 1970s grew up hearing about the population explosion and global environmental crisis, and many remain firmly convinced that

---

[169] Herbert F. Smith, 392-393.
[170] Eberstadt, 38.
[171] Kathleen Gilbert, "Co-Creator of the Pill Laments Results," *LifeSiteNews* (January 9, 2009), http://www.catholic.org/international/international_story.php?id=31473 (accessed December 30, 2011).
[172] Ibid.
[173] Ibid.
[174] Kainz, "Sexual Mores," 367.

"overpopulation" is one of the chief threats to future human existence. And so it may be for many parts of the Third World. But for any developed country, the problem is exactly the opposite: they are in the process of depopulating themselves.[175]

Overpopulation will only be used as an excuse in developed countries to our further detriment—it must no longer be tolerated. However, those who promote contraception with overpopulation arguments will be quick to point to the situation in developing countries.

At the same time as the population has declined in developed countries, areas like India, China, parts of Africa, and Latin America are having some authentic issues with overpopulation. Where problems about overpopulation genuinely threaten the well-being of families and nations, NFP is a perfectly viable option, and may present the best option among all alternatives (as was discussed in the previous chapter). Nevertheless, attempting to throw contraceptives at a population crisis misses the underlying problem. These issues go deeper than mere population control, and simply providing contraceptives does not help the situation. If we want to truly solve such problems, we must go to the root.

The World Food Conference has recognized the "irony" behind the fact that "development programs" for Third World countries actually increase populations as will be explained below.[176] Moreover, the World Food Conference stated, "These programs reduce social life to economic value; they assume that 'progress' means industrialization, and they place too much confidence in purely technological solutions (which ultimately serve already 'advanced' nations)."[177] McCarthy notes, "Six years before the World Food Conference, Paul VI articulates the same critique in reference to artificial regulation of births. Contraception is a false solution that diminishes the lives of those who purportedly will be helped the most."[178]

---

[175] Fukuyama, 38.
[176] McCarthy, "Procreation," 701.
[177] Ibid.
[178] Ibid.

The real issue behind population problems must be resolved through social justice, not contraception. Herbert Smith argues that Malthus was wrong in his assertion that misery could curb population growth as he states, "Today there is extensive evidence to the contrary: The poorer the family, the larger the number of children— its only form of 'social security' in many countries."[179] In developing countries, sufficient offspring are necessary to take care of aging parents, which only adds to an impetus to have more children. Similarly, Kainz affirms, "It is obvious that what is called the 'overpopulation problem' is not a space problem, but more precisely a problem of *distribution* of wealth and resources—a political/social/ethical issue."[180] Just because numbers may drop does not mean people will be any better-off; instead, they will simply continue to have reason to increase their offspring. Kainz further suggests that we must "grapple with the *real* population issue," which he explains as

> Recognizing the injustices and inequities prevailing in domains such as politics, economics, and business. The fact that, for example, the United States, with 5% of the world's population, is consuming 30% of the world's resources, cannot be ignored. Our growing awareness of this imbalance should inspire both individual and communal efforts to right the wrongs, and reduce the gap between the "haves" and the "have-nots". But—"overpopulation" being understood as the excessive numbers of impoverished people—simplistic solutions like global promotion of contraception and abortion will do nothing to alleviate global injustices.[181]

Typical of the American mindset, we want to cover up profound problems by taking the easy route, like postponing the inevitable effects of heart disease with a pill rather than counteracting the effects and correcting the underlying problem through diet and

---

[179] Herbert F. Smith, 388.
[180] Kainz, "Sexual Mores," 367.
[181] Ibid., 368.

exercise. Where family planning must be implemented, NFP is an excellent solution, but simultaneous efforts must be made to correct the social justice issues underpinning the problems in the first place.

Finally, we ought to recognize that large populations are not inherently evil. Herbert Smith argues, "Human resources are the key to unlocking all resources. This populous [twentieth] century has afforded leaps into new realms," because, "'Leisure is the basis of culture,' and every worthwhile idea or invention of one person can—and often did—enrich all the earth's people present and future."[182] He suggests that far from being a burden, people are *de facto* productive. Perhaps a larger population, in itself, is not a problem; perhaps the problems truly are a poor distribution of resources and wealth among that population.

Ecological Considerations

Another issue pertinent to the discussion about contraception and NFP is ecology. Ironically, in an era when living naturally was becoming popular, HV was radically rejected. Reflecting on the times of the 1960s, George Weigel comments, "One has to ask why a position that defended 'natural' means of family planning was deemed impossibly antiquarian at precisely the moment when 'natural' was becoming one of the sacred words in the developed world, especially with regard to ecological consciousness."[183] One might have hoped out of the 1960s at least a few more couples would have appreciated the Church's position on the grounds of its naturalness—in the sense of not chemically altering the body or thwarting fertility. Ternier and Ternier-Gommers saw the light when others did not, and their understanding is all the more consistent with the consideration of modern ecology. They explain, "We are committed to farming without chemicals, so it was logical to choose a family planning method without chemicals."[184] In yet another way the decades following HV have come to support the Church's position—this time from an ecological standpoint. For good reasons, environmentalism and "going green" are gaining prominence in our

---

[182] Herbert F. Smith, 397.

[183] George Weigel, *Witness to Hope: The Biography of Pope John Paul II* (New York: Harper Collins, 2001), 210.

[184] Ternier and Ternier-Gommers, 19.

lives; we cannot be blind to the effects of contraception on the environment as well.

A number of recent articles have considered this topic. An October 2009 issue of *Time* carried the story, "Sex and the Eco-City," by Kathleen Kingsbury. She writes:

> Another big enviro-sex trend: *birth control* that's au naturel. Like all good Catholics, my husband and I had to attend church-run marriage prep before we tied the knot last year. I was surprised, however, during the hard sell on natural family-planning (NFP), that this updated version of the rhythm method was being advertised not only as morally correct but also as "organic" and "green." I was even more surprised when I found out that some of the most popular instructors of NFP—known in secular circles as the Fertility Awareness Method—are non-Catholics who praise it as a means of avoiding both ingesting chemicals and excreting them into rivers and streams.[185]

Kingsbury provides the example of "Nikki Walker, 35, an actress in New York City [who] stopped taking the *Pill* because of concerns about the effects of excess estrogen on her body and the *environment.* 'I do yoga every day and eat vegetarian,' she says. 'Why wouldn't I go green in this area of my life?'"[186] Similarly, a recent article in an environmental magazine by Jessica Rae Patton discusses "bringing environmentalism into the bedroom."[187] Citing one authority, Patton writes, "Jennifer Rogers, the programs and policy director for the Reproductive Health Technologies Project (RHTP), says that considering the impact of contraception on the environment is a new concept for both the scientific community and reproductive rights

---

[185] Kathleen Kingsbury, "Sex and the Eco-City." *Time* 174, no. 16 (October 26, 2009): 51-52.

[186] Kingsbury.

[187] Jessica Rae Patton, "Make Love, Not Waste," *E – The Environmental Magazine* 19, no. 5 (Sep/Oct 2008): 40-41.

advocates."[188] Visiting a natural/organic food store, this author's wife stumbled upon an article in *Better Nutrition: The Shopping Magazine for Natural Living*, which featured a Q & A section written by a medical professional from Alaska who explains natural birth control and such biological markers as basal body temperature as well as cervical mucus, openness, and rigidity as ways of identifying fertile and infertile parts of a woman's cycle.[189] NFP is gaining ground in this vein, even if the Church's credibility is not simultaneously recognized.

The concern about chemically contaminating the environment as a result of birth control is very real and is becoming more thoroughly documented and understood. Hormones from contraceptives are passing from people into the environment through human waste. Patton recounts:

> Hormonal contraception scores high for convenience but has been the focus of some limited, yet worrisome, environmental-impact studies. A 2004 study in Boulder, Colorado, looked at the effect of estrogenic chemicals on fish. One of the principal researchers, Dr. David O. Norris of the laboratory of environmental endocrinology at the University of Colorado at Boulder, says that the birth control pills add to the level of estrogen in wastewater and can contribute to the feminization of fish. "However, considering that these pollution problems are a direct consequence of human population growth coupled with the concentrations of people into small areas, we should not think that suppressing any form of birth control will improve conditions," he cautions. "Although there are a variety of methods for controlling conception, the 'pill' has proven to be the most effective and least expensive, albeit with some risks of its own."[190]

---

[188] Ibid.
[189] Emily A. Kane, "Natural Birth Control," *Better Nutrition* (December 2010): 30.
[190] Patton, 40-41.

Aside from the fact that his statement ignores the proven effectiveness of NFP for both avoiding and achieving pregnancy, Norris advances no solution for the negative impact of birth control on the environment. Sexual license has become so sacrosanct for some, like Norris, that they would not dream of changing even if it means further contaminating the water supply.

Many other studies have also exposed problems with chemicals from contraceptives harming the environment and wildlife. Anil Ananthaswamy states, "Gender-bending chemicals could be interfering with the breeding of songbirds. First alligators and fish were being feminized by synthetic hormones leaking into the environment. Now nightingales, skylarks, and even the humble sparrow seem to be at risk."[191] Ananthaswamy identifies the problem: "Synthetic oestrogen used in birth control pills or hormone replacement therapy (HRT) for women has been finding its way into streams and rivers."[192] While this contaminant may come from some other sources as well, including "the breakdown of pesticides such as DDT," it seems the major concern is from contraceptive products.[193]

The effects are dramatic: "Researchers have found that such chemicals interfere with songbirds' reproduction. They also alter their brains, making females sing when they shouldn't," and, "Finches given oestradiol produced fewer eggs and they had brittle shells. The number of hatchlings fell dramatically."[194] In other species, "Oestrogens are believed to be responsible for male alligators in Florida being born with shrunken penises[, and] male fish have also produced yolk protein—something usually only female fish do."[195] An article from *Environment* discusses a chemical contraceptive patch that leeks ethinylestradiol into water sources, despite being processed by sewage treatment facilities, and even running-off from landfills, thereby feminizing fish.[196] Even trace amounts can have a significant effect on the fish, as researchers have demonstrated and reported: "[The] FDA does not require an environmental risk assessment of

---

[191] Anil Ananthaswamy, "Sing Out Sister," *New Scientist* 173, no. 2336 (March 30, 2002): 8.

[192] Ibid.

[193] Ibid.

[194] Ibid.

[195] Ibid.

[196] A. T., "Not Quite Worry-Free," *Environment* 45, no. 1 (Jan/Feb 2003): 6-7.

products that contribute to drug concentrations in the environment at less than one part per billion—but according to [Joakim] Larsson, ethinylestradiol is biologically active in fish at one ten-thousandth of that concentration."[197] Our contraceptive choices are having effects we could not have imagined decades ago.

Even governmental agencies have become increasingly aware of and concerned with these issues. In a 2008 report, Dr. Matthew C. Larsen, Associate Director for Water with the U.S. Geological Survey for the U.S. Department of the Interior, noted, "The observed presence of emerging contaminants in the environment has prompted public interest regarding potential adverse ecological effects and potential contamination of drinking water."[198] The chemicals under consideration come from "human and animal wastes," and, "Many of these chemicals are a new focus for environmental research, because they are used in relatively small quantities and, therefore, were not expected to be of significant environmental concern."[199] Interest in these trace elements and possible effects upon the environment, wildlife species, and humans was "spurred by the findings of European colleagues, who, looking for a pesticide, detected a heart medication in the North Sea (Buser et al., 1998). The realization that chemical-use and waste-handling practices had resulted in detectable concentrations of a drug in such a large water body suggested the need for further research," states Larsen.[200]

By 2008 the U.S. Geological Survey has compiled over 150 reports on trace animal and human chemicals contaminating the environment, and some reports have shown that "these chemicals are assimilated by organisms" and "cause adverse ecological health effects."[201] Furthermore, Larsen states, "Chemical mixtures can act

---

[197] Ibid.
[198] Matthew C. Larsen, "Statement of Dr. Matthew C. Larsen, Associate Director for Water, U.S. Geological Survey, U.S. Department of the Interior Before the Committee on Transportation and Infrastructure Subcommittee on Water Resources and Environment," (September 18, 2008), http://www.usgs.gov/congressional/hearings/docs/Larsen_18sept08.doc (accessed December 18, 2009), 1.
[199] Ibid.
[200] Ibid., 2.
[201] Ibid., 3.

collectively to cause adverse effects, even when each component is below its individual level," and, "Significant uncertainty remains regarding the effects of long-term exposure to levels found in environmental settings."[202] Larsen's report also substantiates the concerns indicated in the studies mentioned above:

> Endocrine disruption is one adverse health effect of concern because it may occur as a result of exposure to very low levels of hormonally active chemicals. One form of endocrine disruption observed in environmental settings affects fish reproductive systems, where fish have been found to be "feminized" by exposure to a range of chemicals that act similarly to the natural hormone estrogen. ... A recent study (Kidd et al., 2007) demonstrated that the addition of ethinylestradiol (one of the active ingredients in birth control pills) at observed environmental concentrations to an experimental lake in Canada caused feminization and near extinction of fathead minnows in the lake.[203]

Other studies, such as from the British Environmental Agency, suggest that increased levels of such hormones in tap water may have caused "the 30 percent decrease in the sperm count among British males from 1989-2002," and could also "be responsible for the earlier and earlier onset of menarche in young women."[204] Clearly, time and science have demonstrated the harmful effects of chemical contraceptives like OCPs on numerous parts of our ethics, society, and relationships—now we may also include the environment in that list.

AIDS and Condoms

It is not fair to say that the Catholic teaching regarding contraception is *completely* ignored by the public. However, what makes headlines lately are stories of an authoritarian Catholic Church

---

[202] Ibid., 4.
[203] Ibid.
[204] Popcak, 31.

stubbornly clutching archaic sexual ethics in the midst of a dynamic global social landscape. A prime example stems from comments Pope Benedict XVI made while traveling on his first visit to Africa on March 17, 2009. Asked about the AIDS epidemic on the continent—which constituted seventy-five percent of worldwide AIDS mortality cases in 2007—he stated, "You can't resolve it with the distribution of condoms," and, "On the contrary, it increases the problem."[205] Benedict affirmed past teachings of Pope St. John Paul II and other Vatican officials that the only cures for the AIDS epidemic are "fidelity in marriage and abstinence from premarital sex."[206] These statements met with fierce opposition in the media including from some Catholic organizations. One such response was in the *Washington Post* from Rebecca Hodes, the head of policy, communication, and research for the Treatment Action Campaign in South Africa, who accuses: "[Pope Benedict XVI's] opposition to condoms conveys that religious dogma is more important to him than the lives of Africans."[207] Such cynicism was evident from many sources.

However, a few days later the *Washington Post* published a response article by Edward C. Green, the director of the AIDS Prevention Research Project at the Harvard Center for Population and Development Studies and senior research scientist at the Harvard School of Public Health. Green, a self-identified liberal and advocate of condom use as a last resort, affirms that despite popular opinion, "empirical evidence supports [Pope Benedict XVI]," in an article the title of which includes, "The Pope Was Right."[208] In a lengthier article almost a year earlier, Green and Allison Herling Ruark noted that ideology and bias had infiltrated the thinking of AIDS organizations and even peer-reviewed articles on the subject stating, "The mainstream HIV/AIDS community has continued to champion

---

[205] Victor L. Simpson, "Pope Says Condoms Worsen HIV Problem," *Washington Post* (March 18, 2009), http://www.washingtonpost.com/wp-dyn/content/article/2009/03/17/AR2009031703369.html (accessed April 3, 2012).

[206] Ibid.

[207] Ibid.

[208] Edward C. Green, "Condoms, HIV-AIDS and Africa – The Pope Was Right," *Washington Post* (March 29, 2009), http://www.washingtonpost.com/wp-dyn/content/article/2009/03/27/AR20090327.2825.html (accessed April 3, 2012).

condom use as critical in all types of HIV epidemics, in spite of evidence."[209] Green does note that Thailand and Cambodia have been able to reduce the spread of HIV with condoms; however, in these countries, "most HIV is transmitted through commercial sex and … it has been possible to enforce a 100 percent condom use policy in brothels."[210] Circumstances in Africa, on the contrary, cannot be helped by simply promoting condom use. Green and Ruark list several studies since 2000 indicating that an increase in condom use has not led to decreases in HIV infection.[211] In fact, condom use in Africa can counter-intuitively *increase* the spread of HIV due to what Green calls "risk compensation," which is explained as, "The tendency to take more sexual risks out of a false sense of personal safety that comes with using condoms some of the time."[212] Green and Ruark note that "Even consistent condom use reduces risk by, at best 80 to 90 percent," so a person with an HIV infected spouse is likely to contract the virus over time even if they correctly and consistently use a condom.[213]

The solutions to the problem are exactly those proposed by Pope Benedict XVI, however unpopular such a truth may be. The major problem in Africa is the number of sexually active single people and unfaithful married couples. Green notes, "In Botswana, which has one of the world's highest HIV rates, 43 percent of men and 17 percent of women surveyed had two or more regular sex partners in the previous year."[214] Consequently, the two most effective—not to mention simple and cost efficient—solutions to the AIDS epidemic in Africa are abstinence and faithfulness.[215] Such strategies have been successful in many places such as, "Uganda, Kenya, Haiti, Zimbabwe, Thailand, and Cambodia, as well as urban

---

[209] Edward C. Green and Allison Herling Ruark, "AIDS and the Churches: Getting the Story Right," *First Things* (April 2008), http://www.firstthings.com/article/2008/03/002-aids-and-the-churces-getting-the-story-right-27 (accessed April 3, 2012).

[210] Edward C. Green.

[211] Green and Ruark; Edward C. Green.

[212] Ibid.

[213] Green and Ruark.

[214] Green.

[215] Green and Ruark; Edward C. Green.

areas of Ivory Coast, Ethiopia, Zambia and Malawi."[216] Green and Ruark explain that faith-based groups offer a unique blend of charity and moral ethics so as to fight the epidemic in ways secular groups cannot. They recognize, "What the churches are called to do by their theology turns out to be what works best in AIDS prevention," though they affirm that the most effective programs teach, "abstinence and faithfulness but also include accurate information on condoms"—a position not entirely in conformity with Papal teaching due to the promotion of condom use as a last resort.[217] Nonetheless, the information provided by Green and Ruark affirms the Catholic position and roots it in empirical evidence.

Critiquing a Georgetown report from 2007, which advocates condoms as the solution in Africa, Green and Ruark explain, "One must ask whether they are more concerned with upholding a Western notion of sexual freedom or with saving lives. The Georgetown report's concern over any prevention approach that might be 'moralistic' caused them to miss entirely the evidence for the remarkable success of sexual-behavior change in reducing HIV infections."[218] Perhaps there are ulterior motives behind the condom lobby in Africa. Green and Ruark note, "Simple behavior changes such as mutual fidelity do little to contribute to a robust and ever-expanding multibillion-dollar 'risk-reduction' AIDS industry focused on medical services, drugs, and devices such as condoms while leaving the true driver of the pandemic, sexual behavior, alone."[219] Green and Ruark are an independent voice of support for the Church's logic on condoms. While they support condoms as a last resort, they see simple behavioral change as the only feasible answer to this deadly epidemic.

In 2010, one year following his visit to Africa, Pope Benedict gave an interview in which he was questioned about the African AIDS epidemic. Benedict indicated that he felt "provoked" by people who opposed the Church's work against AIDS, because he believes the Church to be doing the most to help those struggling with the

---

216 Green and Ruark.
217 Ibid.
218 Ibid.
219 Ibid.

illness, "both before and after they contract the disease."[220] He further indicated that a reliance on the condom, even as a "last resort" as Green and Ruark would have it, "implies a banalization of sexuality, which, after all, is precisely the dangerous source of the attitude of no longer seeing sexuality as the expression of love."[221] He went on to make a comment that would be twisted by the media:

> There may be a basis in the case of some individuals, as perhaps when a male prostitute uses a condom, where this can be a first step in the direction of a moralization, a first assumption of responsibility, on the way toward recovering an awareness that not everything is allowed and that one cannot do whatever one wants. But it is not really the way to deal with the evil of HIV infection. That can really lie only in a humanization of sexuality.[222]

Benedict's interviewer asked for clarification whether this meant the Church is not "opposed in principle to the use of condoms," to which the Holy Father replied, "There can be nonetheless, in the intention of reducing the risk of infection, a first step in a movement toward a different way, a more human way, of living sexually."[223]

Reactions to these statements included everything from an assertion that the Catholic Church is now allowing condoms to reaffirmations that nothing had changed. However, as Fr. Martin Rhonheimer, professor of ethics and political philosophy at the Pontifical University of the Holy Cross in Rome, affirms, Pope Benedict did not suggest that condoms are a lesser evil in the prevention of HIV and pregnancy.[224] Since Pope Benedict's comments concerned the use of condoms by prostitutes, it should be obvious that prostitution and condom use are condemnable.

---

[220] Pope Benedict XVI, *Light of the World: The Pope, the Church, and the Signs of the Times – A Conversation with Peter Seewald*, trans. Michael J. Miller and Adrian J. Walker (San Francisco: Ignatius Press, 2010), 118.

[221] Ibid., 119.

[222] Ibid.

[223] Ibid.

[224] John Norton, "Ethicist: Pope Intended Condom Use/AIDS Reflection," *OSV Newsweekly* (December 19, 2010).

However, it at least demonstrates that the prostitute who may be infected with HIV, albeit engaged in gravely disordered sexual activity, is beginning to develop the seeds of compassion.

In regards to Benedict's comments, and the disingenuous reactions to them, Rhonheimer notes, "The Holy Father has said that in certain cases (in the sex business, for example), [condom] use can be a sign of or first step toward responsibility (at the same time making it clear that this is neither a solution for overcoming the AIDS epidemic nor a moral solution; the only moral solution is abandoning a morally disordered life-style, and living sexuality in a really humanized way)."[225] That settled, Rhonheimer turns to the question of prophylactic use of condoms for spouses, which he is clear to say is beyond Benedict's statement, as he only addressed condom use in the case of prostitution. Rhonheimer indicates, "The question is under study and I have no problems accepting whatever solution the Church proposes."[226] Were the Magisterium to allow condoms as a prophylactic for married couples, Rhonheimer suggests that abstinence during fertile times would be advisable so as to rule out any contraceptive orientation.[227] In addition, Rhonheimer concludes:

> I think complete abstinence would be the morally better choice, not only for prudential reasons (condoms are not entirely effective in preventing virus transmission, even when used consistently and correctly), but also because it better corresponds to moral perfection—to a virtuous life—to abstain completely from dangerous acts, than to prevent their danger by using a device that helps to circumvent the need for sacrifice. Christian spouses should be exemplary in always choosing the path of perfect virtue.[228]

---

[225] Ibid.
[226] Ibid.
[227] Ibid.
[228] Ibid.

Pope Francis and Contraception

Since Bl. Paul VI's pontificate, each time a new pope is elected there are some who anticipate the possibility that a new pope will change the Church's teaching on contraception, as if he could. As demonstrated earlier, when a pope speaks on contraception and family planning, he is often misunderstood. In August 2013, Pope Francis offered an interview in which he discussed a number of his thoughts and visions for the Church. In an often quoted paragraph, Francis brought up some controversial moral issues stating:

> We cannot insist only on issues related to abortion, gay marriage and the use of contraceptive methods. This is not possible. I have not spoken much about these things, and I was reprimanded for that. But when we speak about these issues, we have to talk about them in a context. The teaching of the church, for that matter, is clear and I am a son of the church, but it is not necessary to talk about these issues all the time.[229]

Here Francis makes evident that the teaching is not something he is questioning. Rather, his point in bringing up such subjects and noting that they need not be discussed at all times appears in a particular context. If Pope Benedict XVI's vision of the Church was that it might become smaller and more faithful to the teachings of Christ through the Magisterium, Pope Francis's vision is distinctly missionary. In a missionary Church the foundations of the Gospel must be properly laid first, and that is most important throughout the life of a Christian. Later in the interview he explained, "The proclamation of the saving love of God comes before moral and religious imperatives."[230] Francis is not suggesting that we avoid talking at all about such issues, or even more, that he disagrees with the teachings of the Church on such issues. He is working instead to make clear that we cannot draw souls to Christ if we start with anything other than the salvific Gospel message.

---

[229] Antonio Spadaro, "A Big Heart Open to God," *America* (September 30, 2013).
[230] Ibid.

These comments in the interview are located in a section in which Pope Francis explains that he considers the Church to be a field hospital. He elaborates:

> "I see clearly," the pope continues, "that the thing the church needs most today is the ability to heal wounds and to warm the hearts of the faithful; it needs nearness, proximity. I see the church as a field hospital after battle. It is useless to ask a seriously injured person if he has high cholesterol and about the level of his blood sugars! You have to heal his wounds. Then we can talk about everything else. Heal the wounds, heal the wounds.... And you have to start from the ground up.

This is the context in which Pope Francis says such issues should not be the first things we might bring up in a conversation with an unbeliever, or even a fallen-away Catholic. In a missionary Church, the fundamental issues must be settled before people will be able to hear God's call in these other issues. He further clarifies his vision:

> **Proclamation** in a missionary style focuses on the essentials, on the necessary things: this is also what fascinates and attracts more, what makes the heart burn, as it did for the disciples at Emmaus. We have to find a new balance; otherwise even the moral edifice of the church is likely to fall like a house of cards, losing the freshness and fragrance of the Gospel. The proposal of the Gospel must be more simple, profound, radiant. It is from this proposition that the moral consequences then flow.[231]

It is also necessary to intellectually maintain and physically put into practice the teachings of the church on moral issues like homosexuality, abortion, and contraception, toward which Pope Francis directed his attention. In fact, one day after Pope Francis's

---

[231] Ibid.

interview was published, the Holy Father condemned abortion at a gathering of Catholic gynecologists.[232] He is obviously firm on these issues; he simply reminded us in his interview that the essential Gospel of Jesus Christ must be primary.

Permitted Uses of Contraception

It is important to note that the Church does not consider contraceptives themselves as objectively intrinsically evil. Pope Bl. Paul VI made clear in HV that medical necessity could justify recourse to contraceptives, provided they were not being used primarily as a contraceptive.[233] In this sense, contraceptives are not being used as contraceptives, *per se*. Rather, they are justifiable by the principle of double effect—wherein a person may perform an action that has an unintended secondary evil effect, provided that the primary action is (1) not objectively evil in its own right, (2) a necessary action, and (3) is proportionate to the secondary evil effect.

The Principle of Double Effect should not be confused with situation ethics, which holds that the primary action can be evil if it achieves some relative good. It is commonplace for physicians to violate the *necessity* condition of double effect, by prescribing OCPs for menstrual cramps and cycle irregularity, or to violate the proportionality condition by prescribing it for acne. In reality, contraceptives like OCPs rarely if ever function to truly *"cure* bodily diseases" (emphasis mine), as Bl. Paul VI wrote. Instead, they merely *mask* symptoms.

There are often other alternatives that can at least as effectively mask, if not truly treat and cure, bodily maladies. Dr. Chris Kahlenborn indicates that menstrual cramps and migraines can be relieved in much less risky ways than OCPs with simple doses of calcium and magnesium.[234] Some Catholic NFP organizations—like

---

232 Francis X. Rocca, "Pope Condemns Abortion as Product of 'Throwaway Culture," *Catholic News Service* (September 20, 2013), http://www.catholicnews.com/data/stories/cns/1303991.htm (accessed September 30, 2013).

233 Pope Paul VI, Humanae Vitae, http://www.vatican.va/holy_father/paul_vi/ encyclicals/documents/hf_p-vi_enc_25071968_humanae-vitae_en.html (accessed July 14, 2009), §15.

234 Chris Kahlenborn, *Breast Cancer: Its Link to Abortion and the Birth Control Pill* (New Hope, KY: One More Soul, 2000), 38.

the Pope Paul VI Institute in Omaha, Nebraska—are proficient in treating and often healing underlying health concerns that are frequently merely masked by OCPs. Another resource is Marilyn Shannon's *Fertility, Cycles and Nutrition*, which explores the relationship of fertility to quality of nutrition, including ideas for how to adjust diet to improve fertility. Such services and resources have been dramatically underappreciated and underutilized, largely to the detriment of authentic healing and true medicine. It seems symptoms like acne, cramps, and cycle irregularity—which may be more effectively treated by other means—may oftentimes serve as an excuse by both Catholic doctors and patients to justify contraception.

Even if such prescriptions are started "morally" before marriage, they are often carried into the marriage under the same pretenses, though they have now taken on a clearly contraceptive role. A single woman may morally use a contraceptive as a therapeutic medicine, but the whole situation changes with marriage and subsequent sexual activity. The abortifacient nature of OCPs alone would make them illicit for spouses to utilize. Using a contraceptive as a contraceptive is not justifiable.

Many people are surprised to learn that the Church may sometimes permit the use of contraceptives in the case of rape. The *Ethical and Religious Directives for Catholic Health Care* Services by the United States Conference of Catholic Bishops (USCCB) in 2001 states, "A female who has been raped should be able to defend herself against a potential conception from the sexual assault. If, after appropriate testing, there is no evidence that conception has occurred already, she may be treated with medications that would prevent ovulation, sperm capacitation, or fertilization."[235] However, abortion or any means that would operate as an abortifacient and "have as their purpose or direct effect the removal, destruction, or interference with the implantation of a fertilized ovum," are morally evil and prohibited.[236] Even in a case of rape, directly attacking an innocent human life, as through abortion or abortifacient procedures, is not morally acceptable. Lawler, Boyle, and May explain that an essential

---

[235] United States Conference of Catholic Bishops, "Ethical and Religious Directives for Catholic Heath Care Services," 4th ed. http://www.usccb.org/bishops/ directives.shtml (accessed December 11, 2009), Directive #36.
[236] USCCB, "Ethical and Religious Directives," Directive #36.

difference exists here between the Church's teaching on contraception between spouses and victims of sexual assault, because a sexually assaulted woman has not consented to the sexual action.[237] Therefore, her action is not a violation of the union between the unitive and procreative goods. As with the approval of using a contraceptive for necessary medical purposes, which is not truly using it as a contraceptive as the Church understands it, so too in this case the use of a contraceptive is not immoral in light of the Church's teaching.

Furthermore, women, such as religious sisters working in a hostile foreign country, "who [are] in real danger of rape," may take contraceptive precautions so as not to conceive should they fall victim to sexual assault, according to some conservative theologians.[238] Echoing Lawler, Boyle, and May; Ashley, Deblois, and O'Rourke explain why this situation is not violating the necessary connection between the unitive and procreative dimensions as they state, "A woman who has consented to intercourse takes responsibility as a free person to use the sexual act in keeping with its intrinsic significance of love and procreation. The arguments of *Humanae Vitae* against contraception are based on this responsibility."[239] Consequently, such a victim has a right to contraceptive measures, provided they are truly contraceptive and not abortive. It would be immoral for a woman to assert and protect her own rights, "at the expense of the rights of a child already in existence."[240]

---

[237] Ronald Lawler, Joseph Boyle Jr., and William E. May, *Catholic Sexual Ethics: A Summary, Explanation, & Defense*, 2nd ed. (Huntington, Indiana: Our Sunday Visitor, 1998), 195.

[238] Benedict M. Ashley, Jean Deblois, and Kevin D. O'Rourke, *Health Care Ethics: A Catholic Theological Analysis*, 5th ed. (Washington D.C.: Georgetown University Press, 2006), 84.

[239] Ibid.

[240] Ibid.

Chapter 3
Changes in the Church

As any nominal Catholic with sufficient life experience can easily recognize, the American Catholic landscape this far into the twenty-first century has changed since 1990, even more considerably since 1965, and quite dramatically since 1940. Each generation has been forged under different circumstances. The situation of the Church today is lamentable, regardless of with which camp one's allegiances lie. Revisionists rejoice in the fact that most Catholics feel free to follow their consciences while remaining in the Church and consider themselves "good Catholics."[1] However, they are perpetually frustrated by a Magisterium that continuously persists in holding to and defending the teaching of HV.[2] Conversely, traditionalists appreciate the minority of Catholics who support and promote the teaching, but they bemoan the majority of Catholics, including many theologians, who believe they can live in a way incompatible with the position the Church believes she is compelled to maintain as God's truth and plan.[3] As the Church has rolled over the clock on this new millennium, we find ourselves persistently locked in polarized camps on the issue of contraception, and all else that has sprung from the issue's history and development.[4] Despite this gridlock, winds are changing, and signs of resolution may be glimmering through the clouds.

---

[1] Charles E. Curran, forward to *The Sexual Person: Toward a Renewed Catholic Anthropology*, by Todd A. Salzman and Michael G. Lawler (Washington D.C.: Georgetown University Press, 2008), xiv.

[2] Charles E. Curran, "Humanae Vitae: Still Controversial at 30." *National Catholic Reporter* 34, no. 35 (June 1998): 12-13.

[3] Germain Grisez, "How to Deal with Theological Dissent," in *Readings in Moral Theology No. 6: Dissent in the Church*, ed. Charles E. Curran and Richard A. McCormick (New York: Paulist Press, 1988), 455.

[4] Francis A. Sullivan, "The Authority of the Magisterium on Questions of Natural Moral Law," in *Readings in Moral Theology No. 6: Dissent in the Church*, ed. Charles E. Curran and Richard A. McCormick (New York: Paulist Press, 1988), 45.

Twenty-First Century American Catholic Landscape

The National Study of Youth and Religion (NSYR) provides a glimpse into 21st century challenges.[5] What the NSYR discovered about Catholic youth is disappointing and should serve as a wake-up-call for the Church. Recognizing some "very religiously engaged" U.S. Catholic teens—as witnessed by one of the researchers at the 2003 National Catholic Youth Conference (NCYC)—they maintain that such vibrant young Catholics "are not typical."[6] Christian Smith and Melinda Lundquist Denton report that Catholic teens are lagging significantly behind their Protestant counterparts in areas such as "religious faith, belief, experience, and practice."[7] The report confirms that many young Catholics are "living far outside of official Church norms defining true Catholic faithfulness," and they "tended to be rather religiously and spiritually indifferent, uninformed, and disengaged."[8] Whereas the report does not deal directly with attitudes toward contraception, it does reveal how little today's youth think with the mind of the Church.

What are the causes of this Catholic deficiency in America's teens? Smith and Denton suggest several. First, the NSYR indicates that teens' attitudes, practices, and beliefs are most significantly impacted by their parents.[9] In other words, today's crisis is rooted significantly in the previous generation—a point that was evident in the NSYR's interviews with the parents of surveyed teens.[10] The problem is therefore intergenerational. Second, Smith and Denton believe that Catholic education is deficient. Traditional Catholic means of propagating the faith, such as CCD/religious education/faith formation programs, seem less effective than those being employed by Protestant congregations.[11]

Finally, demographic changes are believed to have contributed to the issue. Throughout much of American history, Catholics have not

---

[5] Christian Smith and Melinda Lundquist Denton, *Soul Searching: The Religious and Spiritual Lives of American Teenagers* (New York: Oxford, 2005), 4, 6.

[6] Ibid., 194.

[7] Ibid., 216.

[8] Ibid., 194, 195.

[9] Ibid., 208, 210.

[10] Ibid., 210.

[11] Ibid., 210-214.

held a high social position, and they "were recurrently maligned, persecuted, and socially excluded" in decades past, while in the last sixty years "U.S. Catholics made remarkable gains in socioeconomic status, which helped to facilitate their eventual social acceptance in U.S. culture and institutions."[12] American Catholics' socio-economic status improved considerably in the middle of the twentieth century. As a result, the way Catholics practiced their faith changed. Sociologist James Davidson explains:

> U.S. Catholics have gone from being a relatively small, working class, and highly segregated population of largely white Europeans who trusted social institutions, especially their pre-Vatican II Church, and stressed the importance of obeying church teachings, to being a larger, more privileged...population that is more highly integrated into American society and culture, more skeptical of all social institutions, including the post-Vatican II Church, and more inclined to stress the importance of thinking for themselves.[13]

The shifts that took place in the middle of the twentieth century certainly had a major impact on the U.S. Church. Smith and Denton suggest that the "upward mobility and acculturation" of Catholics, combined with the Vatican II climate, resulted in lower Mass attendance, fewer vocations, and an apathy toward the Catholic faith.[14] As a result, Smith and Denton conclude that Catholic teens' social and economic status is a major factor in their (and their parents') lack of adherence to elements of the Church, especially traditional requirements and moral teachings.[15] The situation of the youngest in the Church, also reflective of their parents' beliefs and attitudes, suggests a bleak future for the Church, but what does this all have to do with contraception?

---

[12] Ibid.
[13] Ibid., 214-215.
[14] Ibid.
[15] Ibid., 215.

The implications of the NSYR are certainly important for the topic of contraception. It serves to illustrate the level of commitment found among U.S. teens and their parents, as well as the sociological and ecclesial issues of the twentieth century that have shaped and have been shaped by the contraception debate, among other issues. The changes going on in American Catholics' social situation last century contributed to the way they received, or rejected, HV in 1968 and thereafter. However, the rejection of that teaching easily led to the rejection of Church authority on all kinds of issues, even beyond morality. Catholic theologian Julie Hanlon Rubio notes that the position of the Church on sexual morality became less and less important to many Catholics during this time, and Andrew Greeley has gone so far as to directly suggest one major factor behind lower Mass attendance in recent decades is the poor reception of HV, as reported by Rubio.[16] All of these factors played into the resulting "cafeteria Catholics" phenomenon in the American Catholic Church today. Judging from the current moral laxity, the next generation is poised to inherit a legacy of apathy, relativism, and errant pluralism.

New Appreciation for Church Teaching

This is not to say that dissident influences have won out. In the 1985 *Ratzinger Report*, Joseph Cardinal Ratzinger stated, "At the beginning of the great debate following the appearance of the encyclical *Humanae vitae* in 1968, the demonstrative basis of the theology faithful to the Magisterium was still relatively slim. But, in the meantime, is has been broadened through new experiences and new reflections so that the situation is beginning to reverse itself."[17] The tide has continued to shift, and people are finding credibility in the Church's position.[18] John D. Hagen summarizes a few reasons why things are changing: "Here are a few important points that we've

---

[16] Julie Hanlon Rubio, "Beyond the Liberal/Conservative Divide on Contraception: The Wisdom of Practitioners of Natural Family Planning and Artificial Birth Control," *Horizons* 32, no. 2 (Fall 2005): 275.

[17] Joseph Ratzinger, "The Drama of Morality," in *Readings in Moral Theology No. 6: Dissent in the Church*, ed. Charles E. Curran and Richard A. McCormick (New York: Paulist Press, 1988), 311.

[18] Janet E. Smith, introduction to *Why Humanae Vitae Was Right: A Reader*, ed. Janet E. Smith (San Francisco: Ignatius Press, 1993), 12; John D. Hagen Jr., "Humanae Vitae's Legacy," *Commonweal* 131, no. 11 (June 4th, 2004): 8-9.

learned in the intervening years: Natural family planning works. ...
Artificial contraception has abortifacient properties. ... Artificial
contraception poses serious risks to women's health. ... Pope Paul
VI was an accurate prophet."[19] We have reason to hope that if the
faithful come to fully understand the Church's teaching, they may live
lives in tune with it, and the rest of the world will begin to see the
wisdom of properly ordered sexuality with its concomitant effects.

Interest in the Church's teaching is also growing. In 2008, an
article by Dennis Sadowski of Catholic News Service ran the
headline, "On 40th Anniversary, 'Humanae Vitae' Starts to Gain More
Attention," and he noted that the encyclical "seems to be finding new
life across the country."[20] The article quotes Janet Smith stating,
"While the numbers may not be overwhelming, a growing number of
people are beginning to understand the connection between the
sexual freedom that emerged in the 1960s and today's violence,
depiction of women as sex objects and high incidence of divorce."[21]
The article also includes a quote from renowned revisionist Charles
Curran who stated, "In fairness, the strongest argument in favor of
'Humanae Vitae' was the argument the pope himself gave, that this
has been a constant teaching of the church and (he) can't change it.
... In a sense you can understand that. How can the Holy Spirit guide
the church all these centuries and then make a mistake on a rather
significant issue?"[22] Father Tadeusz Pacholczyk, director of education
at the National Catholic Bioethics Center recognizes, "There's a
whole beauty to marriage that is at stake. ... To the extent we can
communicate that, people say 'Wow, the church is relevant and
maybe I shouldn't be so dismissive.'"[23]

---

[19] Hagen, 8-9.
[20] Dennis Sadowski, "On 40th Anniversary, 'Humanae Vitae' Starts to Gain More
    Attention," *Catholic News Service* (July 18, 2008)
    http://www.catholicnews.com/data/stories/cns/0803746.htm (accessed
    October 14, 2009).
[21] Ibid.
[22] Ibid.
[23] Ibid.

Theology of the Body Movement

Another development worth noting is an increasingly popular Theology of the Body movement[24], which is based on Pope St. John Paul II's 1979-1984 Wednesday audience series on human dignity and the revelatory nature of human sexuality. One of the most popular contributors in this area is the author and speaker Christopher West, who was interviewed on national television in 2005 regarding Pope St. John Paul II's teachings in the days following his death. Strongly supportive of the Magisterium, West is an advocate for St. John Paul II's personalism, and has written a full, scholarly commentary on the Theology of the Body (TOB), the goal of which is to "unpack the entire catechesis from start to finish."[25] West has also produced a beginner's version for the "average Catholic" on the topic, the first and second editions of which have been among the most popular books in Catholic publishing. West distills St. John Paul II's ethics down to four principles of divine love, which we are called to imitate: "free, total, faithful, and fruitful."[26] He suggests that since various sexual acts like contraception, homosexuality, masturbation, fornication, and adultery fail to meet one or more of the four criteria listed above, they fail to adequately imitate God's love and his plan for our sexuality to reflect his love.[27] Furthermore, West suggests, couples make promises to love this way in the questions of intent to marry and their marriage vows. To deny any of the four ideals is to shortchange one's wedding vows.[28]

West notes, "People hate being told what to do and what not to do, especially when it comes to sex. ... We don't want anyone, not even God, telling us that something we want to do is wrong. We want to determine what is good and evil for ourselves. It's the

---

[24] The history of *Theology of the Body*, including its impetus, is discussed in Chapter 6.

[25] Christopher West, *Theology of the Body Explained: A Commentary on John Paul II's "Gospel of the Body"* (Boston: Pauline, 2003), xviii.

[26] Christopher West, *Theology of the Body for Beginners: A Basic Introduction to Pope John Paul II's Sexual Revolution* (West Chester, Pennsylvania: Ascension Press, 2004), 96.

[27] Ibid.

[28] Ibid., 105.

problem of pride."[29] The Language of the Body was instrumental in West's whole outlook. "Embracing this teaching changed the way I see, well, *everything*," he writes; "The Church's teaching against contraception is where the rubber hits the road (pun intended). ... Indeed, the entire Christian sexual ethic...either stands or falls on this point."[30] Taking up the question of whether the hierarchical Church has lost touch with the laity and lost credibility on sexual (if not all moral) issues, West states, "If the Church is wrong about this issue, I would agree. She is 'out of touch' and loses all credibility right here. But if the Church is right about contraception, then it's the rest of the world that's 'out of touch,' and the Catholic Church *gains* all credibility right here."[31] While West's influence has faded in recent years, his work has represented a new grass roots movement for integrated sexuality that signifies God's overall call to love.

Author and speaker Jason Evert—frequently teamed with his wife Crystalina—offers a similar approach, but for teenagers. They have co-authored a book with Brian Butler called *Theology of the Body for Teens*, spoken internationally on chastity, established a chastity club and website, and authored a number of practical booklets on God's plan for sexuality. Their chastity talks and websites have attracted thousands of teenagers throughout the country, including non-Catholics.[32] For a decade Jason and Crystalina have spoken to over a million people and have shared authentic chastity and respect for sexuality learned from Catholic sexual morality and St. John Paul II's TOB. These popular authors and speakers are a couple of the highlights among many who are part of the turning tide at work in the Church.

A New Type of Catholic

While many young Catholics are imitating popular society's views (likely also their parents' views) on family planning, a new type of Catholic is emerging within the Church as well. Some of these are

---

[29] Christopher West, *Good News about Sex & Marriage: Answers to Your Honest Questions about Catholic Teaching* (Ann Arbor: Servant, 2000), 31.
[30] Ibid., 106.
[31] Ibid., 118.
[32] Colleen Carroll, *The New Faithful: Why Young Adults are Embracing Christian Orthodoxy* (Chicago: Loyola Press, 2002), 135.

laypeople, some are becoming theologians and contributing to the family planning discussion, and some are joining the ranks of the clergy and religious. The coming of this new type of Catholic has been in the making for decades, but they have only recently come to the fore. Already in 1988, Bishop John J. Myers observed that many people, including religious and clergy, had made up their minds on sexual teachings of the Church; however, many young couples and clergy are reversing this trend.[33] He notes, "They have grown up in a different age. ... They have a *predisposition for assent* to the teaching of the Church."[34] Living through the history of the issue, Hagen recognizes the new signs of the times as younger generations of Catholics are finding credibility in the Church's teachings, while those who remain stuck in the older arguments are "aging and dwindling," and their ideals are headed for extinction.[35] As one example, we might consider the differences between religious orders and dioceses that are growing in vocational recruits, versus those that are fading away. Orders and dioceses boasting expansion are the ones meeting the needs of this often younger, more magisterially oriented generation of Catholics. They are not interested in dissent; they are interested in Catholic identity and something more than secularism and pluralism have to offer.

A new subgroup of young Catholics has emerged. Borrowing a phrase from David O'Brien, William L. Portier calls them "evangelical Catholics" and describes them in the following way:

> By the 1990s, a new breed of student started turning up in my theology classes. Far from a majority, their small number often includes the most intellectually gifted. These students are interested in Catholic-specific issues. They want meat. They love the Pope. They are pro-life. They do service trips during breaks and gravitate toward "service" upon

---

[33] John J. Myers, "The Rejection and Rediscovery by Christians of the Truths of *Humanae Vitae*," in *Trust the Truth: A symposium on the Twentieth Anniversary of the Encyclical Humanae Vitae*, ed. Russell E. Smith (Braintree, MA: The Pope John XXIII Medical-Moral Research and Education Center, 1991), 75.

[34] Ibid.

[35] Hagen, 9.

graduation. All during this time as well, I observed the 150 or so seminarians at Mount Saint Mary's Seminary on our campus. Often dismissed as "conservative" throwbacks to the 1950s, they strike me as undeniably contemporary. ... Neither liberal nor conservative, they confound the categories of my fifty-something friends.[36]

Evangelical Catholics break the polarized molds of the late 20th century. They are looking for the best in Catholicism, as they understand it, which often means utilizing elements from "conservatives" and "liberals." In terms of contraception, their minds are much more open, having missed the divisive debates following HV and having grown up in a very different world and Church than their parents and grandparents. Janet Smith recognized an increasing interest among such youth in the early 1990s when she wrote, "Recently a student group at a major Catholic university in the Midwest wanted a speaker to explain the Church's teaching on contraception. They were most astonished to find that in a theology department of over thirty, not one professor could be found who was willing to give a public lecture explaining and defending the Church's teaching on contraception."[37]

We may continue by asking, what is the cause of this new group of young Catholics in the late twentieth and early twenty-first centuries? Portier explains that it has a lot to do with the changes in society and the Church in the second half of the twentieth century. The primary catalyst is the move from a strong Catholic subculture within the U.S. to religious pluralism. Portier explains,

> It is pluralism, fragmentary and unstable, that makes evangelical forms of Christianity sociologically possible. ... If we have no subculture to buffer so many Catholics from pluralism's ordinary dynamics, we can expect to see more "evangelical Catholics." ...

---

[36] William L. Portier, "Here Come the Evangelical Catholics," *Communio* 31 (Spring 2004): 37.

[37] Janet E. Smith, "Paul VI as Prophet," in *Why Humanae Vitae Was Right: A Reader*, ed. Janet E. Smith (San Francisco: Ignatius Press, 1993), 502.

They will not only embrace Catholic identity voluntarily, but will also have to struggle to differentiate the freedom of faith from the culture of choice encouraged by contemporary pluralism.[38]

Portier recognizes that the most significant event of the twentieth century that is usually credited with shifts in American Catholicism is Vatican II; however, when we consider that the council has not had the same effect on younger generations in other countries, there must be more to it.[39] The shift from subculture to pluralism helps to fill in these gaps and explain what else contributed to the polarization found within the U.S. Catholic Church. It is this pluralism to which the evangelical Catholics are reacting, as it was the Catholic subculture of the mid-20th century to which many Vatican II Catholics reacted. In the same vein as the NSYR, Portier notes, "As the twentieth century advanced, American Catholics continued to move up the sociological escalator. But as they did, many experienced the subculture as more of a confine than a haven," to the point that some began to see the subculture as a "ghetto."[40] By the time of HV, Catholics were more assimilated into American culture.[41]

The reality is that such a changed worldview has dramatically altered how evangelical Catholics exercise their religious liberty. David McCarthy compares the experience of living in a pluralistic society to that of a strong Catholic subculture, which provides some insight into the situation:

Evangelical Catholics are immersed in American pluralism. Conversing with others in a field of cultural diversity is a regular habit of life, not an epistemological problem. Sharing time and interests with those who do not share one's "values" comes naturally. Being a self-ruled individual with an ironic conception of life is not hard to imagine. The pressing question is not the possibility of responding,

---

[38] Portier, 41.
[39] Ibid., 47.
[40] Ibid., 46.
[41] Ibid.

interacting, and breaking bread with the "other" in a pluralistic world, but what we Catholics, as a people, bring to the table. What can we give? This is an evangelical question. Pluralism and a diversity of worlds are taken for granted, and in the Church's theology, liturgy, and social practice, the evangelical finds a coherent, reasonable, and persuasive account of human life.[42]

Identity is a key issue for the evangelical Catholics. Having been raised within a pluralistic culture, they are now seeking something that their parents and grandparents took for granted—something *unique* about their Catholic faith, something that sets them apart from typical society and unites them as a group, something that speaks to them on a deeper level than the world has to offer.[43] Portier relays a story of disconnect between a Catholic professor who was trying to teach his young students about dissent: "The students said they needed a deeper sense of what the Church stood for. Instead of permission to dissent from the Church, this particular group of young Catholics wanted to learn about the Catholic tradition and its significance in their lives."[44] For the most part, dissent does not make sense, or at least is not a significant issue to young Catholics, because they are used to it, and they are now looking for the truths the Church has to teach them.[45] The changing times, social and ecclesial structures, as well as a longing for eternal truths have produced this novel type of young Catholic.

As the previous example of the teacher and his students illustrates, this new group is typically misunderstood by their elders in the faith. Passionate about service trips, Catholic social teaching, and legitimate diversity, many "liberals" warm up to such youth while "conservatives" dismiss them. Then the same youth may also pray the rosary, attend Eucharistic adoration, and talk warmly of the pope,

---

[42] David M. McCarthy, "Shifting Settings from Subculture to Pluralism; Catholic Moral Theology in an Evangelical Key," *Communio* 31 (Spring 2004): 86.

[43] Portier, 49, 51.

[44] Ibid., 57.

[45] "Paul VI Vindicated, Denver Bishops Says," *National Catholic Reporter* 34, no. 35 (July 31, 1998): 12-13.

thus provoking an opposite reaction. The new evangelical Catholics simply cannot be categorized by the old caricatures; this new wine will only break the old wineskins. "Evangelical Catholics are willing to submit to a tradition and a way of life that is deeply reasonable. This kind of submission sounds retrograde to both personalist natural lawyers and to revisionists. But for a generation reared amid pluralism this turn to a continuing tradition of thought and action is necessary to ground reason," explains McCarthy.[46] There is no other way to see these evangelical Catholics than as a new generation of the Church, reacting to the social and ecclesial background of their lives, not so different in the stimulus for their origin than previous generations.

Both McCarthy and Portier recognize the influence these evangelical Catholics are likely to have in the future. Portier sees evangelical Catholics taking a leadership role in the near future:

> Surely [evangelical Catholics] are not the majority. But…they look more like the future than the past. In my experience, admittedly anecdotal, it is from among this thirty-seven percent that undergraduate theology majors, parish youth ministers, and graduate students in theology and ministry are more likely to come. If true, this is most significant for the future of the Catholic Church in the United States.[47]

McCarthy notes, "An evangelical future marks a return to the rosary, but it may very well be held during a protest of the World Bank."[48] Admittedly, evangelical Catholics do not all agree on all of the Church's official teachings, but perhaps they are capable of finding the best of both sides in the deadlock between traditionalists and revisionists, reopening the lines of communication, appreciating the changes of the past several decades, and helping the Church move forward in the third millennium. In some ways this has already begun. Magisterial teachings on contraception may well carry more weight with future generations of Catholics, and not as an isolated

---

[46] McCarthy, "Shifting Settings," 102.
[47] Portier, 53.
[48] McCarthy, "Shifting Settings," 110.

subset of Catholic doctrine, but as a sign of the larger wisdom of Holy Mother Church.

A New Generation of Theologians

Despite the apathy and other problems evident in the American Catholic landscape, a new generation of theologians—some of whom resemble evangelical Catholics—has begun making contributions on the issue of family planning. They come to the issue with new perspectives, concerns, insights, and needs. Curran introduces the up-and-coming generation in the following:

> These scholars—such as Florence Caffrey Bourg, David Matzo McCarthy, and Julie Hanlon Rubio—have no living memory of Vatican II and *Humanae vitae*. In general these married people emphasize that marital morality involves much more than just sexual issues. … In many ways they are trying to move beyond the paralyzing debates of the last forty years of the twentieth century.[49]

The sociological and ecclesiological changes of the past half-century have also influenced moral theology. A young theologian himself, David McCarthy explains:

> The story of post-Vatican II debates is not only about a radical transition in moral thought, but also about an attempt to buttress moral reason without the kind of theological and practical stability that a subculture can take for granted. Moral theologians raised in a subculture do not have to go looking for theological sources or formation systems. Theologians reared on pluralism and postmodernism are looking for connections, not only between practices of piety and the moral life, but also between theology and socio-economic questions.[50]

---

[49] Curran, forward to *The Sexual Person*, xiv.
[50] McCarthy, "Shifting Settings," 89.

McCarthy believes the revisionist approach to morality, which often employs proportionalism[51], is incapable of functioning outside of a subculture mentality that inherently provides some structure and boundaries. He argues,

> Proportionalism has not been able to sustain a structure of goods from which it can weigh proportionate benefits and harms. It is a response to an institutionally established set of norms but it cannot count on them within its own methodology. In other words, it is not a system but a corrective to a (subculture's) system. As a theory in itself, it lacks clear criteria to judge and determine benefits and harms, so that insofar as it is successful in undermining the system of institutional obligations that it reacts against, the theory loses its legs. ... It fails to ask basic questions about identity: who am I, and what kind of person ought I to become?[52]

Consequently, it lacks popularity among younger Catholics, because the milieu upon which it depends no longer exists. Thus, he notes, "These questions about identity are fundamental in a pluralist culture, and for this reason, the debate about proportionalism has receded."[53] Evangelical Catholics are looking for stability—a stability older Catholics formed in a subculture take for granted. For this reason, they are interested in positions revisionists adamantly rejected, such as moral absolutes.[54]

The title of a recent article by Julie Hanlon Rubio, "Beyond the Liberal/Conservative Divide on Contraception: The Wisdom of Practitioners of Natural Family Planning and Artificial Birth Control," is indicative of young theologians' desire to move beyond the current theological impasse. She expresses legitimate disapproval

---

[51] Proportionalism holds that an action is morally permissible as long as the good it pursues is proportionately greater than the evil inherent in the act. See part II for the origins of this moral philosophy, its deficiencies, and Magisterial condemnation in *Veritatis Splendor*.

[52] Ibid., 104.

[53] Ibid.

[54] Ibid., 95, 102.

of the current theological situation in which "liberals" rarely continue to discuss the issue and basically "indicate by their silence that the issue has been settled," while the "conservatives" who are still addressing it do so "in forums removed from mainstream academic conferences."[55] It is as if this issue has crippled unitive and creative work amongst Catholic theologians. Her critique is shared by another young theologian, Christopher Ruddy. In a discussion of young theologians looking at the current theological situation, he notes that many Catholic universities and colleges are "dominated by some older theologians, whose intellectual clocks stopped in 1968 with the ecclesial politics of Humanae vitae, and a middle generation whose theology is often uprooted and diffuse."[56] McCarthy concurs, "It is the post-Vatican II debates that depend upon a bygone world, and evangelical Catholic theologians are as indifferent to these debates as they are distant from the Catholic subculture of the 1940s and 50s."[57] This new generation is already beyond the setting from which the issue erupted; now it's a matter of moving the Church and moral theology forward.

The situation of two polarized camps incapable of intercommunication and mutual appreciation seems to be changing with these younger theologians. Ruddy explains they are "not interested in fighting the old battles: in hearing the war stories of liturgical abuses of either the Left or the Right, and the seminary horror stories of the 1950s or 1970s; in practicing a theology obsessed with liberal and conservative camps and shooting down those who dare to see merit in the 'opposition's' thought."[58] Rubio echoes this point-of-view and adds, "A new sort of sexual ethics that fails to fit in to the usual categories is beginning to emerge."[59] The times have changed, as Ruddy notes, "Younger theologians are concerned with how to grasp more fully the sources of our tradition, address the consumerism of our culture and the cheapness of all life in it, and pass on the church's liturgical and social riches to our own

---

[55] Rubio, 270.
[56] Christopher Ruddy, "Young Theologians—Between a Rock & a Hard Place," *Commonweal* (April 21, 2000), http://findarticles.com/p/articles/mi_m1252/is_8_127/ai_61795234/ (accessed December 17, 2009), 4 of 5.
[57] McCarthy, "Shifting Settings," 86.
[58] Ruddy, 4 of 5.
[59] Rubio, 271.

and future generations that are so sadly ignorant and in need of them."[60] Rubio suggests this "new generation of scholars and lay people ... cannot be easily categorized as liberal or conservative," and they promote "a counter cultural focus on self giving in sexual relationships [that] sharply contrasts with a cultural backdrop of promiscuous sex for personal pleasure."[61] This new generation may be coming to the situation enough removed from the immediate post-Conciliar Church and its debates to find a way to move toward an authentic resolution, or even beyond the need for resolution. Although the issue will likely take many more generations to resolve, the beginning to middle of the twenty-first century may witness a new era beyond the schism currently still rending the Church.

Different ideas on how to move forward may be proposed; however, the younger theologians tend to share more in common and are much less polarized. Rubio mentions, "Younger writers both embrace the relational-focus of contemporary culture and maintain a counter-cultural understanding of sexuality as a dimension of Christian discipleship. This is a good place for a new conversation to begin."[62] Her goal is to demonstrate the "common ground" shared both by users of contraception and users of NFP.[63] Her approach, therefore, tends to be one of recognizing the best of both sides in an attempt to keep the conversation alive and make it more productive than it has been in previous decades. Rubio suggests that there is much to be learned from both sides, as a "groundswell of popular literature" has erupted in recent years on NFP, as well as a bit of a riposte from couples using contraception.[64] She observes that for most practitioners of NFP, "The experience is extremely positive," and, "The problems of couples in the Crowleys' study seem largely absent," largely due to significant advances in the last several decades.[65] On the other hand, contracepting couples' positions "are deeply rooted in experiences of Christian spouses who want their sexual lives and their faith to be of one piece, and find contraception

---

[60] Ruddy, 4 of 5.
[61] Rubio, 293.
[62] Ibid., 272.
[63] Ibid., 276.
[64] Ibid., 271.
[65] Ibid., 276.

to be helpful rather than harmful," and evidence "finds in the lives of couples who use contraception desire for and experience of many of the very same goods NFP advocates value."[66]

Rubio continues by highlighting important elements of each side that deserve more attention in order to move the issue beyond the current standstill. She suggests the emphases of "total self-giving", abstinence, as well as the importance and priority put on the good of children (typical of NFP couples) are significant contributions to the discussion and "cry out for imitation."[67] She recognizes that "boredom is a recurring theme" in contemporary sexuality, and periodic abstinence has been shown to significantly increase "sexual desire and pleasure" among females.[68] On the other hand, Rubio also notes the insights that contracepting couples bring to the discussion, such as the "self-giving" contemporary couples are called to beyond the family that may not allow for additional pregnancies.[69] Rubio's primary suggestion for continuing the discussion involves "developing an experientially-based theological vision that can serve as a guide for the sexual relationships that are central in the lives of most Christians."[70] Rubio has suggested admirable goals in terms of continuing the discussion, crossing over the typical polarized boundaries, and recognizing the best things from both side. A point of caution: her emphasis on an "experientially-based theological vision" may prove to be inherently susceptible to relativism if insufficiently grounded in objective morality.

Virtue Ethics

Some argue that contemporary moral theology has taken a positive turn with the recovery of virtue ethics, catalyzed by a return to virtue ethics in philosophy that has spilled into other disciplines like theology. A major cause of this was Alasdair MacIntyre's *After Virtue*. D. Vincent Twomey suggests that consideration of the human vocation to eternal beatitude and holiness, as well as the topics of the

---

[66] Ibid., 278.
[67] Ibid., 291.
[68] Ibid., 292.
[69] Ibid., 292.
[70] Ibid., 294.

passions and virtues, has been largely ignored.[71] "Thanks to a return to the ethics of Aristotle in philosophy and of Aquinas in theology…," Twomey explains, "The most exciting discovery in the past two decades has been the recovery of virtue not only as a concept but as providing the context for moral reflections."[72] According to Twomey, *Veritatis Splendor* (VS) worked to end the debates of moral theology erupting after HV, while the promulgation of the CCC, with its renewed discussion of passions and virtues, marked a "new beginning", which Twomey believes has finally answered the call of Vatican II for renewal in moral theology.[73]

Moral theology that emphasizes virtue has emotional and aesthetic appeal without sacrificing truth. "Virtue ethics," says Twomey "is essentially about human character, about our integrity as human beings."[74] When moral theology is taken out of the context of the Christian calling to holiness, it loses its lifeblood. A focus on Christian holiness and virtue for the purpose of love of God and neighbor must once more become the center of moral theology. Recently, Twomey has suggested, "Moral theology…will cease to be *existentially* peripheral to the inner life of the Church once moral theologians realize that what is truly 'specific' to moral theology is its humble (but daunting) role in helping to define (and continually to refine the definitions of) what constitute the moral conditions for the acquisition of holiness."[75] Morality must be at the core of the Christian life, yet in recent decades it has faded in importance to the point that living as a Christian has lost its meaning and purpose for many.

In his book *Rediscovering Catholicism*, Catholic author and speaker Matthew Kelly encourages what he calls "singleness of purpose" to achieve success—this means for a person to have a "clearly defined goal," and thereafter to form "habits that [enable] him to achieve his goal."[76] Kelly identifies the significance of singleness of purpose in

---

[71] D. Vincent Twomey, *Moral Theology after Humanae Vitae: Fundamental Issues in Moral Theory and Sexual Ethics* (Dublin: Four Courts Press, 2010), 87.

[72] Ibid.

[73] Ibid., 97.

[74] Ibid., 103.

[75] Ibid., 122.

[76] Matthew Kelly, *Rediscovering Catholicism: Journeying Toward Our Spiritual North Star* (Cincinnati: Beacon, 2002), 122.

the following: "When you have singleness of purpose, everything else is embraced or discarded according to whether or not it moves you in the direction of your goal. When you don't have this singleness of purpose, you get lost in the tossing and turning of daily life."[77] Kelly's idea of singleness of purpose relates closely to St. Ignatius of Loyola's "First Principle and Foundation", which serves as an outstanding guide to morality:

> Man is created to praise, reverence, and serve God our Lord, and by this means to save his soul. The other things on the face of the earth are created for man to help him in attaining the end for which he is created. Hence, man is to make use of them in as far as they help him in the attainment of his end, and he must rid himself of them in as far as they prove a hindrance to him. ... Our one desire and choice should be what is more conducive to the end for which we are created.[78]

"Singleness of purpose" might be the key to an integral sexual morality in which marital relations are portrayed and understood as signifying the divine calling to mutual self-gift. To assist us in the challenges of living such a lifestyle, Twomey refers to the saints as the "living 'authorities' of tradition, the great exponents of virtue within certain historical situations and cultural conditions," who like "their model...Jesus Christ, *the* exemplar," are available "to inspire us and to prompt us to imitate them."[79]

The theme of virtue is also a key component of Martin Rhonheimer's treatment of the Church's teaching on family planning. By respecting the body-spirit unity of each lover's beloved, the couple that practices periodic abstinence is capable of utilizing both the acts of intercourse and the abstentions to grow in deeper relationship with one's beloved and in holiness. He explains:

---

[77] Ibid., 123.
[78] St. Ignatius of Loyola, *The Spiritual Exercises of St. Ignatius*, trans. Louis J. Puhl (Chicago: Loyola Press, 1951), 12.
[79] Twomey, 105.

By abstaining from possibly fertile intercourse, spouses relate virtuously to sexual acts, to themselves, and to each other as a possible cause of new life. This respecting of their sexual activity as such a cause—and provided that they feel obliged not to beget a baby—is precisely the reason why they abstain from intercourse. By acting together in their restraint, the spouses moreover act as two persons "united in one flesh": their behavior proceeds from procreatively responsible love and serves this love.[80]

Yet, he does not stop there. Rhonheimer goes on to address the challenges with which NFP couples sometimes struggle and recognizes in them an opportunity to grow in virtue and holiness and fulfill the essence of sacramental marriage. Such opportunity is itself integral to the purpose of the marriage itself—to lead the spouses to greater sanctification together. He continues:

The problems, burdens, and difficulties possibly involved in a practice of periodic continence, to which its critics so often refer, have to be considered as the burdens and difficulties involved in faithfully carrying out marital commitment and *not*—as critics usually do—as something interfering with marital love. These burdens and difficulties may be overcome precisely by the fact that continence *is* an act of marital love in itself. The very nature of responsible abstinence includes the dynamic principle for overcoming these difficulties: this principle is precisely "marital love," which must be continually deepened, in this case through renunciation *for the sake of love* and responsibility. ... What may seem like a burden changes into a source of maturing in love and increasing in mutual self-giving.[81]

---

[80] Martin Rhonheimer, *Ethics of Procreation and the Defense of Human Life: Contraception, Artificial Fertilization, and Abortion*, ed. William F. Murphy Jr. (Washington D.C.: Catholic University of America Press, 2010), 97.

[81] Ibid., 97-98.

He summarizes, "Contraception is problematic precisely because of the fact *that it renders needless a specific sexual behavior informed by procreative responsibility; it also involves a choice against* virtuous *self-control by continence.*[82]

How does one make this apparent to couples? Rhonheimer suggests in order to demonstrate the vice and sin a contracepting couple enters into, it is necessary to show the virtue opposed to such a vice as he notes, "If one explains to contracepting people what they are doing when they contracept, precisely by making them aware of what they *would* do *instead* if they practiced periodic continence, then they are enabled to immediately grasp what they are *failing* to do by adopting contraception. To explain vices, one has to talk about the virtues to which they are opposed."[83] To do this, he recounts HV §21:

> [Such discipline] demands continual effort yet, thanks to its beneficent influence, husband and wife fully develop their personalities, being enriched with spiritual values. Such discipline bestows upon family life fruits of serenity and peace, and facilitates the solution of other problems; it favors attention for one's partner, helps both parties to drive out selfishness, the enemy of true love; and deepens their sense of responsibility. By its means, parents acquire the capacity of having a deeper and more efficacious influence in the education of their offspring; little children and youths grow up with a just appraisal of human values, and in the serene and harmonious development of their spiritual and sensitive faculties.[84]

Rhonheimer believes the depth of these virtues as articulated by Bl. Paul VI may be possessed by the couple practicing periodic abstinence as a result of and coming forth from their continence. He reflects on contraceptive consequences in the following:

---

[82] Ibid., 100.
[83] Ibid., 108.
[84] Ibid., 109.

All of these are endangered, if not completely lost, by contraception. Indeed, these goods might even begin to be experienced subjectively as evils, because of the effort and sacrifice required to attain them. The state of marriage in contemporary society (especially the incapacity of the young to form marriages, and the increase of separation and divorce) reflects in fact a situation *opposite* to one marked by the above goods, which derive from responsible love and the corresponding "self-discipline" of the spouses.[85]

Catholic Social Teaching

One thing "evangelical Catholics" can bring to the discussion about Church teaching on contraception and family planning is its link to Catholic social teaching. More immune to tendencies of polarization among their elders, evangelical Catholics are less likely to fall into the situation Raymond Brown rightly criticized over thirty years ago, yet still rings true in the Church:

> Catholics are in a strange state of schizophrenia about Church pronouncements. Those who inhabit the extreme right of the Catholic spectrum are eager to burn at the stake any theologian who disagrees with Church pronouncements on sexual morality; but the necessity of accepting Church positions becomes very vague if the bishops suggest returning the Canal to Panama or come out in support of the farmworkers, or if Rome comes to an agreement with an Iron Curtain country. For this group, obedience is required in matters of faith and morals—and "morals" means sexual morals—but not in matters of social and political justice. On the other side of the spectrum, Catholic liberals taunt conservatives with non-observance of the social encyclicals, but preserve a glacial silence when the Pope or the bishops speak

---

[85] Ibid.

about sexual morality. For them, bishops should be listened to if they say something progressive, but when they repeat tradition, that is just the party line. A reference to infallibility in faith and morals is looked on as archaic.[86]

Today's evangelical Catholics may be in a position to conjoin the Church's teaching on contraception with its social justice ethos.

McCarthy hopes to show the link between the anti-contraceptive stance of the Church and its social teaching, and he has proposed the value of seeing HV as both theological *and* social in its approach, function, and purpose.[87] He explains:

> It is not merely coincidental that reductionist proposals for economic progress depend upon contraceptive technology as a means for advancement, for the upward mobility of citizens, and for the development of nations. To this degree, HV's opposition to artificial contraception parallels Paul VI's arguments in documents such as *Populorum Progressio* and *Octogesima Adveniens*. The teaching on contraception is a social teaching, and the social teaching is founded on theological claims about human solidarity and upon the continuity between our natural and supernatural, or eschatological, fulfillment.[88]

One great concern here is the ability of issues related to procreation to undermine the good of the family and therefore destabilize society itself, of which the family is an essential building block. The CCC states, "The family is the *original cell of social life*. It is the natural society in which husband and wife are called to give

---

[86] Raymond E. Brown, "The Magisterium vs. the Theologians: Debunking Some Fictions," in *Readings in Moral Theology No. 3: The Magisterium and Morality*, ed. Charles E. Curran and Richard A. McCormick (New York: Paulist Press, 1982), 291.

[87] David M. McCarthy, "Procreation, the Development of Peoples, and the Final Destiny of Humanity," *Communio* 26 (Winter 1999): 699.

[88] Ibid., 700.

themselves in love and in the gift of life."[89] When families are not healthy, society will not be healthy. Furthermore, the mentality of children as a burden (if not worse) is detrimental to society as a whole. McCarthy explains, "Contraceptive practices promise relief in a culture where child rearing is an economic liability and a risk to one's personal lifestyle, but Paul VI warns that we will undercut the basic structure of social life if we abdicate our common calling to bear and raise children."[90] Practices that undermine marriages and families are a threat to society and ought to be condemned. In this way the Church's teaching on contraception is related to Catholic social teaching.

Also pertinent to the cooperation of the Church's family planning teaching and its teaching on social justice, is the issue of protecting the human right to fertility. Bl. Paul VI warned about the activities of some government authorities who might be inclined to solve problems of families, populations, natural resources, or economics by promoting or even imposing contraceptives. In HV he stated, "Who will blame a government which in its attempt to resolve the problems affecting an entire country resorts to the same measures as are regarded as lawful by married people in the solution of a particular family difficulty?"[91] Within a couple of decades of HV this prediction came to realization. Janet Smith attests, "In Third World countries many undergo sterilization unaware of what is being done to them. The forced abortion program in China shows the stark extreme to which governments will take population control programs."[92] Other examples include "coercive" emergency contraception in India (1976-1977) and the "bullying implantation" of contraceptive devices and drugs by the government of Indonesia in the 1970s and 1980s.[93] Furthermore, it is not uncommon today for

---

[89] *Catechism of the Catholic Church: Modifications from the Editio Typica*, 2nd ed. (Washington, DC: United States Catholic Conference, Inc.—Libreria Editrice Vaticana, 1997), §2207.

[90] McCarthy, "Procreation," 701.

[91] *Pope Paul VI, Humanae Vitae, http://www.vatican.va/holy_father/ paul_vi/encyclicals/documents/hf_p-vi_enc_25071968_humanae-vitae_en.html (accessed July 14, 2009), §17.*

[92] Janet E. Smith, "Paul VI as Prophet," 527.

[93] Austin B. Vaughan, "*Humanae Vitae* and Respect for the Dignity of the Human Person," in *Trust the Truth: A symposium on the Twentieth Anniversary of the*

"foreign aid" granted to impoverished countries to have strings attached that require receiving governments to "promote contraceptives—and abortion—under the guise of 'family planning' or 'reproductive rights'."[94] Even Charles Curran has recognized the fulfillment of Bl. Paul VI's prediction that impoverished countries and peoples could suffer "exploitation" by the rich and powerful through contraceptives.[95] When methods of family planning are absolutely necessary, we must also keep in mind that NFP has been demonstrated to be very effective, especially among the poor.

Imposing contraception on poorer, less-developed nations carries with it the imposition of the problems related to contraceptives as well. Not only does this involve the problems of side-effects, but also the social and economic issues discussed in the previous chapter. McCarthy draws this parallel:

> Common sense formulae for economic growth pit money-making and childbearing against each other not only in terms of a global equation for developing countries, but also for the American middle-class couple who secure their own bit of economic and social advancement (along with their careers) with what has become a requisite access to contraceptives. ... Controlling births is risk management. Bearing and raising children (and domestic life as a whole) is no longer considered a productive venture, but a practice of consumption that drains rather than accrues resources.[96]

This approach is incompatible with true progress and a Christian attitude about family and sexuality. McCarthy continues, "Could so-called progress place a burden upon families because it is not real

---

Encyclical Humanae Vitae, ed. Russell E. Smith (Braintree, MA: The Pope John XXIII Medical-Moral Research and Education Center, 1991), 20; Mary Eberstadt, "The Vindication of Humanae Vitae," *First Things*, no. 185 (Aug/Sep 2008): 38.

[94] Twomey, 22.

[95] Janet E. Smith, *Humanae Vitae: A Generation Later* (Washington D.C.: Catholic University of America Press, 1991), 191.

[96] McCarthy, "Procreation," 704.

progress at all? … Put another way, is childbearing set against money-making because the system of money-making is itself set against human solidarity and true social development?"[97] McCarthy further asserts, "When pursued outside of God's design for human community, human advancement contradicts itself. … Paul VI situates human development within the context of the Creator's design. … Both *Populorum Progressio* and *Humanae Vitae* hold economic and cultural progress up to the test of human fulfillment."[98] In this way, there is much more shared between the Church's teaching on family planning and Catholic social teaching than has been commonly realized. This is not the type of argument one finds in traditionalist defenses of HV, but it needs to be an argument going forward. Evangelical Catholics, who seem most able to bridge the gap between entrenched conservatives and liberals, are in a unique position in today's Church to bring this connection to light.

McCarthy makes further connections between contraception and Catholic social teaching. He explains, "Paul VI argues against contraception on the same terms that he critiques global economic planning and reductively technological (impersonal) solutions to problems of human community."[99] "Contraception is certainly a question about the beginning of life," he continues, "but primarily it is an issue of human solidarity, in accord with the end of creation and our community with God. … The teaching against contraception is a call for instituting the practices of an authentically generative economy and a procreative way of life."[100] By comparing HV to the Church's social doctrines, we are able to appreciate the Church's teaching on contraception and family planning in a new way. McCarthy concludes:

> If a contraceptive economy and culture set economic advancement against childbearing, if the social and economic equality of women is defined in terms of the non-procreative activity of men, if

---

[97] Ibid., 705.
[98] Ibid., 705-706.
[99] Ibid., 715.
[100] Ibid.

"making love" is set over against "making children," then the procreative character of human sexuality has become detached from social and economic life. It is for this reason that it becomes necessary to insist upon the procreative goods of sexuality and of human life. ... Paul VI holds that technology and economics must serve human nature—must complete and perfect God's creation (*PP*, nos. 22, 27), build authentic human community (no. 47), and fulfill human life in light of our supernatural destiny (nos. 14-18). This principle applies as much to the use of private property (nos. 23-24) as it does to procreation (no. 37).[101]

In this way, McCarthy works to show how social justice and Catholic social teaching are intertwined with the issue of contraception and family planning. These issues cannot remain separated as earlier generations of theologians have allowed, because both will be furthered by realizing the connection between them.

McCarthy is not alone in linking contraception with social justice, though. In Pope Benedict XVI's 2009 social encyclical, *Caritas in Veritate*, he too notes the connection between social justice and contraception. Benedict XVI suggests, "One of the most striking aspects of development in the present day is the important question of *respect for life*, which cannot in any way be detached from questions concerning the development of peoples."[102] The Holy Father lays out the threats posed to the human family by aggressive contraception policies:

> Not only does the situation of poverty still provoke high rates of infant mortality in many regions, but some parts of the world still experience practices of demographic control, on the part of governments that often promote contraception and

---

[101] Ibid., 719, 721.
[102] Pope Benedict XVI, *Caritas In Veritate* (2009), http://www.vatican.va/holy_father/benedict_xvi/encyclicals/documents/hf_ben-xvi_enc_20090629_caritas-in-veritate_en.html (accessed August 15, 2009), §28.

even go so far as to impose abortion. In economically developed countries, legislation contrary to life is very widespread, and it has already shaped moral attitudes and praxis, contributing to the spread of an anti-birth mentality; frequently attempts are made to export this mentality to other States as if it were a form of cultural progress. ... Moreover, there is reason to suspect that development aid is sometimes linked to specific health-care policies which *de facto* involve the imposition of strong birth control measures.[103]

The encyclical, likewise, extols the social benefits of a pro-family culture:

Openness to life is at the centre of true development. When a society moves towards the denial or suppression of life, it ends up no longer finding the necessary motivation and energy to strive for man's true good. If personal and social sensitivity towards the acceptance of a new life is lost, then other forms of acceptance that are valuable for society also wither away. The acceptance of life strengthens moral fibre and makes people capable of mutual help. By cultivating openness to life, wealthy peoples can better understand the needs of poor ones, they can avoid employing huge economic and intellectual resources to satisfy the selfish desires of their own citizens, and instead, they can promote virtuous action within the perspective of production that is morally sound and marked by solidarity, respecting the fundamental right to life of every people and every individual.[104]

---

[103] Ibid.
[104] Ibid.

Ecumenism

Following HV, some revisionists lamented the perceived negative effects the encyclical may have on ecumenical dialogue. Although up until 1930 all Christians forbid contraception as immoral, following the 1930 Lambeth Conference (when Anglicans permitted contraception for married couples for serious reasons) other Christians followed suit. By the time of Vatican II, Catholics stood, for all practical purposes, alone among Christians as officially condemning the practice. During and following the council, the Church became more ecumenically focused, and walls began to break down between Catholics and other denominations. Those who wanted to see the Church's teaching on contraception change had hoped such a change would decrease the differences between Catholics and other Christians. This was another revisionist hope that came crashing down with HV. Instead, fear began to take hold that the Church's "stubborn" position would make ecumenical dialogue more difficult.

Obviously, considering the developments on the issue that had been taking place within Protestantism prior to Vatican II, we could have guessed that many Protestants would not be happy about HV. Robert McAfee Brown, for example, makes bold statements similar to the revisionists when he writes the following soon after HV:

> *Humanae Vitae* is a tragedy for the Catholic Church and for the contemporary world. It is not only its content that upsets me, although I think it objectively wrong on almost every score, from its lack of contact with the modern world to its limited understanding of the psychology of marriage and its faulty understanding of the place of sexual intercourse in that relationship. It is also the manner of its issuance that upsets me; it not only fails to produce convincing arguments to support its thesis and to go counter to the overwhelming majority opinion of the papal commission that was presumably to guide its final content, but it also flies in the face of the collegial principle that I thought had been established

149

by Vatican II and implies, possibly by intent, that papal authority is once again to be understood along the most reactionary lines of nineteenth-century Catholic thought.[105]

These are certainly strong words, yet Brown is passionately interested in this situation, because he knows what happens in Catholicism is also important for Protestants, like himself, and the world.[106] Consequently, he does not believe other Christians can simply disregard the official Catholic Church's teaching on this topic as insignificant.

In the last few years, however, things even in the area of ecumenism have been changing. Young journalist Colleen Carroll explored a general movement within Christianity of young believers growing in appreciation for traditional Christianity, including a more strict morality, in her book *The New Faithful: Why Young Adults are Embracing Christian Orthodoxy*. Echoing what we have discovered about evangelical Catholics above, Carroll recognizes that although it is not the only cause, "A reaction against today's moral relativism and religious pluralism surely accounts for much of the inverse appeal of orthodoxy."[107] Among young Christians, Carroll has recognized, "A growing number of young adults are rebelling against their elders by embracing tradition in the way they dress, date, marry, and mate. Repulsed by the sexual license, moral confusion, and social chaos they see around them, these young adults are embracing conventional morality and an orthodox faith that gives meaning to their countercultural choices."[108] The soil is ripening for reconsideration of contraception and NFP among Christians, not only Catholics. Moreover, it is an issue that has the ability to bind them ecumenically together as Christians, together becoming a sign of contradiction to worldly values and trends.

---

[105] Robert McAfee Brown, "*Humanae Vitae* a Protestant Reaction," in *Contraception: Authority and Dissent*, ed. Charles E. Curran (New York: Herder and Herder, 1969), 193-194.

[106] Ibid., 196-197.

[107] Carroll, 9.

[108] Ibid., 124.

One of the major groups reconsidering HV is Protestant evangelicals. A "symposium" on contraception in *First Things* relays the insights of two major evangelicals: R. Albert Mohler, Jr., President of the Southern Baptist Theological Seminary in Louisville, and evangelical theologian Harold O. J. Brown. On this topic Mohler states, "The effective separation of sex from procreation may be one of the most important defining marks of our age—and one of the most ominous. This awareness is spreading among American evangelicals, and it threatens to set loose a firestorm."[109] Reflecting on how things were at the time of the release of HV, Harold Brown notes, "While most Protestant leaders regarded artificial contraception with some misgivings, in the absence of a foundation in natural law they had not developed good and principled arguments for dealing with it. To the extent that contraception was regarded as a Catholic preoccupation Protestants tended to be tolerant of it."[110] Similarly, Mohler writes, "Most evangelical Protestants greeted the advent of modern birth control technologies with applause and relief. … Indeed, birth control became fixated in the Protestant mind as a 'Catholic issue.' That is, until recently."[111] Today, Harold Brown notes, Protestants are being "forced" to reconsider Rome's "outmoded values" in the wake of the sexual revolution and a loss of respect for "both the Bible and natural law."[112] Considering the changing times, Mohler explains, "In an ironic turn, American evangelicals are rethinking birth control even as a majority of the nation's Roman Catholics indicate a rejection of their Church's teaching. … A new evangelical assessment of *Humanae Vitae* is in order."[113] If evangelicals are finding reason to reconsider the issue, certainly Catholics ought to do so as well.

Reflecting on HV, Harold Brown explains the reasons why HV failed to convince Catholics and other Christians was not that it was "unsound," but rather it impinged upon what people wanted to do, "as all divine law, both natural and revealed will do," and it "came

---

[109] "Contraception: A Symposium." *First Things* 88 (December 1998), http://www.firstthings.com/article/2007/01contraception-a-symposium-28 (accessed December 21, 2009).

[110] Ibid.

[111] Ibid.

[112] Ibid.

[113] Ibid.

too late," as social and scientific developments had already brought the sexual revolution into full swing.[114] Mohler speaks of the problems contraceptives like OCPs created:

> As Pope Paul VI warned, widespread use of birth control would lead to "serious consequences," including marital infidelity and a general erosion of morality. In reality, The Pill allowed a near-total abandonment of Christian sexual morality in the larger culture. Once the sex act was severed from the likelihood of childbearing, the traditional structure of sexual morality collapsed. ... Thirty years of sad experience demonstrate that *Humanae Vitae* sounded the alarm, warning of a contraceptive mentality that would set loose immeasurable evil as modern birth control methods allowed seemingly risk-free sex outside the integrity of the marital bond.[115]

It is remarkable to consider that a comment such as this is coming from someone other than a staunch traditionalist Catholic, let alone the president of a Southern Baptist seminary, three decades after HV.

In 2006, Mohler gave an interview for the New York Times in which he stated, "I cannot imagine any development in human history, after the Fall, that has had a greater impact on human beings than the pill."[116] In recent years, the issue has intensified among evangelicals, and like the evangelical Catholics, younger evangelical Protestants are reconsidering the question of contraception. Mohler indicates, "I detect a huge shift. Students on our campus are intensely concerned. Not a week goes by that I do not get contacted by pastors about the issue. There are active debates going on. It's one of the things that may serve to divide evangelicalism."[117] Early revisionists might have been surprised to hear of the turmoil among young

---

[114] Ibid.
[115] Ibid.
[116] Russell Shorto, "Contra-Contraception." *New York Times* (May 7, 2006), http://www.nytimes.com/2006/05/07/magazine/07 contraception.html (accessed December 21, 2009).
[117] Ibid.

evangelicals and a prominent Protestant like Mohler finding credibility in Catholicism's position on this subject, which leads naturally to opportunities for ecumenism with Catholics. If such changes in perspective on contraception become more common within Protestant circles, as men like Mohler believe is already happening, young twenty-first century Catholics may find themselves in considerable agreement with some young Protestants, and even non-Christians, on this issue. Rather than causing a problem for ecumenism, the Church's sexual teaching adds credibility to the Church's position.

Famous Protestant converts to Catholicism, Scott and Kimberly Hahn, found their way to the Catholic teaching on contraception while they were still evangelicals. Kimberly came from a family of Presbyterian ministers, and Scott was staunchly Calvinist and self-identified as unreservedly anti-Catholic. Scott was not quiet about his firm conviction that "The Pope was the Antichrist and…the Church of Rome was the whore of Babylon."[118] Kimberly was the first to wrestle with the issue of contraception, though. She recalls, "I had not thought it was an issue to be studied until I became involved in pro-life work. For some reason, birth control kept creeping in as an issue. Being a Protestant, I did not know any friends who did not practice birth control."[119] Exploring the Catholic side of the issue and becoming convinced of its legitimacy, Kimberly was able to share with Scott the Catholic Church's position, which they found to be not only remarkably convincing, but also strongly grounded in Biblical values.[120] Kimberly shares, "In reading *Humanae Vitae*, I came to appreciate the balance of the Church in her understanding about contraception. There was a godly way to experience the act of marriage and to be prudent in serious circumstances by practicing continence during times of mutual fertility."[121] Based upon their findings, Scott admits, "I grew disturbed. The Roman Catholic Church stood alone as the only 'denomination' in all the world with the courage and integrity to teach this most unpopular truth. I did

---

[118] Scott Hahn and Kimberly Hahn, *Rome Sweet Home: Our Journey to Catholicism* (San Francisco: Ignatius Press, 1993), 25.

[119] Ibid., 33-34.

[120] Ibid., 27, 34-37.

[121] Ibid., 39.

not know what to make of it."[122] This discovery was part of a chain of events by which they eventually fully embraced Roman Catholicism. Since then they have both written on a variety of Catholic theological topics and have traveled throughout the world sharing their conversion story.

The work of Charles D. Provan is also a significant ecumenical contribution. A Protestant opposed to contraception on Biblical and historical grounds, he affirms, "Some may say to themselves as they read this, 'Why this is just a Roman Catholic custom, and so may be discarded.' But, dear readers, this is not so."[123] He takes a hard line when he writes, "Christians of today have been so influenced by our godless materialistic culture that their view of children is the same as that of the world: 'children are an economic drain—they make you poor—they limit economic progress—they prevent women from reaching their potential.'"[124] He goes on to cite Luther, Calvin, and numerous other Protestants throughout the centuries since the Reformation along with countless Biblical references to demonstrate to his Protestant audience that contraceptives and a contraceptive mentality are not the will of God for his people. Catholics will find in contributors like Provan a great asset for ecumenical progress against such evils.

The examples of ecumenism go even beyond Protestants. A committed Mormon, Joseph B. Stanford M.D. has found the position of Roman Catholicism absolutely convincing. He and his wife were trained in NFP by a Catholic organization while he was in medical school, and later he learned another method of NFP in a Catholic setting. He relates, "I began to feel that any form of contraception had its unintended detrimental effects on the marital (or non-marital) relationship, whether recognized or not," largely due to the separation of procreation from the unitive dimension of sexual intercourse, by which the meaning of the action is contradicted, and the husband becomes ever more capable of objectifying his own wife

---

[122] Ibid., 28.
[123] Charles D. Provan, *The Bible and Birth Control* (Monongahela, PA: Zimmer Printing, 1989), 14.
[124] Ibid., 7.

154

for the sake of his own pleasure.[125] Stanford recognizes the value of NFP as a husband and doctor:

> I find that the following benefits come to those couples who use NFP: 1) they come to a deeper appreciation of fertility as a gift from God, rather than a biological phenomenon to be manipulated or a curse to be avoided; 2) they are usually able to consciously and rapidly achieve pregnancy when they choose to ("surprise" pregnancies are rare for NFP users); 3) they consider their choices about their fertility on an ongoing basis; 4) in their relationship, each spouse sends to the other the implicit and powerful message: "I accept all of you, including your fertility"; 5) they learn to assume and exercise joint responsibility for decisions about their fertility; and 6) they learn that times of abstinence from genital contact can strengthen their relationship.[126]

Remarkably, after study of HV and the Catholic position, Stanford testifies, "I believe that the insights of [HV] could only have come from divine inspiration."[127] In this way Stanford has come to appreciate the Catholic position, study it intently, and implement it into his own life while also recommending it to his patients and other physicians.

Even leaders of cultures in the East have champions who have taken a stand against contraceptives. Consider for example a quote from Mahatma Gandhi as cited in Coffin:

> As it is, man has sufficiently degraded [woman] for his lust, and artificial methods, no matter how well meaning the advocates may be, will still further degrade her. I urge the

---

[125] Joseph Stanford, "My Personal and Professional Journey with Regard to Moral Issues in Human Procreation," in *Physicians Healed: Personal, Inspiring, and Compelling Stories of Fifteen Courageous Physicians Who Do Not Prescribe Contraception*, ed. Cleta Hartman (Dayton: One More Soul, 1998), 114-115.

[126] Ibid., 116.

[127] Ibid., 122.

advocates of artificial methods to consider the consequences. Any large use of the methods is likely to result in the dissolution of the marriage bond and in free love. Birth control to me is a dismal abyss.[128]

Through the use of reason, people of all cultures are capable of discovering God's natural law and its inherent objection to contraception.

Ecumenism is fostered by truth, not compromise—however compassionate it may be. A comment by convert Kimberly Hahn is well conveyed: "Other Christians are under the same obligations we are to follow truth; there isn't one standard for Catholics and another for other Christians, In fact, we have important information they need to have that will give them the clarity to live according to truth."[129] As more and more of the Church's separated brethren accept the truth of the Church's wisdom on contraception, the Church's openness to children is reaffirmed and the prospects for a larger unification become brighter.

U.S. Bishops

Like many others discussed in this chapter, the U.S. Bishops have moved further from revisionist sensibilities and have more strongly supported the official teaching of the Church. If the aftermath of HV showed an international episcopal college in conflict over the issue of contraception, it is significantly less so today. In 2006 the United States Conference of Catholic Bishops (USCCB) published "Married Love and the Gift of Life." Recognizing the social context in which they wrote, the bishops note the prevalent thinking: "Being responsible about sex simply means limiting its consequences—avoiding disease and using contraceptives to prevent pregnancy," to which they reply, "This cultural view is impoverished, even sad. It fails to account for the true needs and deepest desires of men and women. Living in accord with this view has caused much

---

[128] Patrick Coffin, *Sex au Naturel,* (Steubenville, OH: Emmaus Road, 2010), 78.
[129] Kimberly Hahn, *Life-Giving Love: Embracing God's Beautiful Design for Marriage* (Ann Arbor: Servant, 2001), 232-233.

loneliness and many broken hearts."[130] Steeped in St. John Paul II's personalism, the bishops affirm: "That 'body language'—what a husband and wife say to one another through the intimacy of sexual relations—speaks of *total* commitment and openness to a future together. So the question about contraception is this: Does sexual intercourse using contraception faithfully affirm this committed love?"[131] In reply they state, "When married couples deliberately act to suppress fertility, however, sexual intercourse is no longer fully *marital* intercourse. ... Suppressing fertility by using contraception denies part of the inherent meaning of married sexuality and does harm to the couple's unity."[132] As pastors, the bishops recognize the challenges this teaching presents, "Many couples today, through no fault of their own, have not heard (or not heard in a way they could appreciate and understand)," this teaching on family planning.[133] Finally, while being acquainted with the challenges of the teaching, they remind Catholics of the strength and grace they can find in God, the sacraments, and the Church. Near the end they recall a pertinent verse, "You are not your own; you were bought with a price. So glorify God in your body. (1 Cor 6:19-20, RSV)"[134]

At the end of 2009, the USCCB released another document significant to our discussion. Echoing the subtitle of St. John Paul II's *Theology of the Body*, it is called "Marriage: Love and Life in the Divine Plan." Within an overall discussion of marriage, the bishops identify four "fundamental challenges to the nature and purposes of marriage;" contraception is listed first among these.[135] The bishops reaffirmed the inseparable connection between the unitive and procreative dimensions of each sexual act in marriage, as stated in

---

[130] United States Conference of Catholic Bishops, "Married Love and the Gift of Life," (November, 14, 2006), http://www.usccb.org/laity/marriage /MarriedLove.pdf (accessed December 17, 2009), 2.

[131] Ibid., 3.

[132] Ibid.

[133] Ibid., 3, 4.

[134] Ibid., 3, 9.

[135] United States Conference of Catholic Bishops, "Marriage: Love and Life in the Divine Plan," (November 17, 2009), http://www.usccb.org/laity/ LoveandLife/MarriageFINAL.pdf (accessed 11/19/09), 17.

HV.[136] The bishops characterized contraception as an obstacle to the mutual love of spouses:

> [Contraception] is objectively wrong in and of itself and is essentially opposed to God's plan for marriage and proper human development. It makes the act of intercourse signify, or speak, something less than the unreserved self-gift intended in the marriage promises. The language of the body that is meant to express self-gift becomes mixed with another message, a contrary message—namely, the refusal to give oneself entirely. Thus the unitive meaning of the language is falsified.[137]

Recognizing that many spouses believe they are doing what is best by using contraceptives, the Bishops counter, "The deliberate separation of the procreative and unitive meanings of marriage has the potential to damage or destroy the marriage. Also, it results in many other negative consequences, both personal and social."[138] Finally, the Bishops recognize the legitimacy of NFP and promote its use when couples need to postpone or avoid pregnancy.

Recent years have witnessed an escalating confrontation between Catholic bishops and the White House. The Obama administration released health care plans in 2011 as part of the Affordable Care Act that would require all employers' health insurance plans to provide FDA approved contraception and sterilization services to their employees—known as the Health and Human Services Mandate. Religious exemptions were in place, however, they were not broad enough to include Catholic hospitals, charities, and educational facilities like schools, colleges, and universities. Such a proposal has been in the works since 1997, introduced to Congress as "the Equity in Prescription Insurance and Contraceptive Coverage bill or EPICC

---

136 Ibid., 18.
137 Ibid., 18-19.
138 Ibid., 19.

bill."[139] According to Teresa Wagner, contraceptives are not healthcare, as she explains in the following: "Contraception is different from other prescription drugs, in that they do not treat or prevent disease and therefore are *not truly health care*."[140] Confusion is rampant—being fertile is healthy, while infertility is what needs to be fixed through authentic health care.

This ethical-political situation erupted into a firestorm with dissenters on both sides. Archbishop of New York and then President of the United States Conference of Catholic Bishops, Timothy Cardinal Dolan led the opposition from the Catholic side, primarily arguing that such requirements impinge upon religious freedom and constitute a government mandated violation of conscience. For instance, in early March 2012 Dolan stated, "Don't impose your teaching upon us and make us do as a church what we find unconscionable to do!" and, "It is a freedom of religion battle. … We are talking about an unwarranted, unprecedented radical intrusion into the interior life of integrity of a church's ability to teach, serve, and sanctify in its own."[141] Some Catholics have disagreed with the bishops, such as "Sister Carol Keehan, president and CEO of the Catholic Health Association of the United States," who approves of women's access to contraception, though even she was "'disappointed' that the administration did not affirm an 'appropriate conscience protection' for religiously affiliated employers."[142]

The White House is no more united. Jake Tapper with ABC News reports of the situation in 2011, "For months, Vice President Joe Biden and then-White House chief of staff Bill Daley argued

---

[139] Teresa Wagner, "Contraception, Natural Family Planning, and Women," In *Integrating Faith and Science Through Natural Family Planning*, ed. Richard J. Fehring and Theresa Notare (Milwaukee: Marquette UP, 2004), 51.

[140] Ibid.

[141] Kevin Sheehan and Gary Buiso, "Dolan Blasts White House Contraception Plan as 'Freedom of Religion Battle'," *New York Post* (March 3, 2012), http://www.nypost.com/p/news/local/dolan_blasts_white_house_contraception_tlOdFvb1saw2qldwedIUpL?utm_medium=rss&utm_content=Local (accessed April 5, 2012).

[142] Devin Dwyer, "Obama Rejects Contraception Exemption for Catholic Hospitals, Schools," *ABC News* (January 20, 2012), http://abcnews.go.com/blogs/politics/2012/01/obama-rejects-contraception-exemption-for-catholic-hospitals-schools/ (accessed April 5, 2012).

internally against the rule, sources tell ABC News. Biden and Daley didn't think the rule was right on either the policy or the politics."[143] According to ABC News sources, while Biden and Daley thought the "policy was wrong," and, "the Obama administration couldn't force religious charities to pay for something they think is a sin," their discussion of the issue was centered more around how the situation would affect the administration, especially the Catholic vote going into an election year.[144] Biden and Daley, both Catholics, are among other Catholics in the administration such as Defense Secretary Leon Panetta and other staffers including: "senior advisor David Plouffe and Human Services Secretary Kathleen Sebelius, senior White House advisers Vallerie Jarrett and Pete Rouse, and then-domestic policy council director Melody Barnes."[145] That said, these top officials are not united for or against the mandate. Kathleen Sebelius, for instance, has remained a top promoter of the Act and mandate.

As the conflict persists, more exemptions have been granted by the administration; however, conflict still remains as the current exemptions do not include commercial enterprises with more than 50 employees. The nationally widespread arts and crafts store Hobby Lobby, which is touted as a Christian business, and others have been pushed to the point of challenging the legislation in court. In 2014 the U.S. Supreme court agreed to evaluate cases on this issue, including Hobby Lobby's appeal. In that case, they ruled 5-4 that family-owned corporations, like Hobby Lobby, could not be required to provide coverage for contraceptives to which they morally objected based upon their rights to religious freedom.

Regardless of where allegiances lie, Cardinal Dolan and the U.S. bishops know that truth is not determined by a majority vote, either by those inside or outside of the Church. Consequently, they continue to stand firm against these measures as a matter of freedom of religion and conscience as well as continuing to affirm that separating the unitive and procreative dimensions of a sexual act with

---

[143] Jake Tapper, "Policy and Politics of Contraception Rule Fiercely Debated Within White House," *ABC News* (Februrary 9, 2012), http://abcnews.go .com/blogs/politics/2012/02/policy-and-politics-of-contraception-rule- fiercely-debated-within-white-house/ (accessed April 5, 2012).
[144] Ibid.
[145] Ibid.

contraception is inherently evil. With repeated affirmations of Church teaching on family planning, it seems the U.S. bishops' resolve could not be firmer.

PART II
BACKGROUND

Chapter 4
Considering Contraception

The Church's teaching on family planning has stood the test of time, but it has not gone unchallenged or undeveloped. It was primarily in the twentieth century, namely during and following Vatican II, in which the issue was reconsidered in unprecedented ways, though years of development had contributed to this period of reconsideration.

History of the Church's Teaching

The Church's moral teaching on contraception throughout history has been generally agreed upon by opponents of the teaching (revisionists), as well as supporters (traditionalists[1]). For example, as even two recent revisionist authors state, "No Catholic theologian has ever denied that, before the appearance of *Humanae Vitae*, the Catholic Church's condemnation of artificial contraception was recurrent and consistent. No Catholic theologian aware of history ever could."[2] Scholars on both sides recognize the consistent testimony of the Church throughout history. A popular summary comes from historian John T. Noonan, Jr.'s classic text on the subject published in 1965, in the midst of the debate:

> Since the first clear mention of contraception by a Christian theologian, when a harsh third-century moralist accused a pope of encouraging it, the articulated judgment has been the same. In the world of the late Empire known to St. Jerome and St. Augustine, in the Ostrogothic Arles of Bishop Caesarius and the Suevian Braga of Bishop Martin, in the Paris of St. Albert and St. Thomas, in the

---

[1] Those supportive of Magisterial Church teaching may be identified by a number of labels, such as "orthodox"; however, this group has acquired the label of "traditionalist" in the years following *Humanae Vitae*. Its use here is intended to be consistent with other works on this subject, not to be pejorative.

[2] Todd A. Salzman and Michael G. Lawler, *The Sexual Person: Toward a Renewed Catholic Anthropology* (Washington D.C.: Georgetown University Press, 2008), 174.

Renaissance Rome of Sixtus V and the Renaissance Milan of St. Charles Boromeo, in the Naples of St. Alphonsus Liguori and the Liege of Charles Billuart, in the Philadelphia of Bishop Kenrick, and in the Bombay of Cardinal Gracias, the teachers of the Church have taught without hesitation or variation that certain acts preventing procreation are gravely sinful. No Catholic Theologian has ever taught, "Contraception is a good act." The teaching on contraception is clear and apparently fixed forever.[3]

This witness to unbroken history on the subject is "particularly forceful," because Noonan not only played a significant role as a historian in the discussion on the topic during the period from Vatican II through HV, he also held a "conviction that a change would and should be forthcoming."[4] Revisionists appreciate Noonan's support for change while traditionalists appreciate his testimony to the constancy of the Church's teaching throughout history. All things considered, the Church's condemnation of contraception has been consistent; this does not mean, however, that its teaching on family planning has not experienced development.

Many modern readers are surprised to learn that contraceptive techniques in the Mediterranean world, or at least the will to employ them, are as ancient as the foundations of Judaism with Abraham. As early as 1900 BC, Egyptian papyri provide examples of contraceptive concoctions utilizing a variety of things from crocodile feces to honey mixed with things like dates or sodium carbonate and placing them around the vulva or inside the uterus.[5] The Egyptians were not an isolated case; cultures utilizing contraceptive measures would prevail throughout Jewish and early Christian times. Noonan explains, "The means of contraception known to the Jewish communities included not only coitus interruptus, but postcoital ejection, occlusive pessaries, sterilizing potions, and sterilizing

---

[3] John T. Noonan Jr., *Contraception: A History of Its Treatment by the Catholic Theologians and Canonists* (Cambridge: Harvard University Press, 1965), 6.

[4] Janet E. Smith, *Humanae Vitae: A Generation Later* (Washington D.C.: Catholic University of America Press, 1991), 3.

[5] Noonan, *Contraception*, 9-10.

surgery."[6] For the purposes of this study it is also interesting to note the Greek "Hippocratic school" proposed a theory about periods of natural fertility and infertility in women, suggesting that a period of fertility followed menstruation.[7] Therefore, we ought not to consider the desire for and various means of contraception and family planning merely a modern concern.

What direct reference Scripture offers on this topic is a contested issue. A traditional interpretation of Gen 38:8-10 may provide the only direct reference to a contraceptive practice in the Bible—an act of coitus interruptus (i.e. "withdrawal" or "pulling out"). It is the story of Onan who was obligated to have intercourse with his deceased brother's wife, Tamar, in order to continue the family line. Onan chose to prevent procreation through coitus interruptus, because the child(ren) would not be credited to him, and God subsequently killed him. Noonan posits, "Was Onan punished for his disobedience, for his lack of family feeling, for his egotism, for his evasion of an obligation assumed, for his contraceptive acts, or for a combination of these faults?"[8] From an exegetical perspective Noonan suggests, "There is explicit post-Exilic legislation against homosexuality, against bestiality, and against temple prostitution (Lv 18:22, 20:13, 20:15-16, Dt 23:18). If these acts had to be prohibited by law, it seems unlikely that, in the absence of clear prohibition, the Jewish people would have believed that coitus interruptus or the use of contraceptives was immoral."[9] For centuries, early Jewish and Christian writers identified contraception as the root of Onan's sin, though it fell into disuse by the time of Aquinas.[10] Noonan is in fair company, as modern Catholic condemnations of contraception have centered on natural law and are largely silent with regard to Scripture. Even *The New Jerome Biblical Commentary* states, "Onan's offense is obvious; he selfishly refuses the responsibility of fulfilling his duty to

---

[6] Ibid., 11.
[7] Ibid., 16.
[8] Ibid., 35.
[9] Ibid.
[10] Ibid., 36.

167

his brother, as the law provided. That is the point of his offense (not what is popularly called onanism today)."[11]

Nonetheless, a defense of the traditional interpretation has resurfaced. Protestant author, Charles D. Provan, released a text in 1989 titled, *The Bible and Birth Control,* in which he addresses various Biblical and historical points to condemn contraceptive practice for a Christian. Provan contests that the penalty of death must be a consequence of the contraceptive act, as opposed to other reasons like failing to fulfilling the law, because the penalties for such alternative breeches were not so severe (e.g. the penalty for not fulfilling the law in this case is humiliation, see Dt 25: 5-10).[12] Provan's position is supported by Kimberly Hahn (a Presbyterian convert to Catholicism) in 2001 as well as Patrick Coffin as recently as 2010.[13] Coffin argues, "Onan went through the motions of fulfilling his family duty, and yet withheld the very element that would have made him faithful to it."[14] This correlates with the Ananias and Sapphira situation in Acts 5:1-11 where they are put to death by God for withholding something while their actions communicate a deeper offering.[15]

Regardless of the Onan incident, the Scriptures definitely teach foundational principles about sexuality and marriage from which the traditional condemnation of contraceptives would arise. Many threads important to our subject are present in the Bible. Throughout the Old Testament exists an appreciation for fecundity flowing from Genesis' prescription to "be fertile and multiply" (Gen 1:27-28, 9:1, and 35:11).[16] Coffin notes, "Any teaching repeated by God three times should give us pause."[17] Furthermore, children are constantly

---

[11] Richard J. Clifford and Roland E. Murphy, "Genesis," In *The New Jerome Biblical Commentary,* ed. Raymond E. Brown, Joseph A Fitzmyer, and Roland E. Murphy (Englewood Cliffs NJ: Prentice Hall, 1990), 38.

[12] Charles D. Provan, *The Bible and Birth Control* (Monongahela, PA: Zimmer Printing, 1989), 13.

[13] Kimberly Hahn, *Life-Giving Love: Embracing God's Beautiful Design for Marriage* (Ann Arbor: Servant, 2001), 66-67; Patrick Coffin, *Sex au Naturel* (Steubenville, OH: Emmaus Road, 2010), 44-45.

[14] Coffin, 44.

[15] Coffin, 50

[16] Noonan, *Contraception,* 31; Coffin, 33.

[17] Coffin, 33.

seen as a blessing (e.g. Ps 127:3-5; Gen 16:10, 17:2, 17:20, 22:17, 26:4, 26:24, 28:3, 41:52; Lv 26:9; Dt 30:5; Ps 105:24; Jer 30:19; and Jer 33:22).[18] Conversely, sterility is related to a curse, misfortune, and God's ill favor (e.g. Jer 18:21; Hos 9:10-11, 14; Lv 21:17; and Dt 23:1).[19] Joseph Sommer identifies an additional thread as the value of marital union stemming from Adam and Eve: "The Lord God said: 'It is not good for the man to be alone. I will make a suitable partner for him.' ... The man said: 'This one at last is bone of my bones and flesh of my flesh' ... and the two of them become one body" (Gen 2:18, 23, 24).[20] There is also a "spiritual union" thread in which the union and fidelity of man and woman is supposed to operate as mirror of the covenant between Yahweh and Israel (e.g. Song of Songs).[21]

The New Testament has valuable information as well. The spiritual union model will become more sacramental, and the relationship between man and woman will be called to mirror the relationship between Christ and the Church, for example. Within the New Testament, Sommer sees a reinforcement of each of the earlier values of "fidelity, mutual love and support, and the bearing and raising of children," coupled with a new value for virginity.[22] Similarly, Noonan provides an extensive list of New Testament values that would have a significant impact on later theology regarding marriage, sexuality and contraception: "the superiority of virginity; the institutional goodness of marriage; the sacral character of sexual intercourse; the value of procreation; ... the evil of extramarital intercourse and the unnaturalness of homosexuality; the connection of Adam's sin and the rebelliousness of the body; the evil of 'medicine' [to prevent conception]."[23] Traditionalist Janet Smith provides four themes from throughout the Bible of note:

---

[18] Ibid., 34, 38-40.
[19] Ibid., 40-41.
[20] Joseph Sommer, *Catholic Thought on Contraception through the Centuries* (Liguori: Liguorian, 1970), 9.
[21] Ibid.
[22] Ibid., 12-13. In this case, "virginity" means virginity for the sake of the Kingdom, as in avowed celibacy, consecrated virginity, and consecrated religious life.
[23] Noonan, *Contraception*, 37.

There are at least four themes in Scripture that provide strong evidence that contraception does not fit within God's plan for human sexuality. These are (1) the extreme value given to procreation, (2) the portrayal of sterility as a great curse, (3) the condemnation of all sexual acts that are not designed to protect the good of procreation, and (4) the likening of Christ's relationship to His Church to that of a bridegroom to his bride, a union that is meant to be a fecund relationship, one that will bring forth many sons and daughters of God.[24]

These foundational principles provided in Divinely inspired Scripture would be the building blocks from which later theologians would further construct the Church's position on contraception and family planning as God's will.

Throughout the centuries, the Church upheld procreation as the primary purpose of marriage in opposition to numerous heretical sects who either considered sexuality to be so profane as to be irreconcilable with spirituality or overemphasized the love of the couple to the point of undermining procreation. Such groups included the Gnostics, Manichees, Troubadours, and Cathars.[25] However, scholars within the Church have also pointed to other values and goods of marriage and marital intercourse.[26] For example, St. Augustine developed his three goods of marriage: (1) the procreation, formation, and education of offspring; (2) "fidelity," meaning both avoiding adultery and paying the "marital debt"; and (3) the sacramental value by which God's love for Israel and Christ's love for the Church are reflected in a married couple's love.[27] These three goods strongly influenced the Church's understanding of marital intercourse for the rest of history. St. Thomas Aquinas also recognized and used them while identifying procreation as *primary*—a

---

[24] Smith, *A Generation Later*, 130.

[25] Sommer, 18, 20-21; Noonan, *Contraception*, 46, 55, 75, 120, 138, 136, 181-184.

[26] Noonan, *Contraception*, 78; Salzman and Lawler, 175.

[27] Noonan, *Contraception*, 127-129; Salzman and Lawler, 175.

contribution that would stand for seven centuries.[28] The other values would occasionally surface with procreation throughout the centuries, yet procreation held pride-of-place well into the twentieth century. Gradually, as heresies and attitudes like those of the Gnostics, Manichees, Cathars, and Troubadours remained absent in later parts of Church history, she was free to explore these other goods, including pleasure in the sexual act, all the while maintaining an uncontested, strong condemnation of contraception. However, the most recent centuries would witness the beginning of developments that led to a revolution regarding the issue.

Contraception gained ground on nearly all fronts from the late 18th century through the start of the 20th century. The Church lagged behind addressing the growing issue among the general populace, and at times, the Church's exact position on the subject, or at least how to handle the subject in the confessional, proved elusive. In the 1800s birthrates in Western Europe began to fall, especially in Catholic France, as people readily utilized contraceptive practices such as *coitus interruptus*.[29] It was not until the early 20th century that the Church's aggressive stance against contraception was forced into public view.[30]

Simultaneously, "open advocacy" for contraceptives as a "socially desirable practice" was propagated and diffused in both the United States and England, largely based upon the overpopulation predictions of Anglican minister, Thomas Malthus, who suggested that human population growth would exceed that of food supplies.[31] In the latter half of the nineteenth century, more and better contraceptive options also became available, including barriers like diaphragms and condoms, as well as anti-fertility chemicals such as spermicides. The production of these contraceptives became a viable business.[32] Fueled by the new contraceptive industry, activist organizations, and an overpopulation scare, contraceptives were seen as a product of wisdom to secular society.[33] By the 1920s Margaret Sanger was creating an environment in which Catholics were pitted

---

[28] Salzman and Lawler, 175.

[29] Noonan, *Contraception*, 387-390, 394; Sommer, 44.

[30] Sommer, 47.

[31] Noonan, *Contraception*, 387, 392, 406-408.

[32] Ibid., 394, 408

[33] Ibid., 407-409.

against the rest of America for their stance against contraceptives, calling it "a dictatorship of celibates."[34] While conservative Protestants agreed with the Catholic (still really the Christian) position, they "were also apt to be the most anti-Catholic," so Sanger's attacks were not countered by other Christians.[35]

Before the turn of the century, evidence suggests that the more affluent American Catholic families were having fewer children, and by 1928 Fr. Joseph Nevins published his article, "Birth Control is Now a Practice with Catholics".[36] Way ahead of his time, Catholic University anthropologist Fr. John Montgomery Cooper published a tract in 1923, the content of which historian Leslie Woodcock Tentler explains:

> To "isolate sex passion from love and parenthood," as contraceptive practice did, was to "dethrone love and parenthood and enshrine physical self-regarding pleasures in the central and dominating place of personality." The inevitable consequences included an erosion of marital fidelity, the undermining of women's status, and dangerous vulnerability for the young. Society as a whole would suffer irreparably. The Catholic teaching on contraception, then, "is the one position that can adequately and in practice safeguard individual and collective welfare."[37]

The Magisterium was hard-pressed to offer a response to the situation; however, no weighty, direct statement was made. The U.S. bishops discussed it at their 1929 annual gathering but "declined to do more than commission a new generation of anti-birth control pamphlets."[38] It was not until the shifting of a brother ecclesial community's official teaching on the subject proved to be the last

---

[34] Leslie Woodcock Tentler, "Catholics and Contraception: An American History" (Ithaca: Cornell UP, 2004), 53.

[35] Ibid.

[36] Ibid., 17, 43.

[37] Ibid., 50.

[38] Ibid., 70-71.

straw, that Rome was finally forced to muster a novel campaign against contraception.

Until the 20th century the Catholic Church was united with all other Christian communities who had also condemned contraceptives as immoral.[39] Protestant opponent of contraception, Charles Provan, has written, "We have found not one orthodox theologian to defend Birth Control before the 1900's. NOT ONE! On the other hand, we have found that many highly regarded Protestant theologians were enthusiastically opposed to it, all the way back to the very beginning of the Reformation."[40] Remarkably, in the 20th century this situation would be turned on its head so that by Vatican II (1962-1965) the Catholic Church virtually stood alone. According to Tentler, "Four liberal denominational bodies in the United States," including branches of Universalists, Unitarians, Methodist Episcopals, and American Rabbis, "had by June of [1930] given public endorsement to marital contraception."[41] More popularly, in August of 1930 the Anglican Lambeth Conference allowed married couples to use contraceptives "for grave reasons."[42] Later that year Pope Pius XI released his encyclical *Casti Connubii*, or *On Christian Marriage*. The encyclical was motivated not only by the change in the Anglicans' moral position but also by rising Catholic disobedience. Some Catholics even began to publicly call for a similar statement from Rome as was given by the Anglicans.[43]

In *Casti Connubii*, Pius XI reaffirmed procreation as the "principal end" of marriage; however, he also recognized the three goods of marriage, "offspring, conjugal faith, and the sacrament," like Augustine and Aquinas, noting that there is more to married sexual intercourse than simply procreation.[44] Nonetheless, he stood firm in the Church's tradition against contraception declaring, "Any use whatsoever of matrimony exercised in such a way that the act is deliberately frustrated in its natural power to generate life is an

---

[39] Ibid., 5.
[40] Provan, 63.
[41] Tentler, 73.
[42] Janet E. Smith, *A Generation Later*, 5; Tentler, 73.
[43] Sommer, 49.
[44] Pope Pius XI, Casti Connubii, http://www.vatican.va/holy_father/pius_xi/encyclicals/documents/hf_p-xi_enc_31121930_casti-connubii_en.html (accessed July 14, 2009), §8, 13, 43.

offense against the law of God and of nature, and those who indulge in such are branded with the guilt of a grave sin."[45] The encyclical was well publicized and cleared any confusion on the issue, allowing confessors a more firm approach, leading to more preaching on the subject, and convicting the consciences of Catholics.[46] It was generally regarded as an infallible teaching and therefore carried considerable weight in Catholics lives—a status that was not called into question for another three decades.[47] Nonetheless, Catholics were still using contraceptives and perhaps even increasing usage as evidenced by it becoming "an increasingly frequent problem in confession."[48] While many Americans were using contraceptives, conservatives (Catholic or not) did not officially approve of them, and "laws in most states restricting or even prohibiting access to the various means of birth control" remained in effect.[49] *Casti Connubii* was and would remain the most direct and important contribution from Rome on the subject until HV almost forty years later.[50]

Impetus for Reconsideration

Following *Casti Connubii*, developments in theology, the Church, and society laid the groundwork for the issue to be reconsidered by the Church's highest authorities. Dietrich von Hildebrand, a noted theologian, contributed to the theology of marital love prior to *Casti Connubii*. Building on the traditional idea of fidelity as a good of marriage, he was among the first to suggest that love is not merely a side-element of marital intercourse, but an integral element.[51] Von Hildebrand did not intend to subvert procreation as the primary good but rather to highlight the value of love, and it seems no coincidence that the Church may have needed a married layman such as von Hildebrand to make this contribution to the subject. Rather than focusing so much on the action, von Hildebrand took a more personalistic or relational approach. A new concept at the time of *Casti Connubii*, von Hildebrand's ideas were not explicitly condemned

---

[45] Ibid., §56.
[46] Tentler, 74, 86.
[47] Ibid., 74.
[48] Ibid., 84.
[49] Ibid., 75.
[50] Sommer, 49-50.
[51] Noonan, *Contraception*, 495.

or condoned, though Noonan suggests the encyclical seemed to favorably reflect elements of it.[52]

German priest Herbert Doms followed von Hildebrand in highlighting the importance of love and marital union, but Doms suggested that the procreative dimension of marital intercourse was on par with the unitive good of the spouses.[53] According to Noonan, Doms's theory helped to explain many practices and laws in the Church that did not make sense if procreation stood alone as the end of marriage such as sex during pregnancy, sex between the sterile, the practice of annulments for "unconsummated marriages," and the indissolubility of sterile marriages simply due to lack of procreation.[54] Rome, however, did not seem to look upon Doms as favorably as it may have von Hildebrand, reiterating that procreation must remain primary in a 1944 statement.[55] John Gallagher has suggested Rome's concern involved the idea that recognition of two equal ends could lead to sexual activity devoid of procreation.[56] Consequently, Doms's ideas faded for a few years until Rome's struggle with another sexual issue would bring attention back to his position.[57]

As artificial insemination became possible during the pontificate of Pope Pius XII in the 1950s, the importance of the unitive good of sexual intercourse was needed to explain the problems with this new reproductive technique. In his "Address to Midwives on the Nature of Their Profession" in 1951, while still maintaining that procreation was primary, Pius XII condemned artificial insemination because it violated the good of marital union. He stated, "To reduce the common life of husband and wife and the conjugal act to a mere organic function for the transmission of seed would be but to convert the domestic hearth, the family sanctuary, into a biological

---

[52] Ibid.

[53] John Gallagher, "Magisterial Teaching from 1918 to the Present," in *Readings in Moral Theology No. 8: Dialogue about Catholic Sexual Teaching*, ed. Charles E. Curran and Richard A. McCormick (New York: Paulist Press, 1993), 78.

[54] Noonan, *Contraception*, 497-498.

[55] Gallagher, 78.

[56] Ibid., 79.

[57] Sommer, 54.

laboratory."[58] Other goods of marriage could not be pursued when procreation was deliberately impeded, and now procreation could not be pursued when the good of marital union/bonding was circumvented.

Other issues were also discussed by Pius XII. Sterilization procedures had become more common at this time, and Pius XII condemned them saying, "Direct sterilization—that is, whose aim tends as a means or as an end at making procreation impossible—is a grave violation of the moral law and therefore unlawful."[59] This condemnation, however, still allowed for the possibility of sterilization where it may be medically necessary. Theologians posited the licitness of removing diseased (or disease associated with) reproductive organs when they may be threatening the overall health of a person; on the other hand, if pregnancy would constitute the threat to health, sterilization would not be permitted.[60]

Furthermore, the "Address to Midwives" also made a significant pronouncement on the practice of avoiding conception through use of periodic abstinence, the acceptability of which had been debated for many years.[61] While there was immediate recognition that periodic abstinence was distinct from what had formerly been condemned as contraception, the possibility of periodic abstinence involving a contraceptive mentality caused concern. However, Pius XII made the Church's position on the matter clear when he stated, "Observance of the natural sterile periods may be lawful."[62] Nonetheless, he provides conditions: "Serious motives, such as those that not rarely arise from medical, eugenic, economic and social so-called 'indications,' may exempt husband and wife from the obligatory, positive debt [of procreation] for a long period or even the entire period of matrimonial life."[63] Therefore, periodic abstinence was condoned, with conditions—it cannot be used indiscriminately. Pius XII's address was significant, because this was the first time a

---

[58] Pope Pius XII, *Address to Midwives on the Nature of Their Profession* (1951). http://www.papalEncyclicals.net/Pius12/p12midwives.htm (accessed October 2, 2009), 10 of 13.
[59] Ibid., 5 of 13.
[60] Noonan, *Contraception*, 457-458.
[61] Ibid., 444.
[62] Pope Pius XII, *Address to Midwives*, 6-7 of 13.
[63] Ibid., 7 of 13.

Magisterial authority recognized a method of family planning to have the potential to be used morally.

Finally, Pius XII also affirmed the good of pleasure to be enjoyed by spouses in the conjugal union, which was essentially unheard of from an authoritative source like the pope. This affirmation, however, carried with it two conditions. First, he rejected any form of hedonism, by which one would seek pleasure as a highest good.[64] Second, Pius XII was clear that this licit enjoyment of pleasure was not to be separated from procreation.[65] Pleasure is therefore recognized as a good of the sexual act, willed by God, which may serve as a motivation for intercourse, but is not among the ends themselves. It may *motivate* people to engage in intercourse, but it cannot be the sole *purpose* of the act.

In the years immediately preceding Vatican II, a number of other issues coalesced in support of the need for the Church's teaching to be discussed. At this time a new form of contraception—oral contraceptive pills (OCPs), known more popularly as "the pill," became available. OCPs functioned in three ways: to prevent ovulation, reduce the ability of cervical mucus to aid the function of sperm, and prevent sufficient buildup of the uterine lining (endometrium) necessary for the successful implantation of a fertilized egg.[66] The question raised early on was whether these new "anovulant" (preventing ovulation) OCPs should be considered contraceptives as the Church had traditionally understood the term. What made the OCP different was that "it did not violate the integrity of the sexual act," as will barriers or withdrawal, "and served only to delay ovulation, a process also effected by nature."[67] The question was whether it truly only delayed ovulation or was a contraceptive by preventing ovulation in that cycle entirely. As more was known about OCPs, there were two more questions: whether it acted as a contraceptive by rendering cervical mucus so thick as to

---

[64] Ibid., 11 of 13; Sommer, 52.

[65] Pope Pius XII, *Address to Midwives*, 11 of 13.

[66] Noonan, *Contraception*, 460-461.

[67] Janet E. Smith, *A Generation Later*, 9; see also Ronald Lawler, Joseph Boyle Jr., and William E. May, *Catholic Sexual Ethics: A Summary, Explanation, & Defense*, 2nd ed. (Huntington, Indiana: Our Sunday Visitor, 1998), 147.

become a barrier and whether it acted as an abortifacient by preventing implantation.

Pius XII's reaction to OCPs was not absolute condemnation. In 1958 he recognized that there could be some licit medicinal or therapeutic uses for OCPs that induced artificial sterility, based upon the cases of medical necessity that would also justify indirect sterilization by principle of double effect, yet he maintained that they could not be utilized as a contraceptive, *per se.*[68] Thereafter, theologians discussed things related to this teaching but not directly mentioned by Pius XII, like using OCPs "to regulate the menstrual period, during pre-menopause, during lactation, after childbirth, for psychological sicknesses, and even to cure sterility."[69]

Unfortunately, OCPs did more than simply delay or prevent ovulation; they are also abortifacients. By preventing a fertilized embryo from implanting in the uterus, OCPs caused a conceived life to be lost. As early as 1965, Noonan recognized, "Prevention of nidation [implantation] would be described by most modern Catholic theologians as abortion."[70] Kimberly Hahn explains:

> When it was first used, the Pill always suppressed ovulation as well as altered the lining of the uterus so that new life would not thrive. However, there were many serious side effects, … [and] physicians discovered that these risks were lower if the dosage of the hormone in the Pill was lowered. Once the pharmaceutical companies altered the levels of hormones, creating low-dose Pills, there was a new consequence: abortions began to occur.[71]

At this time, though, most theological discussion about OCPs revolved around the presumption that they were simply anovulants and were strangely oblivious to the abortifacient potential.

Many other developments also contributed to the perceived need for the Church to reexamine its position against contraception.

---

[68] Sommer, 54-55; Noonan, *Contraception*, 466.
[69] Sommer, 55.
[70] Noonan, *Contraception*, 461.
[71] Kimberly Hahn, 76.

Among these were continued Malthusian concerns about global overpopulation, the change of women's roles in society and the workforce, and shifting dynamics in society and education that raised the costs of educating and raising children.[72] Certainly, population was on the rise, and projections indicated that global populations would increase if left unchecked.[73] The most significant contributor to this fact was the increase in medicine and health care, which reduced mortality rates and extended life expectancies.[74] The concern was that humans would outgrow the food supplies and natural resources necessary to support larger numbers of people. Second, the role of women in society had changed. They had gained ground in terms of property rights, suffrage, and education.[75] Furthermore, women were now contributing their own valuable perspectives on issues like contraception, and divorce had become more socially acceptable and easier to obtain.[76] Third, education became more thorough, lengthy, and expensive, so bringing one child to adulthood cost much more than in the past.[77] Fourth, by 1955, some laity were beginning to express public dissent. Tentler reports, "By the mid-1950s, lay views on family planning were making their way into print in notably larger numbers, mainly through readers' letters. These letters were increasingly blunt and increasingly apt to challenge the teaching, though support was plentifully evident, too."[78]

The practice of American Catholics was in flux. In a survey of "currently married white women between the ages of 28 and 39, roughly 30 percent of the Catholic respondents admitted to having employed a means of family limitation other than abstinence or rhythm" by 1955.[79] A 1960 survey indicated that the number had risen to nearly 40 percent.[80] Interestingly, Tentler reports, "As late as 1965, college-trained Catholic women were significantly less likely to

---

[72] Janet E. Smith, *A Generation Later*, 9; Noonan, *Contraception*, 476, 478, 479, 480, & 483.

[73] Noonan, *Contraception*, 476.

[74] Ibid., 476-477.

[75] Ibid., 478.

[76] Ibid., 478-479.

[77] Ibid., 479-480.

[78] Tentler, 200.

[79] Ibid., 133.

[80] Ibid., 134.

defy their church on this score than Catholic women who had not completed high school"—a statistic that would reverse thereafter.[81]

Lastly, with a greater appreciation for separated ecclesial communities (i.e. Protestant denominations) exemplified by Pope John XXIII, their testimonies on the subject made an impact. Following the Anglican Lambeth Conference, most other Christian groups shifted their moral positions to permit at least some form of contraceptives.[82] It would take until the 1950s for the most conservative Protestant denominations, such as the Missouri Synod Lutherans, to officially change their position on contraceptives, but change they did.[83] Noonan explains the overall situation: "These developments produced new data on the question of contraception; they brought into being new attitudes; they created a demand for greater clarity and rationality in the rules against contraception."[84] As the world moved into the 1960s, this was the cultural, societal, and theological world within which Vatican II commenced.

Second Vatican Council

It was at the Second Vatican Council that the Catholic Church employed *aggiornamento* (updating or renewal) to propel the People of God into a new ecclesial era. By the mid-twentieth century many pots were brewing in the Catholic Church's kitchen, and among them was the issue of contraception. The council did not convene to deal with contraception and discuss methods of family planning, though. Its most significant theme was discussion about the Church herself. It was the discussions about Church and family that made it apparent the issue of contraception demanded attention.

Council deliberations over *Gaudium et Spes* (GS)—or the *Pastoral Constitution on the Church in the Modern World*, which was among the last of the documents ratified by the council—witnessed significant developments and discussions about marriage and marital sexuality. In these critical years the issue would come to the fore as never before in Church history. A draft of GS appeared in 1964 under the name *Schema 13* with a section on marriage, including a

---

[81] Ibid., 133.
[82] Noonan, *Contraception*, 490-491.
[83] Tentler, 5.
[84] Noonan, *Contraception*, 491.

condemnation of contraceptives that took a traditional approach that clearly condemned condoms and withdrawal.[85] It was regarding this section that heated discussions took place. After the discussions revealed no significant majority position, which is generally necessary in order for a conciliar teaching to be adopted, Pope Bl. Paul VI made what Noonan referred to as a "logical" and "wise" decision in which he asked the council to avoid making any conclusive statements and to leave the issue to be reviewed by his "special commission" for the issue, which he inherited from Pope John XXIII.[86] The commission would issue a more definitive statement after the council adjourned.

Nonetheless, significant developments came out of GS regarding marriage that relate to the topic of contraception. Building on decades of theology proposed by theologians like von Hildebrand and Doms, and later built upon by Bernard Haring and Josef Fuchs, the council recognized that conjugal love is to be recognized as an end to marriage.[87] Previously, the Church had always understood procreation as the *primary* end of marriage; however, GS is clear to avoid any discussion of this hierarchy of primary and secondary ends, which caused considerable tensions between bishops of opposing perspectives.[88] This development worried conservatives, because a strong firewall against contraceptives had always been the primacy of procreation in marriage.[89] Authentic development on the Church's understanding of marriage and marital intercourse led to a new balance between these goods having been struck, which was something of a vindication for Doms.

Furthermore, GS also recognized a couple's responsibility for family planning. Balancing the goods and ends of marriage, GS talks about "harmonizing married love with the responsible transmission

---

[85] Sommer, 64; John T. Noonan Jr., *The Church & Contraception: The Issues at Stake*, (New York: Paulist Press, 1967), 17.

[86] Noonan, *The Church & Contraception*, 18.

[87] John T. Noonan Jr., "Contraception and the Council," in *The Catholic Case for Contraception*, ed. Daniel Callahan (London: Macmillan, 1969), 6-7.

[88] *Gaudium et Spes*, In *Vatican Council II*, ed. Austin Flannery (Northport: Costello Publishing Company, 1996), §50; Salzman and Lawler, 171, 182; Noonan, *The Church & Contraception*, 32.

[89] Noonan, *The Church & Contraception*, 32.

of life."[90] Now through GS the Church also took as its official position the teaching, "It is the married couple themselves who must in the last analysis arrive at these judgments [regarding family planning] before God."[91] These two changes in GS were monumental in their novelty and authoritative significance. Such developments led some to believe the door was opening to allow the possibility of changing the Church's teaching on contraception, or at least recognize OCPs as non-contraceptive, yet the council deliberately left these questions unanswered.

Although Bl. Paul VI asked the council not to speak definitively about contraception in GS, this does not mean that the document did not speak of it at all. The council condemned multiple offenses to the dignity of marriage and included, "unlawful contraceptive practices."[92] At this time, though, exactly what constituted such practices was debated, as Bl. Paul VI's commission had yet to propose an answer. Moreover, GS asserts, "In questions of birth regulation the daughters and sons of the church, faithful to these principles, are forbidden to use methods disapproved of by the teaching authority of the church in its interpretation of the divine law."[93] This assertion included footnote 14:

> By the order of the Holy Father, certain questions requiring further and more careful investigation have been given over to a commission for the study of population, the family, and births, in order that the Holy Father may pass judgment when its task is completed. With the teaching of the Magisterium standing as it is, the Council has no intention of proposing concrete solutions at this moment.[94]

Conservatives would look on GS as developing the Church's idea of marriage while maintaining the current teachings, at least until Bl. Paul VI made any pronouncement. Progressives saw the changes

---

[90] GS, §51.
[91] Ibid., §50.
[92] Ibid., §47.
[93] Ibid., §51.
[94] Janet E. Smith, *A Generation Later*, 65-66.

to the way the Church viewed marriage as important steps on the way to allowing contraceptives for married couples.

Papal Commission

Following the council, Pope Bl. Paul VI counted on his commission to assist him with the discernment of contraception, and OCPs specifically. The commission's original intention was to assist John XXIII in 1963 to prepare for a conference with the United Nations and World Health Organization (WHO) in which the major topic of discussion was global overpopulation.[95] Composed of six professionals from the fields of medicine, politics, sociology, economics, and demographics, this group's focus was to help John XXIII support the Church's teaching on family planning at the conference.[96] All of this changed after Bl. Paul VI's succession and the discussions about contraception in the draft of GS.

Given the gravity of the issue, Pope Bl. Paul VI saw fit to expand the size and scope of the commission. In 1963 the commission was enlarged to include two more sociologists and five moral theologians—most of whom publicly expressed adherence to the Church's current teachings on family planning.[97] Mark Graham comments on Bl. Paul VI's intentions: "According to papal advisors, the pope was a thorough and deliberate man who preferred to consider all sides of a question or issue before rendering a judgment. In their view…the pope felt uncomfortable with a lack of theological expertise on the commission and simply desired more input."[98]

The new purpose of this enhanced committee seems to have begun with a limited focus, which quickly ballooned. The commission's assumption that any and all forms of contraception were intrinsically evil, was challenged by debate over the particular design of OCPs and their potential therapeutic value.[99] Following deliberations in 1964, which seemed to make little progress, Bernard Haring and Pierre de Locht, who were advocating for a change in

---

[95] Mark Graham, *Josef Fuchs on Natural Law* (Washington D.C.: Georgetown University Press, 2002), 87.

[96] Ibid., 87.

[97] Ibid., 87-88.

[98] Ibid., 88.

[99] Janet E. Smith, *A Generation Later*, 9-10.

contraceptive teaching, feared that the current commission's indecisiveness would simply lead to a reaffirmation of the current teaching and thus convinced Bl. Paul VI to further expand the commission and intentionally include married couples.[100] Eventually, Bl. Paul VI's commission was expanded to over seventy members, including married couples and laywomen, as well as sixteen bishops (seven of whom were cardinals) as an executive voting committee—these bishops became the official participants of the commission who would report directly to the pope.[101]

The meetings of this commission were lengthy and deliberative. Past meetings of the commission lasted just a few days, but the final meeting of this enlarged commission lasted nearly two months in 1966.[102] Throughout the discussions, the commission was divided on the issue. Men like Haring and de Locht continued to argue in favor of change, while men like Marcellinus Zalba and John Ford contested this conclusion primarily based on the argument that the Church's teaching is historically consistent and irreformable.[103] Interestingly, some significant members of the commission began to sway in favor of change. One of these was the German theologian Josef Fuchs. Even though Fuchs entered the commission supportive of the Church's condemnation of contraception, his encounters with the practical application of such teaching seem to have significantly altered his perspective until he found himself one of the principal advocates of revising Church teaching.

The contributions of Patrick and Patricia Crowley had a significant impact on Fuchs and many others in the commission. As founders of the Christian Family Movement, they conducted two surveys of their members who were described as "active" and "committed" Catholics.[104] The results of their surveys startled Fuchs, the commission, and even the Crowleys themselves. As the Crowleys explained, "[We] have been shocked into realization that even the most dedicated, committed Catholics are deeply troubled by this

---

[100] Ibid., 88-89.
[101] Salzman and Lawler, 45; Graham, 93; Benedict M. Ashley, Jean Deblois, and Kevin D. O'Rourke, *Health Care Ethics: A Catholic Theological Analysis*, 5th ed. (Washington D.C.: Georgetown University Press, 2006), 77.
[102] Graham, 93.
[103] Ibid., 88-90.
[104] Ibid., 91.

problem [of effectively utilizing the calendar rhythm method—the only Church approved method of family planning of the time]. We have gathered hundreds of statements from many parts of the United States and Canada and have been overwhelmed by the strong consensus in favor of change."[105] These surveys presented and quantified the experiences of couples who struggled with how to balance the various goods of marriage in order to determine how best to practice responsible parenthood, including issues like marital intimacy and health, financial and social hardships, quality of rearing and educating current children, and resentment and frustration resulting from periods of abstinence.[106]

Consequently, Fuchs's position on the subject shifted, and this insight required him to significantly adjust his approach to moral theology and natural law theory.[107] In effect, he seems to have made up his mind about this issue and thereafter built a moral theology within which his moral conclusion was able to function. The new moral theology embraced by Fuchs became "proportionalism," which holds that an action is morally permissible as long as the good it pursues is proportionately greater than the evil inherent in the act.[108] Naturally, the theory rejected the possibility of intrinsically evil objects (actions). Fuchs was not alone in his changed position on contraception, and many of the other members of the commission were similarly impacted by the information presented from the Crowleys and others.[109] This also involved another problem, because if the Church could be shown to have been wrong on such a significant moral teaching, its credibility as a moral teacher may be called into question.[110] Now the commission was dealing with something more than a *moral* issue—it was dealing with an *ecclesiological* issue.

---

[105] Ibid.
[106] Ibid., 84.
[107] Ibid.
[108] Ashley, Deblois, and O'Rourke, 77.
[109] Graham., 94.
[110] Janet E. Smith, *A Generation Later*, 10.

The Reports

The discussion on the topic of contraception, which had grown over several years, had witnessed a divergence of advocates and opponents into two camps both in the council itself and thereafter in the commission as well. As a result of several weeks of discussion, the commission composed four reports to present to Bl. Paul VI. The first has been referred to as the Majority Report, due to the number of committee members who signed and supported it—nineteen theologians among others—which argued in favor of changing the Church's teaching to allow contraception for spouses.[111] The second was called "Pastoral Approaches" and supported the Majority Report.[112] The third is known as the Minority Report, which argued that the Church's teaching should remain the same and was signed by four theologians.[113] The last report Gallagher describes as "a working paper" composed by members who agreed with the Majority Report.[114]

The theologians, however, were not the voting members. Bl. Paul VI had placed sixteen bishops on the commission as its official members, which essentially provided a buffer between him and the other members of the commission. The final positions taken by the bishops correlated with the numbers on each side of the argument between the theologians. Most of the bishops voted to say that contraception is not intrinsically evil, nine voted to say that "contraception, as defined by the Majority Report, [is] in basic continuity with tradition and the declarations of the Magisterium," whereas five voted against that proposition, and nearly all suggested that the Magisterium deal with this issue in a timely manner.[115]

Two major points of the Majority Report came from the assertions of GS that conjugal love is an equal end of marriage with procreation, and parents may utilize responsible means of family planning for the good of the marriage and family.[116] The Majority Report went further and proposed that situations may arise in which

---

[111] Gallagher, 83-84.
[112] Ibid., 84.
[113] Ibid.
[114] Ibid.
[115] Salzman and Lawler, 44 & 177.
[116] "Majority Papal Commission Report," in *The Catholic Case for Contraception*, ed. Daniel Callahan (London: Macmillan, 1969), 152-159.

the good of the family, relationship of the spouses, etc. may be endangered by continued procreation, and the good of procreation may thus be subordinated to other goods, yet not dismissed entirely. Thus, in their view, the use of contraceptives must be understood in the proper context of fecundity, while such a "proper context" had not yet been determined by the majority. In addition, while the majority suggested that couples should have the determining say in whether it is in their family's best interests to continue having children, the majority also recognized the possibility of couples "conforming not to Gospel values but to popular opinion and pressure," as Gallagher notes.[117]

Having advocated for a change in official Church teaching, the authors of the Majority Report were forced to explain how such a change would be an authentic and legitimate development in the Church's teaching. The Majority Report argues that the constant teaching of the Church has been against separating the sexual act from its naturally (yet rare) procreative effect, "for motives spoiled by egoism and hedonism."[118] It continues by stating, "The opposition is really to be sought between one way of acting, which is contraceptive and opposed to a prudent and generous fruitfulness, and another way which is in an ordered relationship to responsible fruitfulness and which has a concern for education and all the essential, human and Christian values."[119] Therefore, it suggests that any type of decision not to procreate based upon selfishness or the pursuit of pleasure is incompatible with the Church's consistent teaching, but parents may have recourse to certain contraceptive means for the good of other elements of marriage and the family such as the spouses' relationship and the upbringing and education of already present offspring. This assertion is known as the argument from the principle of totality, which suggests that the *marriage as a whole* needs to be open to the good/end of the transmission of life, as opposed to *every* act of intercourse.

The Minority Report, on the other hand, contained three primary arguments.[120] First, the ban on contraceptives cannot be

---

[117] Gallagher, 85.
[118] "Majority Papal Commission Report," 162.
[119] Ibid.
[120] Sommer, 68.

dropped, because it has always and everywhere been taught as true and is therefore unalterable. The first argument depends on the definition of contraception provided by the Minority Report as, "any use of the marriage right in the exercise of which the act is deprived of its natural power for the procreation of life through the industry of men."[121] The report contends that this teaching has been ever constant and remains a fixed teaching of the ordinary Magisterium. Second, if it were possible for this teaching of the ordinary Magisterium to change, it could undermine and throw into question the teaching authority of the ordinary Magisterium on all issues. Third, the Minority Report suggests that the reasoning (specifically the principle of totality) upon which the Majority Report condones contraceptives could be used to condone other illicit sexual activity. For instance, it suggests people may argue for premarital sex on the grounds that it will help "test their mutual adaptability and their sexual compatibility for the good of the family."[122] Oral sex, anal sex, and mutual masturbation may also be considered licit if it can be argued that they exist in the context of an otherwise fruitful marriage and edify conjugal love and/or the wellbeing of the family.[123] The report also notes, "Even further *the door is opened easily to the licitness of masturbation* among youths on the ground that it could be a remote preparation for realizing a harmonious sexual life in marriage."[124] Lastly, sterilization might also be permissible if the couple has had some children yet finds the prospect of any more could disrupt the harmony of conjugal love or the peace and tranquility of the family.[125] Founded on these three points, the Minority Report concluded that the Church's condemnation must stand.

In a rebuttal to the Minority Report's concerns about the principle of totality, the majority addressed this final concern. They agreed that all such sexually deviant activity was gravely sinful and immoral, and they affirmed that licit intercourse requires an "other" who is "a member of the opposite sex and one to whom one is

---

[121] "Minority Papal Commission Report," in *The Catholic Case for Contraception*, ed. Daniel Callahan (London: Macmillan, 1969), 175.

[122] Ibid., 206-207.

[123] Ibid., 207-208.

[124] Ibid., 208.

[125] Ibid.

married," in order to limit how far couples may go with a loosening of the Church's teaching.[126] The weakness of the majority's position here is its lack of a sufficient safeguard to prevent the slippery slope predicted by the minority and that would eventually come to fruition, as the following decades have demonstrated.

Interim

A period of great anticipation followed the end of the commission proceedings. Adding to the anticipation was the leaking of the confidential Majority and Minority Reports to the press in 1967.[127] With the fact that a majority of bishops and theologians of the commission favored change, many Catholics began to assume that Bl. Paul VI would revise the teaching, yet his conclusion was a long time coming.[128] In the interim a large number of Catholic couples changed their practice in anticipation of what they believed was imminent change. A Gallup poll in 1965 revealed that 60% of lay Catholics anticipated a change, most of them within 5 years.[129] By the mid-1960s the number of Catholics disobeying Church teaching was estimated at about 50%, exposing all the more a "major crisis among American Catholics."[130] A speech from Bl. Paul VI in 1964 stated, "Up to now we do not have sufficient motive to consider out of date and therefore not binding the norms given by Pope Pius XII in this regard. Therefore they must be considered valid, at least until we feel obligated in conscience to change them."[131] Following the release of GS in 1965, Bl. Paul VI stated in a 1966 address, "It cannot be considered not binding as if the Magisterium of the Church were in a state of doubt at the present time, whereas it is rather in a moment of study and reflection concerning matters which have been put before it as worthy of the most attentive consideration."[132] This concept, "a state of doubt," had important theological significance.

---

[126] Janet E. Smith, *A Generation Later*, 29.

[127] Ibid., 11-12.

[128] Daniel Callahan, introduction to *The Catholic Case for Contraception*, ed. Daniel Callahan (London: Macmillan, 1969), viii.

[129] Tentler, 220.

[130] Ibid., 2

[131] John F. Kippley, *Birth Control and the Marriage Covenant*, 2nd ed. (Collegeville: The Liturgical Press, 1976), xxiii-xxiv.

[132] Ibid., xxiv.

Much of the discussion that existed among theologians at this time revolved around certainty and doubt, due to the doctrine of probabilism. According to this concept, when a teaching is in a state of doubt, people must make up their own mind on the issue after careful consideration.[133] Consequently, many of those who pushed for a change worked to suggest that this issue was in doubt, largely because, they argued, Bl. Paul VI indirectly indicated that the teaching *could* change. Obviously, clergy dissent, committee diversity, report leaks, and delay led many to conclude the teaching was in doubt and that couples were allowed to decide for themselves.[134]

This line of reasoning was contested, however, even among those who preferred to see a change. For example, prior to the release of HV, John T. Noonan Jr., who argued strongly in favor of change and served on the commission, affirmed, "The Council makes the present law very plain. In the light of this solemn affirmation by a Council and the Pope about the existing law, no theologian has any basis for saying that the law is in doubt."[135] Drawing on GS as well as the pope's speech in 1964, Noonan believed the doctrine of probabilism was inapplicable.

How was one to explain the pope's lengthy deliberations? Based upon some inside information, Noonan believed Bl. Paul VI was taking his time on the issue due to its monumental significance as well as his careful and thorough nature.[136] Noonan's perception seems reasonable. Prior to this situation, Bl. Paul VI revealed the way in which he approached difficult situations in the following:

> Burning questions are also complex ones. Simple honesty demands that they be considered without haste. We should have respect for the complexity of things, listen, weigh them. If the past teaches us anything, it is that it is better to wait, to risk disappointing the impatient, than to make hasty

---

[133] Ibid., xxiii.
[134] Richard A. McCormick, "Notes on Moral Theology: January-June, 1968: Magisterium and Contraception before Humanae Vitae," *Theological Studies* 29, no. 4 (December 1968): 723.
[135] Noonan, *The Church & Contraception*, 36.
[136] Ibid., 40.

improvisations. And the higher the authority the more it must wait. It is easy to study, difficult to decide.[137]

The decision needed to be slow, because the situation was treacherous and the results would be colossal. The fact that the Church was in a state of instability only compounded the momentousness of Bl. Paul VI's decision. The combination of the social upheaval of the 1960s in America with what George Weigel calls "the widespread challenge to all established authority and the breakout into mainstream culture of the sexual revolution," leads him to surmise, "A thoughtful public moral discussion of conjugal morality was going to be very difficult."[138] The difficulty was increased with the leaking of the papal commission's reports to the press in 1967, possibly to "bring more pressure on the Pope."[139] Bl. Paul VI must have known that either decision would have negative repercussions, and he needed time to consider the issue with the greatest care.

Pope Bl. Paul VI did not work alone though. One bishop member of the commission was absent from its final meeting due to problems obtaining a passport from his home country.[140] This absentee, however, would become one of the most significant men in the world of the twentieth century, and he had no intention of missing out on the important work of the commission even though he could not attend. Consequently, Archbishop Karol Wojtyla of Krakow decided to put together his own commission to address the issue.[141] Obviously respected by Bl. Paul VI, Wojtyla's commission was allowed to preview two drafts of what would become HV in order to collect its input, but the two drafts were seen as heavily deficient by the Krakow commission. The first merely restated traditional positions on the subject and even lacked Pius XII's contribution in the "Address to Midwives," which allowed for the possibility of utilizing periodic abstinence.[142] The other draft sided

---

[137] Janet E. Smith, *A Generation Later*, 164.
[138] George Weigel, *Witness to Hope: The Biography of Pope John Paul II* (New York: Harper Collins, 2001), 206.
[139] Ibid., 207.
[140] Ibid.
[141] Ibid.
[142] Ibid., 208.

191

with the Majority Report, which the Krakow commission believed "misread what God had written into the nature of human sexuality, and did so in a way that undermined the structure of moral theology across the board."[143] Working off of Wojtyla's insights in his 1960 book *Love and Responsibility*, the group sought to provide a way for Bl. Paul VI to maintain the Church's traditional teaching yet with an experiential approach intended to have a wide-appeal.[144] Bl. Paul VI took some of the advice of the Krakow commission for HV, but he stopped short of saturating the encyclical with Wojtyla's approach. Weigel has suggested that HV may have been all the more effective if it would have more thoroughly incorporated Wojtyla's personalistic approach to marital love, intercourse, and family.[145] Whether Weigel's belief is true or not, had Wojtyla been able to attend the commission, the results may have been considerably different.

Humanae Vitae

Finally, on July 25th, 1968 Pope Bl. Paul VI broke his silence and issued his encyclical letter, *Humanae Vitae*. It took nearly three years after Vatican II for HV to produce a verdict, and when it did the Church would be shaken for decades. Bl. Paul VI begins by making clear that he is familiar with all of the developments and issues at hand, including the ecclesial, social, economic, demographic, and scientific changes of the times.[146] The next sections are devoted to discussing the conjugal love of husband and wife and the Church's recognition of responsible parenthood, respectively, citing GS in both instances.[147] It was in sections 11 and 12 that Bl. Paul VI would lay down the most hotly debated points of the encyclical. He affirmed, "The Church ... teaches that every marital act must of necessity retain its intrinsic relationship to the procreation of life," and maintained that the Church's consistent teaching, "is based on the inseparable connection, established by God, which man on his own initiative may not break, between the unitive significance and the

---

143 Ibid.
144 Ibid.
145 Ibid., 209.
146 Pope Paul VI, *Humanae Vitae*, http://www.vatican.va/holy_father/paul_vi/encyclicals/documents/hf_p-vi_enc_25071968_humanae-vitae_en.html (accessed July 14, 2009), §2.
147 Ibid., §9-10.

procreative significance which are both inherent to the marriage act."[148] These assertions entirely closed the door on the principle of totality to support contraceptive behavior and thus any hope of significant change in the Church's position.

After making his judgment clear, Bl. Paul VI further explained it. He argued, "An act of mutual love which impairs the capacity to transmit life…frustrates [God's] design which constitutes the norm of marriage."[149] He added, "Just as man does not have unlimited dominion over his body in general, so also, and with more particular reason, he has no such dominion over his specifically sexual faculties, for these are concerned by their very nature with the generation of life, of which God is the source."[150] This assertion suggests that there are limits to appropriate and moral control humans have over themselves, and the design of God must be respected in such areas as our sexuality. Bl. Paul VI identifies as immoral, "any action which either before, at the moment of, or after sexual intercourse, is specifically intended to prevent procreation—whether as an end or as a means," which includes contraception, sterilization, and abortion.[151] He goes on to condemn arguments from the Majority Report, such as the principle of totality, and utilizes arguments from the Minority Report.[152] He therefore upholds the Church's condemnation of all types of previously condemned contraceptive behaviors—such as barrier methods, withdrawal, masturbation, and oral or anal copulation—and clearly sets the boundaries of his condemnation to include OCPs intended to prevent procreation. He does not say that OCPs themselves are intrinsically evil, just that their use for the purposes that they were designed (directly preventing procreation) is immoral.

Bl. Paul VI continued by identifying what is morally permissible. First, he recognizes as legitimate some medical procedures with contraceptive effects. He states, "The Church does not consider at all illicit the use of those therapeutic means necessary to cure bodily diseases, even if a foreseeable impediment to procreation should

---

148 Ibid., §11-12.
149 Ibid., §13.
150 Ibid.
151 Ibid., §14.
152 Ibid.

result therefrom—provided such impediment is not directly intended for any motive whatsoever."[153] Second, he reaffirms the permissibility of recourse to infertile periods; however, this activity is not permissible unconditionally. There must be "well-grounded reasons for spacing births, arising from the physical or psychological condition of husband or wife, or from external circumstances."[154] Therefore, he does not intend to leave couples in a state of hopelessness, though what he has called them to—namely periodic abstinence when legitimately used—may be considered more challenging than taking OCPs.

Reflecting concerns of the Minority Report, Bl. Paul VI identified questions about possible consequences of permitting the use of contraceptives for married couples. His concerns and predictions about what could happen if the use of contraceptives became widespread have proven so accurate that some have come to consider these thoughts prophetic. First, he claimed that contraceptive sexuality may "open wide the way for marital infidelity and a general lowering of moral standards," suggesting that fear of pregnancy works as a deterrent from, or "incentive" to avoid, adultery and fornication.[155] Consequently, sex, removed from its life-giving power, would be reduced to merely recreation. Second, Bl. Paul VI suggested that men who grow "accustomed to the use of contraceptive methods may forget the reverence due to a woman, and, disregarding her physical and emotional equilibrium, reduce her to being a mere instrument for the satisfaction of his own desires."[156] Finally, Bl. Paul VI warned about the activities of some government authorities who might be inclined to solve problems of families, populations, natural resources, or economics by promoting or even imposing contraceptives. He wrote, "Who will blame a government which in its attempt to resolve the problems affecting an entire country resorts to the same measures as are regarded as lawful by married people in the solution of a particular family difficulty?"[157]

---

[153] Ibid., §15.
[154] Ibid., §16
[155] Ibid., §17.
[156] Ibid.
[157] Ibid.

Bl. Paul VI clearly understood that his reaffirmation of the Church's prohibition of contraception would not be popular and necessitated a pastoral approach. Consequently, he encouraged couples in self-discipline and chastity to aid in their adherence to these moral principles. He also appealed to ministers, public authorities, health care providers, and practically everyone to promote these truths and support families in their efforts to live by them. He also suggested a family apostolate by which families might practice these teachings and pass them along with support and encouragement to other families. The Holy Father presaged that just as families would be challenged, so would the Church. He wrote, "It is to be anticipated that perhaps not everyone will easily accept this particular teaching. There is too much clamorous outcry against the voice of the Church… But it comes as no surprise to the Church that she, no less than her divine Founder, is destined to be a 'sign of contradiction.'"[158] Bl. Paul VI was asking families to follow their Christian duty, in imitation of Christ, to be a sign of contradiction and testify to the truth in the midst of the world.

Aftermath

Humanae Vitae garnered a multitude of reactions when it was released the summer of 1968. Representative of the majority position, Daniel Callahan summarized the negative reaction in a statement only a year after HV, which demonstrates the frustration of the time:

> It is impossible to exaggerate the surprise the encyclical caused. It flew in the face of the Pope's own commission, whose conclusions were specifically rejected by the Pope. It flew in the face of an emergent consensus of theologians. It flew in the face of a number of bishops who had asked the Pope not to issue such an encyclical and who had already told their people they should do as their informed consciences dictated. Finally, and most importantly, it flew in the face of a great mass of married lay people. On the basis of their own marital experience and fortified by their knowledge of a change in the

---

[158] Ibid., §18.

thinking of many bishops, priests and theologians, they had decided they could morally use contraceptives for the sake of responsible parenthood. … Clearly the Church had on its hands a crisis of authority the likes of which it had not seen for centuries.[159]

Only a few weeks after the release of HV, Bernard Haring stated, "No papal teaching document has ever caused such an earthquake in the Church as the encyclical *Humanae Vitae*."[160] Even some bishops' conferences hinted that couples could decide for themselves whether contraception was moral.[161] By 1979, Gary Atkinson and Albert Moraczewski said of the laity, "The teaching of the popes on contraception and sterilization seems to be widely disregarded by Catholics."[162]

Most reactions were negative, but there were also a number of positive reactions. The media had a tendency to give greater attention to the negative reactions, because tension and discord are obviously more sensational and newsworthy. At the time a critic of HV, Fr. Berard Marthaler later commented, "There were many positive things in that encyclical, but they were being ignored because of the negative points which the people were interested in."[163] Things may have looked worse than they actually were, and the *mere perception* of an overwhelmingly negative reaction to the encyclical may have fueled the negative momentum. Tentler notes, "Media coverage was not only oversimplified but typically hostile."[164] To suggest that all reactions were negative would be irresponsibly one-sided.

Views from the minority regarding the reception of HV were understandably more positive. While some bishops' conferences were critical, like those of Canada, France, Italy, and some Northern

---

[159] Daniel Callahan, ix.

[160] Bernard Haring, "The Encyclical Crisis," in *The Catholic Case for Contraception*, ed. Daniel Callahan (London: Macmillan, 1969), 77.

[161] Sommer, 71.

[162] Gary Atkinson and Albert Moraczewski, *A Moral Evaluation of Contraception and Sterilization: A Dialogical Study* (St. Louis: Pope John XXIII Medical-Moral Research and Education Center, 1979), 29.

[163] Tentler., 265.

[164] Ibid.

European nations, others like the United States were substantially positive.[165] The *National Catholic Reporter* even ran the headline, "Bishops United Behind Paul."[166] Athenagoras, Orthodox Patriarch of Constantinople, endorsed the encyclical with the following words directed to Bl. Paul VI: "We assure you that we remain close to you, above all in these recent days when you have taken the good step of publishing the encyclical *Humanae Vitae*. We are in total agreement with you, and wish you all God's help to continue your mission in the world."[167] There was also positive reaction from conservative religious leaders of other communities like other Orthodox patriarchs, conservative Protestants, and even other religions.[168] Among them, perhaps Athenagoras put it best including: "I am completely agreeing with the pope. Paul VI could not have pronounced in any other way. The interests and the very existence of families and nations is at stake."[169]

Reactions were certainly polarized. A statement of American Catholic theologians—spearheaded by Fr. Charles Curran and others at the Catholic University of America, which was reportedly signed by over 600 Catholic theologians and philosophers[170] within a few weeks of the promulgation of HV—states, "As Roman Catholic theologians, conscious of our duty and our limitations, we conclude that spouses may responsibly decide according to their conscience that artificial contraception in some circumstances is permissible and indeed necessary to preserve and foster the values and sacredness of marriage."[171] Yet others in significant positions like the president of

---

[165] Janet E. Smith, *A Generation Later*, 163.

[166] Ibid.

[167] E. J. Stormon, ed. and trans., *Towards the Healing of Schism: The sees of Rome and Constantinople, Public statements and correspondence between the Holy See and the Ecumenical Patriarchate 1958-1984* (Manwah, New Jersey: Paulist Press, 1987), 197.

[168] Leo Alting von Geusau, "International Reaction to the Encyclical Humanae Vitae," *Studies in Family Planning* 1, no. 50 (Feb. 1970): 12.

[169] Ibid.

[170] This number of theologians and philosophers has been called into question.

[171] "Statement by Catholic Theologians, Washington, D.C., July 30, 1968," in *Readings in Moral Theology No. 8: Dialogue about Catholic Sexual Teaching*, ed. Charles E. Curran and Richard A. McCormick (New York: Paulist Press, 1993), 136-137.

the American Catholic Theological Society and the general of the Jesuits fully supported the encyclical.[172]

Two-thousand six-hundred American scientists condemned the encyclical, primarily concerned with the population problem, writing, "More than half of the globe suffers from hunger and its social conditions are deteriorating rapidly, perhaps in an irrevocable way. ... Paul VI has sanctioned the death of endless numbers of human beings with his wrongly inspired and immoral encyclical."[173] Due to the statement's strong wording, some withdrew their signature, however. Most health specialists reacted negatively, but interestingly it was the research physicians, especially ones who had worked on OCPs, who showed the most sympathy for Bl. Paul VI's position.[174] They seemed more privy to its consequences. Ironically, HV's integration of the procreative and unitive aspects of marital sex found support in the previous writings of none other than the avowed atheist, Sigmund Freud, as cited by Coffin: "It is a characteristic common to all the perversions that in them reproduction as an aim is put aside. This is actually the criterion by which we judge whether a sexual activity is perverse—if it departs from reproduction in its aims and pursues the attainment of gratification independently."[175] It is fascinating to see how, in just over three decades, the position of someone as hostile to religion as Freud was closer to the Pope's teaching than most of society.

The timing for the delivery of the encyclical, especially in the United States, was hardly in Bl. Paul VI's favor as one historian indicates:

> Distrust of authority grew apace and was frequently melded with a self-absorbed focus on rights—often defined with unprecedented expansiveness—that paid little or no attention to communal needs. The dominant mood turned sour in the latter half of the decade, with the country embroiled in an unpopular war and race-based angers

---

[172] Janet E. Smith, *A Generation Later*, 162-263.
[173] Von Geusau, 9-10.
[174] Ibid., 10-11.
[175] Patrick Coffin, *Sex au Naturel* (Steubenville, OH: Emmaus Road, 2010), 78.

leading to urban rioting. … Various movements for sexual liberation—from the strictures of marriage and the nuclear family, from allegedly outmoded expectations of premarital chastity, from what poet Adrienne Rich dubbed "compulsory heterosexuality"—took root at mid-decade, infecting popular culture. A resurgent feminism challenged conventional gender roles in marriage. The cult of sexual fulfillment—freed, now, from the exclusive context of marriage—invaded even the soberer reaches of the middle class, presumably aided by the now-ubiquitous anovular pill and the apparent medical conquest of venereal disease.[176]

It is difficult to imagine how the Church's position could have been received well under such circumstances. By 1970 the number of Catholic couples using contraceptives had reached nearly 70 percent according to one study and 78 percent according to another.[177] Accordingly, those frequenting the sacrament of reconciliation fell, and those who went were less likely to mention contraception since they did not believe it to be sinful.[178] The clergy, who themselves were divided on HV's conclusions, felt irrelevant and without grounds to speak on the issue due to their commitment to celibacy.[179] Moreover, the falling rates of confession by the late 1960s led to a further lowering of priestly morale since many saw the sacrament as "the most rewarding of their pastoral roles."[180] Avery Dulles stated, "I sensed that public opinion among Catholics had already swung so far in the direction of change that the pope's decision would be vehemently opposed. I was worried about the internal rifts that would arise in the church. My apprehensions were borne out by the events."[181]

---

[176] Tentler., 208-209.
[177] Ibid., 220, 266.
[178] Ibid., 267-268.
[179] Ibid., 268, 4.
[180] Ibid., 4.
[181] Ibid., 265.

Neither the Majority nor Minority Reports were intended to thoroughly treat and defend their positions—it would take the decades following HV for theologians on both sides to unpack what those early reports began.[182] Some of the strongest critiques were laid against HV for lacking convincing argumentation, but it must also be realized that the encyclical was intended to answer the question at hand, not to offer a comprehensive defense.[183] HV was also working out of a specific moral tradition within Catholicism, and it assumed a certain amount of context and understanding—things of which not all laypeople possessed understanding.[184] This conflicted with the fact that the encyclical was addressed to all people of goodwill, many of whom did not share the Catholic tradition and therefore were largely unconvinced by the conclusions of HV. John Coulson summarized the social climate effectively when he wrote, "[The Pope] has spoken out; the bishops and the faithful have started to speak back; and the unfinished business of Vatican II becomes of a more serious and urgent nature than we had supposed."[185] Due to the hostility of the times, Tentler reports, "Not long after *Humanae Vitae*, a great public silence came to prevail with regard to contraception."[186]

---

182 Janet E. Smith, *A Generation Later*, 34, 35.
183 Janet E. Smith, "*Humanae Vitae* at Twenty," in *Why Humanae Vitae Was Right: A Reader*, ed. Janet E. Smith (San Francisco: Ignatius Press, 1993), 506.
184 Janet E. Smith, *A Generation Later*, 35.
185 John Coulson, "Living with Authority—The Nineteenth Century," in *Contraception: Authority and Dissent*, ed. Charles E. Curran (New York: Herder and Herder, 1969), 39.
186 Tentler, 273-274.

Chapter 5
Revisionism

In order to understand the circumstances of the issue today, it is necessary to understand the situation in the 1960s and years following that led so many Catholic couples to the conclusion that they could morally use contraceptives. People's practical experience, which frequently involved frustration with the rhythm method, was combined with mixed sentiments from clergy and statements by hundreds of theologians who suggested that Catholic couples were within their rights to evaluate the situation and follow their consciences in the matter. However, the natural law foundation of HV would not allow for the use of contraceptives. Consequently, those who held that Catholic couples should be permitted to use contraception, because of the failure of problems with the calendar rhythm method and the threat of overpopulation, sought to revise the moral law. Hence the term "revisionist" for those who dissented from Church doctrine.

In recent decades the fruits of revisionist's positions have become evident, and destruction to the Church, marriages, and families are widespread. While the conclusion of this book lies in full support of Magisterial teaching, going through extensive argumentation to achieve this, it is valuable from a historical perspective to understand the revisionist perspective from within its own point-of-view. This chapter seeks to provide a glimpse of this perspective without condoning it.

Critique of Rhythm

One thing both the revisionists and traditionalists can agree on is that certain situations may arise in which married couples find it necessary to plan and space the number of their offspring. However, the two have very different approaches to carrying out this end. Revisionists insisted such family planning needed to be sufficiently "effective" to truly foster the nuptial bond that the sexual union was supposed to foster—something they argued the calendar rhythm method was incapable of promising. While early revisionists went so far as to recognize that "Aesthetically and medically, rhythm far surpasses other methods of fertility control," they maintained that the method was too unreliable and caused great anxiety for couples, which dramatically harmed marriages.[1] Consequently, the revisionists felt compelled to reject the rhythm method as unsatisfactory for most couples.

The effectiveness of the calendar rhythm method was less than ideal. Some claimed that it might only work for less than one-third of all women, because it was based upon charting a woman's fertile period based upon *averages* of a large pool of women's cycles—not a woman's individual cycle.[2] This represents a deficient understanding of rhythm at the time, because various "rules" for observing an individual woman's cycle were possible and advocated decades prior. By the 1960s further improved methods of family planning, based even more significantly upon individual women's fertility cycles, were being developed as the dawn of modern NFP methods. However, the negative stigma and frustrations associated with rhythm led to a rejection of any method based upon periodic abstinence.

Revisionists also alleged that there was little moral difference between what is being done by couples using OCPs and some other contraceptives, versus rhythm or NFP.[3] They argued that since both are means to avoid pregnancy, there was no moral difference—as if a common goal rendered all the different "means" morally the same. Just as the end does not justify the means, so also the end does not homogenize the means, i.e., make them morally the same (see the rebuttal to this position in Chapter 1).

Revisionists believed the use of rhythm was hindering the unitive dimension of marriage and harming spouses' relationships. While occasional, short-term abstinence was recognized to have value, what revisionists saw as "excessive" abstinence was believed to be problematic for relationships.[4] On this point, Bernard Haring drew attention to 1 Corinthians 7:5: "Do not deprive each other [sexually],

---

[1] Sidney Callahan, "Procreation and Control," in *The Catholic Case for Contraception*, ed. Daniel Callahan (London: Macmillan, 1969), 57-59.
[2] Andre E. Hellegers, "A Scientist's Analysis," In *Contraception: Authority and Dissent*, ed. Charles E. Curran (New York: Herder and Herder, 1969), 224.
[3] Ibid., 229, 233.
[4] Sidney Callahan, 56.

except perhaps by mutual consent for a time, to be free for prayer, but then return to one another, so that Satan may not tempt you through your lack of self-control." He explains that evil can gain the upper-hand and temptations become overpowering if abstinence is unduly prolonged, which can harm relationships. Even if the harm simply involves increasing hostility between spouses and may not lead to adultery or other more serious problems, Haring says it is still a problem.[5] Today's NFP practitioners report a heightened level of self-control, which is useful not only in this area, but in the entirety of moral and marital life. Rosemary Radford Ruether further contended that spontaneity is essential to sexuality's function of building and maintaining a marital relationship and is lost with periodic abstinence.[6] Interestingly, NFP couples have since reported that periodic abstinence is followed by a "honeymoon effect" each cycle as well as higher sexual satisfaction, which counteract the sexual boredom found among couples utilizing contraceptives and who are able to be more "spontaneous."

Revisionists have been criticized at times for being overly focused on the value of sexuality, as if abstinence would cause a marriage to fall apart. While some truth to this criticism exists, it would be an unfair caricature to suggest that those couples who struggled with rhythm were hedonistically seeking pleasure from the sexual act or unwilling to bear necessary burdens of living a moral, obedient Catholic life.[7] Daniel and Sidney Callahan are good examples. While frustrated with and opposed to what they identify as a "contraceptive mentality" in the 1960s, they believed contraceptives ought to have a place in the life of Catholic spouses.[8] Their position was supported by pediatrician Thomas F. Draper who explains that in his practice he encountered what he described as Catholic families where periodic abstinence and anxiety from the unreliability of

---

[5] Bernard Haring, "The Encyclical Crisis," in *The Catholic Case for Contraception*, ed. Daniel Callahan (London: Macmillan, 1969), 88.

[6] Rosemary Radford Ruether, "Birth Control and the Ideals of Marital Sexuality," in *Readings in Moral Theology No. 8: Dialogue about Catholic Sexual Teaching*, ed. Charles E. Curran and Richard A. McCormick (New York: Paulist Press, 1993), 150.

[7] Daniel Callahan, introduction to *The Catholic Case for Contraception*, ed. Daniel Callahan (London: Macmillan, 1969), x.

[8] Ibid., xiv-xv.

calendar rhythm caused unnecessary tension between spouses and intense pressures on spousal relationships.[9] As a result of struggles with rhythm, some women experienced psychological disturbances resulting in hospitalizations. Other couples found themselves experiencing great struggles with intimacy and communication, and some found consolation from priests who gave them permission to take OCPs. These were the types of cases that impacted the Crowleys' position, as well as members of the papal commission's majority opinion, like Josef Fuchs. The popular "wisdom" of the age seemed to suggest rhythm was not practical for most couples. Providentially, most of the concerns of revisionists have been alleviated by modern methods of NFP and are no longer valid.

Clergy also struggled with the issue, especially on how to help couples who grappled with rhythm. Many of them left open the decision to use contraception in the years prior to and even following HV. Among them, auxiliary bishop of St. Paul, Minnesota, James Patrick Shannon was a recently ordained bishop in attendance for the discussion of GS at Vatican II.[10] He left the council sincerely believing change was imminent, and his counsel in the confessional reflected this.[11] Within months of HV's promulgation, Shannon became the first bishop to resign his position over the issue, because he could not reconcile his personal belief with the Church's official position as stated in HV.[12] His resignation was newsworthy, and he briefly became a poster-child for the revisionist cause. However, he subsequently married without ecclesiastical approval and left the Catholic Church altogether, thereby damaging the credibility revisionists would have liked to attach to his resignation.

As a result of these circumstances and the situations in which many Catholics found themselves, the revisionists argued the legitimacy of using contraceptives. In order to make this possible, revisionists had to wrestle with the official Church teaching. Considering what was known at the time, Haring suggests that the

---

[9] Thomas F. Draper, "A Catholic Pediatrician on Family Planning," in *The Catholic Case for Contraception*, ed. Daniel Callahan (London: Macmillan, 1969), 130.

[10] James Patrick Shannon, *Reluctant Dissenter: A Catholic Bishop's Journey of Faith* (New York: Crossroad, 1998), 93.

[11] Ibid., 144.

[12] Ibid., 146, 150-152, 166, 178.

only viable option would be a "catholic pill," which could be capable of regulating a woman's cycle and "fix the time of ovulation" so that the rhythm method could be much more effectively practiced.[13] However, in the event that such a pill would be developed, it would be of questionable morality. Couples might refrain from fertile periods under the drug regimen, but the regimen itself, when used to avoid pregnancy would seem to indicate a contraceptive mentality. The close tie between such a drug's manipulation of fertility and the intention not to have children creates similar problems as OCPs. Providentially for later generations of Catholics, a means much more effective than rhythm would permit couples to identify the times of fertility in a woman's cycle without "regulating" it beyond what would be healthy, through good nutrition and hormonal balance. Unfortunately, this option was not yet widely known nor practiced. Of all the options available, therefore, OCPs were clearly the favorite choice of revisionists as an alternative to the Church's teaching.

Critique of Natural Law

The arguments for HV stem primarily from tradition, so that is where revisionists looked for loopholes. Perhaps the most influential American revisionist, Charles Curran, believed the way the Church had come to understand natural law was flawed. He suggested the natural law ought to be understood in a way that is more dynamic and susceptible to a broader range of conditions, like relationships, sin, and experience.[14]

The work of other theologians, like Bernard Lonergan, was also influential in evaluating natural law. Lonergan suggested there are two ways to perceive human nature. First, the "classicist, conservative, traditional" perspective sees human nature as something solid, static,

---

[13] Bernard Haring, "The Inseparability of the Unitive-Procreative Functions of the Marital Act," in *Readings in Moral Theology No. 8: Dialogue about Catholic Sexual Teaching*, ed. Charles E. Curran and Richard A. McCormick (New York: Paulist Press, 1993), 159.

[14] Charles E. Curran, "Natural Law and Contemporary Moral Theology," in *Contraception: Authority and Dissent*, ed. Charles E. Curran (New York: Herder and Herder, 1969), 157.

and unchanging.[15] From this approach, "human nature is always the same," so moral and ecclesial laws may be drawn from such human nature with the help of divine revelation.[16] On the other hand, the "historical consciousness" perspective considers change inevitable, and it approaches morality by beginning with looking at "people as they are," the "hard-won fruit of man's advancing knowledge of nature, of the gradual evolution of his social forms and of his cultural achievements."[17] Lonergan was not a relativist, but rather worked with the connection of psychology and theology. This dynamic perspective of human nature, was picked up by revisionists. It recognizes some consistency between people of different cultures and ages, but as Lonergan notes, "It is to be known only by the difficult art of acquiring historical perspective, of coming to understand how the patterns of living, the institutions, and common meanings of one place and time differ from those of another."[18] In essence, revisionists see human nature, and thus natural law, as changing over time. This, in turn, makes a change in the teaching against contraception possible. Working from this dynamic understanding of human nature, revisionists struggled with the static approach used in HV. This difference in worldview became all the more evident throughout the debates over contraception in the 1960s and decades to follow as the chasm between revisionists and traditionalists widened.

One of the most common critiques of HV's use of natural law is what revisionists have considered an overly "physical" or "biological" approach to sexual morality.[19] By condemning HV's understanding of natural law as being too "physicalist", revisionists hold that it bases morality on the procreative design of sex. Seeing sex as contributing to the marriage as a whole, they might suggest contraceptive sex is life-giving to the spouses, their love, and marriages. More emphasis needs to be placed on the relationship between the spouses and the necessary sexual union to foster that relationship, they suggested.

---

[15] Bernard J. F. Lonergan, "The Transition from a Classicist World-View to Historical-Mindedness," in *A Second Collection*, ed. William F. J. Ryan and Bernard J. Tyrrell (Philadelphia: Westminster Press, 1974), 2.
[16] Ibid., 3.
[17] Ibid., 2-4.
[18] Ibid., 4.
[19] Curran, "Natural Law and Contemporary Moral Theology," 175.

These concerns laid down by revisionists quickly following HV continued to develop into a position at odds with the Church's official teaching.

As a result of the debates over HV's use of natural law, revisionists proposed alternatives that were open to the possibility of contraception based upon more personalist and relational approaches.[20] Revisionists see this personalism developing in the Church following *Casti Connubii*. The work of von Hildebrand and Doms brought out the importance of the spousal relationship in sexuality. Building upon their contributions, revisionists took it a step further so as to emphasize other goods, especially the unitive good, as primary and procreation as secondary. For instance, twenty-first century revisionists Salzman and Lawler state, "The primary end of sexual intercourse in this perspective is the loving communion between the spouses, a communion that is both signified and enhanced, or 'made,' in intercourse."[21] This position is a reversal of the Church's position on the goods of marriage and the understanding of the sexual act prior to and during the first part of the twentieth century, and it is a step beyond what the years leading up to and including Vatican II concluded. The council did not discuss a primary/secondary hierarchy of these two goods, avoiding a perspective where procreation was given pride-of-place. The fact that GS refrained from continuing to mark the procreative end of marriage as primary and the unitive end as secondary has been used by revisionists to support a position that is person and relationship focused, a position wherein marital union may be prioritized over procreation when serious reasons are present. Thus, revisionists have been accused of upsetting the balance of the two goods in the opposite direction, to prefer the relationship, which they saw as a legitimate further development of the teaching following the council.

Like many revisionists, even into the twenty-first century, Salzman and Lawler continue to affirm a moral theology that makes this reversed hierarchy possible. For instance, they suggest, "Human intervention in the process of the marriage act *for reasons drawn from the end of marriage itself*—that is, from the good of the spouses, their

---

[20] Ibid., 173.

[21] Todd A. Salzman and Michael G. Lawler, *The Sexual Person: Toward a Renewed Catholic Anthropology* (Washington D.C.: Georgetown University Press, 2008), 40.

marital relationship, and any children born of their marital intercourse—should not always be excluded, *provided, that the Catholic criteria of morality are always safeguarded.*"[22] What are these "Catholic criteria of morality," who gets to define them, and who is obligated to obey them? A major problem for revisionists who attempt to uphold vagaries like a "Catholic criteria of morality," or other values worthy of respect, seems to be an inherent inability of such criteria to prevent deviant sexual behavior.

Through approaches such as this, revisionists seem to be creating in moral theology what Martin Luther's doctrine of *sola scriptura* created in the Church—breakdown in authority and thus breakdown in unity. When one felt empowered to interpret Scripture for oneself, thanks to *sola scriptura*, there was no authority to tell a person what is true doctrine. Consequently, soon after Luther broke from Rome, he witnessed subsequent other breaks from himself and disunity within his own camp. Luther once commented on those who broke from him, "This one, will not hear of Baptism, that one denies the Sacrament, another puts a world between this and the last day: some teach that Christ is not God, some say this, some say that: there are about as many sects and creeds as there are heads."[23] Similarly, if one can follow his or her conscience on a given moral issue, even boundaries Salzman and Lawler may insist upon can be broken. The same thing happened with the majority position on the papal birth control commission of the 1960s who wanted to allow contraception for married couples in serious situations, while maintaining a ban on other sexual activities. As a fact of history, the revisionist position is hardly able to bridle a subjective morality gone awry that has logically followed from their first step of separating the unitive and procreative goods in every sexual action.

Ontic (Pre-Moral) Evil

A unique perspective taken by revisionists is to draw a distinction between moral evils (sins) and what they call "ontic" or "pre-moral" evils. An ontic or pre-moral evil arises when an action falls short of the ideal and is lacking in some respect, yet it may not be on the level of being *morally* evil, which would make it sinful.

---

[22] Ibid., 189.
[23] Patrick F. O'Hare, *The Facts About Luther* (Rockford: TAN, 1987), 208.

Consequently, one of the most novel contributions of revisionism came to light—the notion that there can be no intrinsic evils. A significant early contributor to this perspective was Louis Janssens. He defines and explains ontic evil in the following way:

> We call ontic evil any lack of a perfection at which we aim, any lack of fulfillment which frustrates our natural urges and makes us suffer. It is essentially the natural consequence of our limitation. Our limitation itself is not an evil—to be created is to be limited— but, because we are thinking, willing, feeling and acting beings, we can be painfully hampered by the limits of our possibilities in a plurality of realities that are both aids and handicaps (ambiguity). ... When we choose a certain action, we must at the same time, at least for the time being, postpone all other possible acts.[24]

Therefore, there is always some level of ontic evil (shortcoming) in every action. There must be a difference between a moral evil (sin) and committing an ontic evil, otherwise any action we commit or omit would be a sin—we could never act morally.[25]

Janssens continues by noting under what circumstances ontic evils may be tolerated and not considered moral evils. He recognizes the maxim that one may not use evil means for a good end, yet he suggests, "*under certain conditions*, it can be right to intend an ontic evil as end of the inner act of the will, if that end is not willed as a final end, but only as *finis medius et proximus* to a higher end."[26] As a result, an ontic evil cannot be "the ultimate end of our intention," writes Janssens, but it will inevitably be involved in all moral actions.[27] In terms of marital copulation, Janssens makes three points: [1] it may be immoral to have intercourse during the fertile time if the couple

---

[24] Louis Janssens, "Ontic Evil and Moral Evil," in *Readings in Moral Theology No. 1: Moral Norms and Catholic Tradition*, ed. Charles E. Curran and Richard A. McCormick (New York: Paulist Press, 1979), 60-61.
[25] Ibid., 66-67.
[26] Ibid., 68-69.
[27] Ibid., 70.

does not have the means to provide for the child, [2] periodic abstinence may also be immoral if a couple lacks serious reason to avoid "responsible parenthood," and [3] contraceptives may be used provided "responsible parenthood" is respected and the ultimate intention of coitus is the fostering of the unitive dimension of marital sexuality.[28] In the third case the couple is not seeking the ontic evil for its own sake, but it may be involved as a foreseeable lack of perfection in the action that is permissible since they are intending to seek the good of marital unity. His perspective resembles the principle of totality. Janssens concludes, "We must make allowance for our human limitations" in moral deliberation and evaluation of actions.[29]

As a significant member of the birth control commission and prominent revisionist thereafter, Fuchs also contributed to this discussion. He compares contraception to killing; both of which fall short of the ideal and are therefore ontic or pre-moral evils. Fuchs also notes, however, that situations exist in which killing may be morally justified (e.g. self-defense or just war); similarly, he suggests contraception may occasionally be justified.[30] The Church's teaching already allows for some flexibility on contraceptives like OCPs for situations like medical treatment or in case of rape, similar to the flexibility the Church has for killing (self-defense or just war).[31] The moral absolutes proposed by the Church then are against murder (directly and unjustly taking an innocent life) as a specific form of killing, and the use of contraceptives specifically for the purposes of separating the unitive and procreative ends of marital sexuality in every act of intercourse. There is already agreement between Fuchs and the official Church teaching, but Fuchs wants to broaden the basis upon which contraceptives might be justified.

Fuchs suggests that no action can be morally considered apart from the intention and circumstances. For example, he offers an

---

[28] Ibid., 72-73.
[29] Ibid., 86.
[30] Joseph Fuchs, "The Absoluteness of Moral Terms," in *Readings in Moral Theology No. 1: Moral Norms and Catholic Tradition*, ed. Charles E. Curran and Richard A. McCormick (New York: Paulist Press, 1979), 118-119.
[31] United States Conference of Catholic Bishops, "Ethical and Religious Directives for Catholic Heath Care Services," 4th ed. http://www.usccb.org/bishops/directives.shtml (accessed December 11, 2009), Directive #36.

instance of killing by which we cannot judge the action on its own without knowing if it was committed in self-defense or out of wrath.[32] Killing itself is an ontic evil, but it can only be considered a moral evil in the case of unjust murder, as opposed to self-defense. Fuchs puts great emphasis on the intention of the acting subject to determine the moral evil of the action. He offers as another example surgery by which an ontic evil (physical wounding) necessarily accompanies an overall action in which the intention and purpose is to heal a worse threat to the health of the person, thereby justifying the lesser evil of physically wounding the patient to perform the surgery.[33] Fuchs rejects the concept of intrinsic evils, *per se*, because he does not believe any action can be morally judged purely based upon what is done.[34] What we consider intrinsic evils can only be stated as *norms*, ideals that are helpful to live by and direct moral action yet are not absolute in *all* cases.[35] Fuchs is accurate that the object must not be considered alone, as the Church would later clarify in the *Catechism of the Catholic Church*; however he fails to recognize that there are defining factors in the object—factors that make it what it is—that make an object intrinsically evil. Nonetheless, it is on these grounds that revisionists worked to suggest that contraception may be permissible in some cases to directly prevent procreation.

Ramifications of Revisionist Theology

As time progressed, the implications of separating the unitive and procreative acts, justified by revisionist approaches, would be carried to other logical conclusions. Writing in 1977, Philip S. Keane recognized the use of contraception as an ontic evil: "Contraceptive measures, both because of their non-openness to procreation in individual acts and because of problems with the various birth control methods, are always ontically evil. They always lack the fullness of human possibility that might be associated with sexual

---

[32] Fuchs, "Absoluteness", 119.
[33] Ibid., 120.
[34] Ibid., 124-125.
[35] Ibid., 125-126.

intercourse."[36] He further critiques modern society, with its "cavalier and indifferent...attitude toward birth and life," and recognizes that people may be overly accepting of ontic evils, even when justified.[37] Keane therefore recognizes the imperfection of contraceptives and a contraceptive mentality. He also seems to indicate the value in avoiding ontic evil as much as possible. However, his moral theology allows for a variety of sexual activities: he essentially condones contraceptives, homosexual activity, masturbation, oral sex, and anal sex as merely ontic evils—and therefore not sinful—if they promote the unitive dimension, or personalist/relationalist value, of a human relationship.[38]

In addition to Keane's contribution, another significant work was published in 1977 that helped advance the revisionist perspective to a new level—*Human Sexuality: New Directions in American Catholic Thought* by Anthony Kosnik et al., which originated as a study for the Catholic Theological Society of America. Curran summarizes the impact, approach, and conclusions of the text when he explains that it further divided revisionists and traditionalists and removed the revisionist position further from Church teaching by suggesting that morality be based upon alternative values than have previously been used—ones that conditionally allowed for all kinds of (what had previously been considered) sexually deviant behavior.[39] As with Keane, revisionist moral theology began to manifest one of the Minority Report's great concerns, namely that other sexual acts could be justified by the same approach used to justify contraception. As a result of *Human Sexuality*, and the significance of its sponsorship, a number of traditionalist theologians founded the Fellowship of Catholic Scholars for the purpose of "supporting and safeguarding the teaching of the hierarchical Magisterium."[40] While ecclesiastical reaction to Keane's book only involved a request to remove its imprimatur, Kosnik et al.'s work brought down condemnation from

---

[36] Philip S. Keane, *Sexual Morality: A Catholic Perspective* (New York: Paulist Press, 1977), 124-125.

[37] Ibid., 133.

[38] Ibid., 125.

[39] Charles E. Curran, forward to *The Sexual Person: Toward a Renewed Catholic Anthropology*, by Todd A. Salzman and Michael G. Lawler (Washington D.C.: Georgetown University Press, 2008), xii-xiii.

[40] Ibid.

both the Congregation for the Doctrine of the Faith in the Vatican and the U.S. Bishops.[41]

Kosnik et al. turned to the latest psychological and sociological evidence for support of the revisionist perspective. They explain that masturbation cannot be immoral, because studies suggest that its effects on a person vary based upon circumstances independent of the objective action of masturbation.[42] They also reject a broad condemnation of various sexual acts, because the data they collected suggest that there is "no universally forbidden behavior" among human cultures, and "animals at all levels engage in sexual behavior that is not always directed to reproduction but often merely to pleasure," like "self-stimulation, homosexuality, and copulation outside the species."[43] In this way, they reject the traditional interpretation of the natural law, and what they see as its overly physicalist approach, as unconvincing, impractical, and not supportable by empirical data.

Considering the developments that have occurred in Catholic teaching on sexuality in the course of the 20th century, Kosnik et al. consider a further development as necessary. They suggest a shift in terminology concerning the ends of marriage from "procreative and unitive to creative and integrative."[44] This shift opens the door to a variety of other actions that they move to consider morally permissible. Their study argues for seven values necessary for a sexual act to be considered morally good: self-liberating, other-enriching, honest, faithful, socially responsible, life-serving, and joyous.[45] As long as a sexual act meets these seven criteria, it is morally good in their view. In this way, Kosnik et al.'s values are meant to replace the former goods of marital intercourse. Furthermore, from just this simple, precursory presentation of their seven values, it is evident great latitude may be taken with many of them to justify considerable sexual license. This conclusion was a new development in the revisionist camp, because the majority position

---

[41] Ibid.
[42] Anthony Kosnik et al., *Human Sexuality: New Directions in American Catholic Thought* (New York: Paulist Press, 1977), 88.
[43] Ibid., 57.
[44] Ibid., 86.
[45] Ibid., 92-95.

had always maintained that these other deviant sexual acts were not morally permissible, and revisionists as influential as Haring had always maintained a position against things like homosexuality.[46] Clearly, the shift away from the purposes of sexuality being unitive and procreative led to the justifiability of innumerable sexual activities. This was a major fear of the Minority Report that the writers of the Majority Report initially dismissed as unfounded. They only wanted to allow contraception among married couples for serious reasons, but these limitations would not be able to stand among revisionists as they carried their theology to its logical conclusions. This result mirrors what also happened among many Protestant denominations that permitted contraception.

Contraceptive Cautions and NFP Possibilities

The revisionist perspective has shown some concern regarding the long-term use of contraceptives, and has remained open to the viability of NFP. For example, in 1969 Sidney Callahan recognized that OCPs have not been used long enough for people to know what kind of problems may accompany them, but she maintained that the principle of totality is acceptable, provided "no new life is attacked."[47] Ironically, not only would many problems surface regarding OCPs in subsequent years, its threat to new life was already apparent. Remarkably, Mrs. Callahan did not seem to realize at the time that OCPs functioned not only to lengthen the infertile phase and prevent ovulation but also functioned as an abortifacient (as recognized by Noonan in 1965).[48] Had she known and/or accepted this fact, she may have rejected OCPs outright, because she believed attacking new life was not acceptable for a contraceptive. There seemed to be some level of inconsistency on this point.

Moreover, in 1977 Keane also began to recognize some disadvantages of various contraceptives and the growing potential for methods of periodic abstinence—his observations are striking. In terms of contraceptives, Keane agrees with Callahan, noting that they had not yet been around long enough to know of long-term side-

---

[46] Haring, "Unitive-Procreative Functions," 164.

[47] Sidney Callahan, 53.

[48] John T. Noonan Jr., *Contraception: A History of Its Treatment by the Catholic Theologians and Canonists* (Cambridge: Harvard University Press, 1965), 461.

effects like cancer.[49] Keane, writing nearly a decade after Callahan, recognizes the abortifacient character of OCPs, and further states, "In some ways, due to our increased knowledge of the limitations of various birth control methods, Paul's position looks somewhat better than when he first formulated it."[50] Keane weighs in on methods of periodic abstinence: "If ways can be found to predict more exactly when, in the female cycle, ovulation and pregnancy are likely to occur, it may well be that the one means of birth control the Church has approved, periodic abstinence, will emerge as the most desirable birth control method."[51] In this statement, he recognizes the potential for a changing tide.

Finally, nine years after HV, the study by Kosnik et al. was able to provide some new information about Church approved methods of family planning as well as contraceptives. Following HV, significant strides were made toward utilizing means of family planning in conformity with the encyclical, which resulted in movement beyond the calendar rhythm method to various approaches of modern NFP. The Kosnik study recognized that both NFP techniques and education had become more reliable, and dangerous side-effects of contraceptives were becoming a greater fear in the minds of many. The IUD and morning after pill raised red flags about the dangers of contraception when their abortifacient properties became known.[52] Kosnik urged caution: "Natural family planning deserves serious consideration among the alternatives for exercising responsible parenthood. The Church would render a considerable service by supporting clinics and organizations where accurate and up-to-date information could be available to interested couples."[53]

It is helpful to keep in mind that the foundations of the revisionist perspective have continually looked for something better than contraceptives in a means conformable to the Church's teaching yet more practical than the calendar rhythm method as it was

---

[49] Keane, 126.

[50] Keane, 123, 126.

[51] Ibid., 127.

[52] Germain Grisez et al., "NFP: Not Contralife," In *Readings in Moral Theology No. 8: Dialogue about Catholic Sexual Teaching*, ed. Charles E. Curran and Richard A. McCormick (New York: Paulist Press, 1993), 128.

[53] Kosnik et al., 127-128.

practiced and criticized in the 1950s and 1960s. Contraceptives have always been considered at least something short of ideal—as evidenced by calling it an "ontic" evil—even to those who suggest it may be used without sin. It was left to traditionalist moral theologians to develop the case explaining why contraceptives could not ever be used to sever the procreative and unitive meanings of the conjugal act.

Chapter 6
Responses to Revisionism and Support for the Church's Teaching

While the revisionist reaction to HV was dramatic, immediate, and well publicized, it seemed to take years longer for noteworthy support to be garnered by those who endorsed HV's position and the official teaching of the Church. From the promulgation of HV until now, adherents to the Church's teaching on contraception have remained a minority, but their voice and numbers have been growing.

Early Contributors to Personalism

In response to revisionist criticism about the Church's position being overly focused on the physical aspects (physicalism) of the act of intercourse and insufficiently attentive to the relational aspects (personalism), traditionalists needed to work on presenting the Church's teaching in a way that was relationally coherent and attractive. Before his election as Pope John Paul II, Karol Wojtyla was a key contributor to this task. While serving as the Chair of Ethics at the Catholic University of Lublin, and as the newly appointed auxiliary bishop of Krakow in 1960, Karol Wojtyla published *Love and Responsibility*, which reportedly "raised a few eyebrows."[1] Wojtyla anticipated objections that he had no experience in sexual matters by pointing to his extensive interactions with couples, "wider" in its understanding than merely one relationship.[2] In this way he establishes his credibility not merely as a theologian and philosopher, but also as a confessor and pastor. According to George Weigel, biographer of Pope St. John Paul II, "*Love and Responsibility* was, its author remembered, 'born of pastoral necessity.'"[3] As early as the 1950s Wojtyla saw times were changing and that the Church needed to grow in its understanding of sexuality, a likely factor in his being selected to serve on the birth control

---

[1] George Weigel, *Witness to Hope: The Biography of Pope John Paul II* (New York: Harper Collins, 2001), 122, 143.
[2] Karol Wojtyla, *Love and Responsibility*, trans. H. T. Willetts (San Francisco: Ignatius Press, 1993), 15.
[3] Weigel, 140.

commission. In fact, Bl. Paul VI's biographer, Paul Johnson, reported that Bl. Paul VI was reading *Love and Responsibility* while writing HV.[4]

Wojtyla condemned utilitarianism, which promotes mutual self-gratification, in favor of love, which consists in mutual self-gift.[5] His concern is that through the lens of utilitarianism, people may feel morally permitted to use each other in order to seek pleasure—a position that he believed was detrimental to morality, society, and even the relationships of those who are seeking pleasure.[6] Instead, Wojtyla proposed his personalistic norm: "The person is a good towards which the only proper attitude is love," and this attitude must be applied to all morality, especially sexuality—a person may never be used as a means to an end, even a good end.[7] In other words, a person must never be objectified. Wojtyla explained that in contraception the "order of nature" (procreative element) is divorced from the "personal order" (unitive element) such that, "the danger arises that objectively speaking there will be nothing left except 'utilization for pleasure', of which the object will be a person."[8] For Wojtyla, the personalistic norm demands in marriage a "reciprocal self-giving" in love, which is hindered, in its fullest sense, by a rejection of the procreative dimension.[9] Contraception makes it impossible to treat one another as we are designed to be treated. While Wojtyla's personalist perspective recast the discussion, it would undergo further development later during his pontificate.

One of the writers who also contributed to the personalistic approach to married sexuality was Paul Quay. Writing in 1961, Quay also focused more on conjugal love than natural law in his explanation of marital sexuality. One of his major contributions, which would be used later by Pope St. John Paul II, is the discussion of language: "Coitus is, consequently, a communication between persons, nonmediated and direct. But it is more. It is a most sensible language and natural sign and symbol of love. ... Sexual activity is

---

[4] Janet E. Smith, "Pope John Paul II and *Humanae Vitae*," in *Why Humanae Vitae Was Right: A Reader*, ed. Janet E. Smith (San Francisco: Ignatius Press, 1993), 232-233.

[5] Wojtyla, 35.

[6] Ibid., 37.

[7] Ibid., 41.

[8] Ibid., 226-228.

[9] Ibid., 99.

not merely symbolic; it is a language."[10] This language can become a lie that the couples make with their bodies when they use contraception. Quay suggests, "[Contracepting couples] perform what appears to be the act of love but [it] is only a sham; they lie to one another in their bodies as in their hearts. They take that which says perfect union and corrupt it till it can express only mutual pleasure. They abuse the symbol of the gift of one's self to another."[11] Quay recognizes that couples may object in defense of contraception based upon their desire to love each other and unite with one another in love.[12] However, he persists in his condemnation with the following:

> That first contraceptive act declares that, much as one loves the other, one does not love enough to forgo that pleasure of intercourse so that he or she might reserve for the other the most fitting expression of that love. ... Their act does not bespeak the desire for the other's fullness of parenthood; it symbolizes a flat rejection of God's intervention. They are two alone at this moment and refuse to transcend themselves.[13]

Elements of Quay's work, especially the notion of "language" of sexual actions, would find its way into the later contributions of St. John Paul II.

Another contributor worthy of discussion is Dietrich von Hildebrand. The first layman theologian to contribute significantly to the subject of marriage, even before *Casti Connubii* (1930), von Hildebrand laid the foundations for a greater recognition of conjugal love as a good of marital sexuality. Stemming from a developing tradition of marriage and sexuality that revisionists valued and used to arrive at their position, von Hildebrand would have been a

---

[10] Paul M. Quay, "Contraception and Conjugal Love," in *Why Humanae Vitae Was Right: A Reader*, ed. Janet E. Smith (San Francisco: Ignatius Press, 1993), 34. Originally published in *Theological Studies*.
[11] Ibid., 39.
[12] Ibid., 40-41.
[13] Ibid.

welcome ally in their camp. However, within one year after HV, von Hildebrand revealed himself as a strong defender of the encyclical. Like Quay, von Hildebrand's work also had a significant impact on the later theology of St. John Paul II.

Von Hildebrand highly esteems marital sexuality and the bonding of the spouses. Unlike revisionists, though, this supports his *opposition* to contraception. He explains, "We must learn to see that the bodily union, destined to be the fulfillment of spousal love and an ultimate mutual *self-donation*, is as such something noble and a great mystery, a sacred land which we should approach with deep reverence and never without a specific sanction of God."[14] Procreation is an integral part of this self-donation in marital intercourse, and withholding the procreative element is tantamount to a reduction in spousal love and the meaning of the action.[15] Von Hildebrand believes contraception violates more than mere biology; it also violates a proper relationship with God, because it involves the creature "usurping a right" that belongs to God alone.[16] According to von Hildebrand, contraceptive actions not only cause injury to the relationships of spouses, they also damage our right relationship with God.

Critics may well ask why humans are morally permitted to intercede medically upon other elements of human nature in ways that seem to do the work of God for the overall well-being of the person. To this von Hildebrand replies that some such actions involve deeply meaningful relations, while others are "purely 'factual'" actions without a relational aspect, like heart transplants or hysterectomies.[17] "A fatal shot through a man's head is not simply a 'biological intervention' but a murder, because a man's life was connected with the physiological processes that were frustrated. Artificial birth control is thus no mere biological intervention but the severing of a bond which is under the jurisdiction of God," he explains.[18] Key to von Hildebrand's position is careful consideration

---

[14] Dietrich von Hildebrand, "The Encyclical *Humanae Vitae*: A Sign of Contradiction," in *Why Humanae Vitae Was Right: A Reader*, ed. Janet E. Smith (San Francisco: Ignatius Press, 1993), 53.

[15] Ibid., 67-68.

[16] Ibid., 71, 77.

[17] Ibid., 74-75.

[18] Ibid., 79.

of the relational aspect of creatures and God as well as the relationship of the spouses.

Pope Saint John Paul II and the Theology of the Body

Likely the greatest personalist/relationalist contribution for traditionalists came from Pope St. John Paul II's *Theology of the Body* (TOB). As Karol Wojtyla attended the conclave that would elect John Paul I in 1978, he brought with him a draft of a book he was composing that he believed was needed to address the issues in the Church following HV.[19] His election as pope later that year interrupted his plans, but St. John Paul II took advantage of the customary Wednesday audiences to deliver 129 talks from 1979-1984 in which he presented this material, which was later published as TOB.[20] Scarcely appreciated in its promulgation, TOB has become increasingly popular within and beyond the traditionalist perspective, especially amongst young adult Catholics in the twenty-first century.

In TOB, St. John Paul II works to approach our being and sexuality from a different angle than most were using. His perspective was that of phenomenological philosophy, which tends to start with the experiences of the person to draw support for its arguments.[21] This opened his audience to the personal relevance of reproductive morality.[22] By elaborating on the human context, personalism was an effective complement to the natural law foundation. St. John Paul II began with his personalistic norm, that all people have intrinsic value and must not be used as a means, but are ends in themselves.[23] Put simply, contraception violates the personalist ethic in that it allows couples to use each other as objects rather than as dignified beings worthy of love. John Crosby explains that St. John Paul II felt the need to express this "truth about man" in such a personalistic way because it helped to bring forth the "underlying truth" of HV in a way that showed it to be a reality of our being rather than an

---

[19] Weigel, 336.
[20] Pope John Paul II, *The Theology of the Body: Human Love in the Divine Plan* (Boston: Pauline, 1997).
[21] Janet E. Smith, "Pope John Paul II," 234.
[22] Ibid., 235.
[23] Ibid., 236.

imposition by the Church.[24] Pope St. John Paul II wove personalism into his reflections on Genesis and Matthew's account of the Sermon on the Mount to show that the Theology of the Body is applicable to the whole Biblical standard of unrestrained self-gift.

One of the major themes of TOB is love as a gift-of-self, echoing von Hildebrand. St. John Paul II frequently references GS §24, "[Man] can fully discover his true self only in a sincere giving of himself."[25] He suggests that to live out the personalistic norm and to find authentic happiness and human fulfillment, one must overcome selfishness and make a gift-of-self to another. Already in the early 1970s, John Kippley contributed the idea of marriage as a covenant and the marital act as a renewal of that covenant. His thesis has been rendered, "Sexual intercourse is intended by God to be at least implicitly a renewal of the faith and love and unreserved gift of self pledged by the couple when they entered the covenant of marriage."[26] Furthermore, as recently as 2010 D. Vincent Twomey has commented, "Since one gives oneself (one's self to another self), this gift must be exclusive and total—that is, life-long—and open to the gift of new life. Only such a gift is fitting as expressive of one's own person and is worthy of the one to whom one gives oneself and the person (child) who may result from such a mutual self-giving."[27] This perspective thus remains alive and well.

However, to make such a gift, one must truly possess oneself. Reflecting on *Genesis*, St. John Paul II suggests that originally Adam and Eve were capable of authentic love as God intended, because they were sinless and incapable of lust. However, when Original Sin entered the world, the resulting concupiscence made it difficult to control lust. Thus, human freedom is restricted; we are incapable of making a full, authentic gift-of-self; and the love due to the beloved other falls short of what is due to him or her. He writes,

---

[24] John F. Crosby, "The Personalism of John Paul II as the Basis of His Approach to the Teaching of *Humanae Vitae*," in *Why Humanae Vitae Was Right: A Reader*, ed. Janet E. Smith (San Francisco: Ignatius Press, 1993), 198.

[25] Pope John Paul II, *The Theology of the Body: Human Love in the Divine Plan* (Boston: Pauline, 1997), 63.

[26] John F. Kippley, *Sex and the Marriage Covenant: A Basis for Morality*, 2nd ed. (San Francisco: Ignatius Press, 2005), 7.

[27] D. Vincent Twomey, *Moral Theology after Humanae Vitae: Fundamental Issues in Moral Theory and Sexual Ethics* (Dublin: Four Courts Press, 2010), 71.

"Concupiscence entails the loss of the interior freedom of the gift. ...
Man can become a gift—that is, the man and the woman can exist in
the relationship of mutual self-giving—if each of them controls
himself."[28] Consequently, St. John Paul II holds self-mastery in high
regard and integral to true love. With these concepts, he attempts to
lay down the requirements of genuine love.

St. John Paul II believes genuine human love is called to reflect
the communion of persons present in the Trinity. It is this concept
from which the terminology of "Theology of the Body" originates.
St. John Paul II teaches, "The body, and it alone, is capable of
making visible what is invisible: the spiritual and the divine. It was
created to transfer into the visible reality of the world the mystery
hidden since time immemorial in God, and thus be a sign of it."[29] If
theology is the study of God, "Theology of the Body" is the study of
God through the human body. St. John Paul II suggests it is possible
to come to a greater understanding of God through our bodies
because we are made in his image. He further states, "Right 'from the
beginning,' [man] is ... essentially, an image of an inscrutable divine
communion of persons."[30] God is a communion of persons, and—
created in the image of God—all people are also called to exist in a
loving communion of persons. Spouses image this in a special way
through their gift of self in marital intercourse. Our very being is
called to reflect the Trinitarian love of God. Some have taken this to
its limits: "Like the Trinity, we have the capability of entering a
communion of persons. We are first called to enter a *communion of persons*
with God and then with other human beings. Failure to form a
communion of persons is an attack, an aggression, against our very
persons. We must love. It is a subjective need that every human being
has," explain Hogan and LeVoir.[31]

Finally, St. John Paul II also discusses the "language of the
body," drawing from Quay. "The human body is...the means of
expressing the entire man, the person, which reveals itself by means

---

28 TB, 127.
29 Ibid., 76.
30 Ibid., 46.
31 Richard M. Hogan and John M. LeVoir, "The Family and Sexuality," in *Readings
in Moral Theology No. 10: John Paul II and Moral Theology*, ed. Charles E. Curran
and Richard A. McCormick (New York: Paulist Press, 1998), 159.

of the language of the body," as St. John Paul II explains.[32] It is through our bodies that we experience, relate to, and contribute to the world and others, and what we do with our bodies must conform to what we intend to mean with our bodies. St. John Paul II maintains that couples must express the truth of their love and gift-of-self in an objectively truthful way, without withholding integral parts of themselves from coitus, like their procreative potential.[33] The language of words spoken in the marital vows is completed by the language of deeds spoken in marital consummation. St. John Paul II states, "By means of marriage as a sacrament of the Church, man and woman are called explicitly to bear witness—by using correctly the language of the body—to spousal and procreative love."[34] In this way, their bodies faithfully proclaim what their lips promised, to be "willing to accept responsibly and with love the children that God may give [them] and to educate them according to the law of Christ and of the Church."[35] Marital love must therefore remain objectively open to procreation.

By approaching human sexuality from a phenomenological and personalist perspective, interwoven with Scripture and theology, St. John Paul II provided a new way of envisioning the Church's teachings on sexuality, especially contraception. Through this approach, he invites people to look at their marital interaction with a fresh perspective—yet on all points St. John Paul II reaffirms the teaching of his predecessors and HV. He elaborates:

> This communion [of persons] demands that the language of the body be expressed reciprocally in the integral truth of its meaning. If this truth be lacking, one cannot speak either of the truth of self-mastery, or of the truth of the reciprocal gift and of the reciprocal acceptance of self on the part of the person. Such a violation of the interior order of conjugal union, which is rooted in the very order of

---

[32] TB, 397.
[33] Ibid.
[34] Ibid., 365.
[35] Ibid., 363.

the person, constitutes the essential evil of the contraceptive act.[36]

St. John Paul II sees contraception as violating the language of the body, gift-of-self, and the communion of persons. By falling short of all of these, he believes it fails to meet the essential requirements of the act of love so important to the marital relationship. In his reaffirmation of HV, St. John Paul II took one of the theological strengths of the revisionists—a personalistic approach that appreciates and incorporates the love of spouses in relation to marital intercourse—and made it his own.

TOB was not the only instance in which St. John Paul II continued to reinforce the Church's position. It would, in fact, become a recurring theme of his pontificate. Therefore, we must consider other texts to further understand his contributions. Following the 1980 Synod of Bishops, where bishops from around the world once more discussed the Church's teaching on family planning,[37] Pope St. John Paul II wrote *Familiaris Consortio*, or *On the Role of the Christian Family in the Modern World*. In this document St. John Paul II explains that the Synod of Bishops affirmed both the information on marriage from *Gaudium et Spes* (GS) §50 and Bl. Paul VI's teachings in *Humanae Vitae* (HV), "particularly that love between husband and wife must be fully human, exclusive and open to new life."[38] With this he seems to be indicating that the bishops of the 1980 Synod are unified in support of the Church's position. While this may be true, revisionists argue that the cards were stacked. On the 25th anniversary of HV in 1993, revisionist Richard McCormick suggested the 1980 Synod that resulted in Pope St. John Paul II's *Familiaris Consortio* was "orchestrated."[39] He also lamented "…the

---

[36] Ibid.
[37] Ronald Lawler, Joseph Boyle Jr., and William E. May, *Catholic Sexual Ethics: A Summary, Explanation, & Defense*, 2nd ed. (Huntington, Indiana: Our Sunday Visitor, 1998), 148.
[38] Pope John Paul II, *Familiaris Consortio* (1981), http://www.vatican.va/holy_father/john_paul_ii/apost_exhortations/documents/hf_jp-ii_exh_19811122_familiaris-consortio_en.html (accessed July 14, 2009), §29.
[39] Richard A. McCormick, "'Humanae Vitae' 25 Years Later," *America* (July 17, 1993), http://www. americamagazine.org/content/article.cfm?article_id=10960 (accessed October 14, 2009): 3 of 7.

well-known fact that for some years now acceptance of *Humanae Vitae* has become one of the litmus tests for Episcopal appointment" and that "bishops do not feel free to state their opinions honestly."[40] McCormick suggests that the situation among bishops is not as unified or approving as St. John Paul II would have it seem.

Echoing his themes of the personalistic norm and communion of persons, St. John Paul II describes our basic human vocation as a calling to love in the following:

> God created man in His own image and likeness: calling him to existence through love, He called him at the same time for love. God is love and in Himself He lives a mystery of personal loving communion. Creating the human race in His own image and continually keeping it in being, God inscribed in the humanity of man and woman the vocation, and thus the capacity and responsibility of love and communion. Love is therefore the fundamental and innate vocation of every human being. As an incarnate spirit, that is a soul which expresses itself in a body and a body informed by an immortal spirit, man is called to love in his unified totality. Love includes the human body, and the body is made a sharer in spiritual love.[41]

The connection between body and soul, combating dualism (i.e. the idea that our spiritual souls and physical bodies are distinct), is essential for St. John Paul II and other traditionalists, because they saw the revisionist position as separating the soul from the body by focusing on the relational aspect and ignoring the physical action in order to justify contraception. Revisionists saw it the other way around, and St. John Paul II sought to unite the two. He explains that all of our being is one with our body, and we communicate our very selves with our bodies. The love of husband and wife who use contraceptives is interrupted and made deficient, because it lacks substantially in its total self-giving and becomes a lie in terms of the

---

[40] Ibid.
[41] Pope John Paul II, *Familiaris Consortio*, §11.

language of the body, as if the body is saying "I give all of myself to you," while fertility is withheld.[42]

In 1994 St. John Paul II released *Gratissimam Sane* (Letter to Families) to commemorate the "Year of the Family." The letter reiterates: "The two dimensions of conjugal union, the unitive and the procreative, cannot be artificially separated without damaging the deepest truth of the conjugal act itself. This is the constant teaching of the Church, and the 'signs of the times' which we see today are providing new reasons for forcefully reaffirming this teaching."[43] As time elapsed following HV, traditionalists believed the truth of Bl. Paul VI's position became ever clearer, as St. John Paul II's comment reflects.

Swiss Philosopher, Fr. Martin Rhonheimer, discusses the pitfalls of dualism: "The acting human subject is always a body-spirit *unity*: Human acts are not *either* spiritual *or* bodily acts; nor are they acts of a spiritual substance that makes use of the body as its 'instrument.' Human acts are always, although in different ways, acts of body *and* spirit *cooperating*."[44] When we understand a human person as the union of body and spirit and connect this truth of our being with the meanings of sexual intercourse, the depth of Rhonheimer's contribution becomes clear. The procreative and unitive meanings are "inseparably connected" (as HV maintains) in each act of intercourse. Since the body and spirit of both persons are united in each lover and then united with both body and spirit united in the beloved, the procreative meaning that the bodies bring to the act cannot be separated from the unitive meaning the spirits bring to the act since the sexual act itself is a sharing in the complete being of each lover. Rhonheimer explains:

> The "inseparable connection" of the two meanings signifies their *reciprocal inclusive correlation*. The bodily reality of procreation receives its fully human

---

[42] Ibid., §11, 32.

[43] Pope John Paul II, *Gratissimam Sane* (1994), http://www.vatican.va/ holy_father/john_paul_ii/letters/Documents/hf_jp-ii/let_02021994 _families_en.html (accessed November 19, 2009), §12.

[44] Martin Rhonheimer, *Ethics of Procreation and the Defense of Human Life: Contraception, Artificial Fertilization, and Abortion*, ed. William F. Murphy Jr. (Washington D.C.: Catholic University of America Press, 2010), 72.

specification from spiritual love; the spiritual love of the married persons receives its specification as a determinate *sort* of love from the procreative function of the body. … Each receives its full intelligibility as a *human* reality—its fully *human* meaning—precisely *from the other*. Procreation considered independently from spiritual love *is no longer the same thing*. And spiritual love tending to the bodily union between male and female, when considered apart from its procreative meaning, *is no longer the same thing*. This precisely is what follows from man's substantial body-spirit unity. … Both meanings are not extrinsically, but *intrinsically* connected: *The very connection constitutes the specifically human content of both meanings.* … The Inseparability Principle, as stated by *HV*, does not simply state that one is "not allowed" to separate these functions. Instead, it says that one *cannot* do so without destroying the very *meaning* of the marital act. The encyclical in fact refers not to "functions," but to "meanings" of the conjugal act, and it claims that one cannot separate these two meanings without destroying *both*, and therefore its *entire* meaning as an act of conjugal love.[45]

At this point, however, Rhonheimer admits that he has not entirely proved his point, because it leaves open an appeal to the principle of totality. He uses the example of truth stating, "Individual lies cannot be justified based on a life dedicated, in its totality, to truthfulness—they remain lies. Instead, individual actions determine and shape the development of a person's life as a whole."[46]

There are critics of St. John Paul II's approach, though. Charles Curran recognizes that with TOB St. John Paul II has "developed

---

[45] Martin Rhonheimer, *Ethics of Procreation and the Defense of Human Life: Contraception, Artificial Fertilization, and Abortion*, ed. William F. Murphy Jr. (Washington D.C.: Catholic University of America Press, 2010), 77-79, 81.

[46] Martin Rhonheimer, *Ethics of Procreation and the Defense of Human Life: Contraception, Artificial Fertilization, and Abortion*, ed. William F. Murphy Jr. (Washington D.C.: Catholic University of America Press, 2010), 89.

more personalist arguments" in order to defend the Church's teaching, but he suggests that TOB's concept of language of the body and gift-of-self "puts too much emphasis on the meaning of each and every single sexual act"—an emphasis that has been criticized by revisionists since the beginning of the debate.[47] Moreover, Curran and a younger theologian, Luke Timothy Johnson, agree that TOB is lacking in its value and meaning for all people, because they suggest it does little for widows/widowers, people living out a single vocation, or those with homosexual inclinations.[48] Furthermore, from a scriptural standpoint, Johnson criticizes TOB for "deriving ontological conclusions from selected ancient narrative texts."[49] Here Johnson is referring to the numerous references to the *Genesis* creation stories, among others, from which St. John Paul II constructs his view of marital sexuality. Moreover, Johnson thinks important omissions were made in St. John Paul II's scriptural selections, especially ones that show an appreciation for pleasure (e.g. 1 Tim 6:17).[50] Johnson concludes that TOB is specifically designed to support HV's teachings, which he believes to be unreasonable, impractical, and untenable in the modern world.[51]

The argument had clearly evolved since the early post-conciliar conflict. While initially personalism was a strength of revisionists and a deficiency of traditionalists, it has now become a strong bulwark of the traditionalists' position and less commonly used by revisionists.[52] It seems the traditionalists, largely thanks to Pope St. John Paul II, have successfully countered one of the primary arguments leveled against them, so much so that they have turned it around and made it one of their strengths.

---

[47] Charles Curran, *The Moral Theology of Pope John Paul II* (Washington D.C.: Georgetown University Press, 2005), 112-113, 116, 117, 176.

[48] Curran, *Theology of Pope John Paul II*, 168; Luke Timothy Johnson, "A Disembodied 'Theology of the Body'." *Commonweal* 128, no. 2 (Jan 2001): 4-6 of 9.

[49] Ibid., 4 of 9.

[50] Ibid., 5 of 9.

[51] Ibid., 5, 8 of 9.

[52] Janet E. Smith, "*Humanae Vitae* at Twenty," in *Why Humanae Vitae Was Right: A Reader*, ed. Janet E. Smith (San Francisco: Ignatius Press, 1993), 502.

Natural Law and New Natural Law Theory

The subject of natural law can be tricky, because the term has been used in a number of different ways throughout history by different theologians.[53] In essence, it is a moral law inscribed in man's heart by God, by which he may discover what is good and evil through reason.[54] Natural law holds that some actions are always intrinsically (by their very nature) wrong. Some classic intrinsic evils that may be found in almost every culture are murder, stealing, lying, and rape. Based upon the premise that human nature constantly changes, the revisionist worldview argues that the morals of one era cannot be compared to those of another. To the contrary, Twomey suggests cultures of various eras and locations can and sometimes must be judged morally by others. This is why, he explains, we can look at events throughout history such as the holocaust, forced abortion in China, and genocide in Darfur—as well as events in the Church's history like the Spanish Inquisition—and condemn them as immoral.[55] He argues, "This is the standard of our common humanity, what is shared by the entire human community and known to the Stoics as natural law or, in our day, as the conscience of humanity, or even natural justice or 'human rights.'"[56] It is the consistency and permanence of natural law that allows us to look at other cultures of diverse lands and times and see actions like slavery and torture as immoral.[57]

Twomey takes his argument a step further. If the worldview of revisionists is correct, "This would mean we could no longer read either the Bible or the pagan classics, such as Sophocles, or even Shakespeare, since our human nature would in important respects— and not just with regard to clothes, manners, technology or language—be radically different from theirs," he argues.[58] In essence,

---

[53] Janet E. Smith, *Humanae Vitae: A Generation Later* (Washington D.C.: Catholic University of America Press, 1991), 70.
[54] *Catechism of the Catholic Church: Modifications from the Editio Typica*, 2nd ed. (Washington, DC: United States Catholic Conference, Inc.—Libreria Editrice Vaticana, 1997), §1954-1960.
[55] Twomey, 37.
[56] Ibid.
[57] Ibid., 37-38.
[58] Ibid., 68-69.

a connection between cultures and ages of history exists among all humanity, and this corresponds to the natural law, our very being and nature as humans. The worldview of human nature as dynamic and shifting amounts to a "denial of a common human nature that underlines...the changes of culture and history in such a way that we can still relate to common human experiences that span the centuries," writes Twomey.[59] He further notes, "The reason we read the classics is for their insight into the universal human condition marked as it is by the same human hopes and fears, loves and hates, vices and virtues, which are common to all people of whatever epoch."[60]

Part of the struggle with discerning natural law, though, is the belief that man has a fallen, or deprived, human nature. Our concupiscence makes it difficult to clearly discern the natural law without assistance. God provides this assistance through the Holy Spirit by means of revelation and grace that come to us through the Scriptures, Magisterium, Church, and sacraments. Here is where the stumbling block of authority crops up. It leads to more questions, like how the Holy Spirit is working in the Church to guide and direct her, and how should the Church's rightful authority be utilized appropriately? For these reasons, discerning the natural law is much messier than a textbook on the subject may admit.

Many natural law arguments have been accused of advocating the idea that a bodily organ's purpose may be deduced from its healthy function.[61] For instance, by observing the fact that ears hear, we may determine that this is also their purpose. This premise has been attacked by revisionists as being too "physicalist" and "biological," and has been dubbed by some as the "naturalistic fallacy." This criticism is frequently credited to David Hume who stated that it is inappropriate to attempt to derive a moral "ought" from an objective "is" (i.e. the moral purpose of things ought not be entirely determined by their physiological function).[62]

---

[59] Ibid., 82.
[60] Ibid., 69.
[61] Janet E. Smith, *A Generation Later*, 75.
[62] Howard P. Kainz, "Sexual Mores, Ethical Theories, and the Overpopulation Myth." *Heythrop Journal* 49, no. 3 (May 2008): 364.

Writing in 2010, Fr. Martin Rhonheimer explains the flaw of the naturalistic argument (fallacy), which proposes that the physical function of something determines its moral use. He laments the number of Catholics who have moved into the revisionist camp because this was their understanding of the Church's objection to contraceptives that they came to believe was absurd.[63] He maintains, "*agree contra naturam* (to *act* against nature) is not equivalent to *peccare contra naturam* (to *sin* against nature). A reason must always be given as to *why* a violation of nature—that is, of the course of the body's natural processes—does or does not have moral relevance. … Thus, an argument against contraception based upon the naturally given structure of the sexual act does not resolve anything."[64]

Traditional natural law theorists have defended their position by trying to explain that Hume's criticism is unfair. For example, they do not morally object to certain deviant sexual actions performed by various animals, so their condemnation is not merely based upon an "ought" being derived from an "is."[65] Some theorists have also sought to buttress traditional natural law with personalism as a way to sustain it, and one traditional natural law theorist has essentially admitted that traditional natural law objections to contraception are insufficient to stand alone against its use; however, they are helpful in presenting a moral barrier to them.[66] Furthermore, Janet Smith turns the "physicalist" critique against the revisionists when she says that they, "treat the generative processes of Man as merely physical, for allowing the use of contraception seems to suggest that only the organs or processes are violated; that the deeper dimensions of the human person do not enter into these generative acts and thus are not harmed by contraception."[67] In this way, the revisionist position comes dangerously close to dualism, seeing the body and soul as separate entities as opposed to inherently intertwined, composing a

---

[63] Martin Rhonheimer, *Ethics of Procreation and the Defense of Human Life: Contraception, Artificial Fertilization, and Abortion*, ed. William F. Murphy Jr. (Washington D.C.: Catholic University of America Press, 2010), 51-52.

[64] Martin Rhonheimer, *Ethics of Procreation and the Defense of Human Life: Contraception, Artificial Fertilization, and Abortion*, ed. William F. Murphy Jr. (Washington D.C.: Catholic University of America Press, 2010), 53-54.

[65] Janet E. Smith, "*Humanae Vitae* at Twenty," 514-515.

[66] Janet E. Smith, *A Generation Later*, 88.

[67] Ibid., 177.

human person. To continue, it will be useful to familiarize ourselves with the different natural law arguments.

According to Janet Smith, there are three versions of natural law whose "foundations" are found in HV.[68] The first suggests that since contraception "impede[s] the procreative power of actions that are ordained by their nature to the generation of new human life," it is immoral.[69] This argument relies upon the idea that human life is so precious that even the process of creating that life deserves respect.[70] Second, contraception is immoral, because intercourse was inherently designed "by [its] nature to assist God" in creating new life, and contraception obstructs this.[71] This argument obviously relies heavily upon premises of respect for God's creative abilities and contribution in acts of sexual intercourse. Twomey argues from this perspective when he explains, "For the spouses to take the initiative to exclude the possibility of new life is to act against the possibility inherent in that union of God's creative action;…it amounts to an attempt to exclude God from that human act where He is most present in the created order."[72] Finally, the third argument is articulated thusly: "It is wrong to destroy the power of human sexual intercourse to represent objectively the mutual, total self-giving of spouses. Contraception [violates this]. Therefore, contraception is wrong."[73] This argument should sound familiar to the reader who is acquainted with traditionalist theologians' discussion of personalism, as discussed earlier. Its presence within HV is likely due to Wojtyla's correspondence and influence with Bl. Paul VI on the issue prior to HV, such as the Krakow commission and Bl. Paul VI's familiarity with *Love and Responsibility* mentioned earlier. However, other traditionalists prefer an entirely alternative approach to natural law.

Traditional natural law approaches have also experienced criticism by some traditionalists who consider it inadequate and therefore have embarked on a revision of the natural law, yet still supportive of Magisterial teachings. These are the architects of New

---

[68] Ibid., 99.
[69] Ibid.
[70] Ibid., 100.
[71] Ibid., 99.
[72] Twomey, 195.
[73] Janet E. Smith, *A Generation Later*, 99.

Natural Law Theory (NNLT), sometimes referred to as Basic Goods Theory, who work to avoid falling victim to the naturalistic fallacy. Therefore, it must be noted that even within the traditionalist perspective there is disagreement about how to understand and utilize natural law. The architects of this position who continue to be associated with it are Germain Grisez, Joseph Boyle, John Finnis, and William E. May. The major difference between their work and the above approach is that they suggest a contraceptive action inherently involves an immoral intent or will. As Lawler, Boyle, and May state, "It is the anti-life *intent* together with the anti-covenantal and the anti-sacramental effects, and not the mere biology involved, which are held to be morally determinative."[74] In this way their position avoids falling victim to the naturalistic fallacy. It shares elements like covenantal and sacramental understandings of marriage with the personalistic approach, but its defining characteristic is a focus on the anti-life intent. NNLT also involves consideration of goods related to marriage. While many revisionists believe in "ontic" or "pre-moral" evils that may violate one good of marriage at the expense of upholding another, NNLT theorists believe all goods (i.e. the unitive, procreative, and sacramental ends of the marital act) must be shown respect—none may be violated at the expense of another. Consequently, the unitive and procreative goods may not be severed from one another. This point is constantly reiterated by the Magisterium.

Arguments from the Minority Report

In an effort to construct the position of traditionalists, it is also necessary to recognize the arguments presented by the Minority Report in 1966, which are inherited by the traditionalists who continue to defend the minority position. First, traditionalists often maintain that the Church's condemnation of contraception is unchangeable. They use the history of contraception to show that the Church's position has always condemned the prevention of conception. However, they also recognize legitimate development has occurred. In the modern period, the work of such theologians as Dietrich von Hildebrand, as it was assimilated into later magisterial teaching, reflects such development. Moving the Church's

---

[74] Lawler, Boyle, and May, 157.

perspective from viewing procreation as the only good of marriage, to seeing it as the primary good, and finally on to an equal level as the unitive good in GS, is clearly a legitimate development. Lawler, Boyle, and May explain that these developments do not challenge the historical stability of the Church's condemnation of contraception, but rather advances what they recognize as, "themes which were suggested by the medieval theologians and present in the Christian consciousness from the start."[75] In addition to the unitive good, the legitimacy of pleasure has also become recognized and more greatly appreciated by the Church's teaching.[76] In these ways development has certainly occurred.

The problem with the revisionist idea of legitimate development is that it goes inordinately beyond the tradition to the point of overturning it. In some sense, their desire to go beyond the equal goods formulation of GS can be seen as reverting back to a primary-secondary approach, except with the unitive good being primary. The Church's teaching revolving around contraception has not remained static as some revisionists would suggest. Culminating in Vatican II and HV, teachings about sexuality and marriage reached new levels of development, yet this dynamic, authentic development simply did not go far enough in the minds of revisionists.

Second, the Minority Report suggested that allowing the use of contraceptives by married couples would compromise the consistency and credibility of Catholic moral teachings. To counteract this, the majority (and subsequently the revisionists) worked to show how allowing contraceptives in some cases could be considered an authentic development of Church teaching. The majority and revisionists suggested that a change would be commensurate with the increasing appreciation for the other goods and elements of the marital act such as the unitive dimension of the spousal relationship and legitimacy of pleasure.[77] On the other hand, they suggested, it

---

[75] Ibid.

[76] Ibid., 66.

[77] J.A. Selling, "Magisterial Teaching on Marriage 1880-1986: Historical Constancy or Radical Development?," in *Readings in Moral Theology No. 8: Dialogue about Catholic Sexual Teaching*, ed. Charles E. Curran and Richard A. McCormick (New York: Paulist Press, 1993), 97; Bernard Haring, "The Inseparability of the Unitive-Procreative Functions of the Marital Act," in *Readings in Moral*

was Bl. Paul VI's teaching in HV that *every* act must be open to life that was truly novel and not in conformity with tradition. At minimum, though, the concept of openness to life has roots in the ancient understanding of sexuality as procreative at its core.

Revisionists also point to the fact that changes have occurred and do occur in theology, as was especially evident with changes following Vatican II, for example the redemption of Doms's views. Avery Dulles provides more examples from history: "Changes in doctrine were linked to new astronomical discoveries (such as the overthrow of the Ptolemaic system), new biological discoveries (such as evolutionism), new methods in historical criticism, and new developments in politics."[78] The classic examples of change are religious liberty, usury, and the changes to the goods/ends of marriage. Dulles notes that there is room in the Church for changing teachings as they seek "to mediate between the abiding truth of the gospel and the sociocultural situation at a given time and place."[79] Therefore, some teachings may be changeable, depending upon if and how they are tied to specific social, environmental, or cultural milieus. Those who cannot appreciate the validity of changes on some level are likely to be scandalized anytime the Church needs to make adjustments due to sociocultural contexts or doctrinal development (see "Hierarchy of Teachings" in Chapter 7). Thus, it must be recognized that changes, at least in some sense, have occurred in the past, and they are bound to continue to occur.

The premiere case of change revisionists use to show that the Church's teaching on contraception could change is that of usury (i.e. money lending with interest, especially at exorbitant rates). John T. Noonan Jr. provides parallels: the Church's teaching against usury had good scriptural support (i.e. Lk 6:35), a long standing history in natural law, was reviewed by a papal commission that reported to the pope, it was repeatedly condemned by the Magisterium, theologians and laity nevertheless continued to disobey the teaching, and

---

Theology No. 8: Dialogue about Catholic Sexual Teaching, ed. Charles E. Curran and Richard A. McCormick (New York: Paulist Press, 1993), 155.

[78] Avery Dulles, "Authority and Conscience," In *Readings in Moral Theology No. 6: Dissent in the Church*, ed. Charles E. Curran and Richard A. McCormick (New York: Paulist Press, 1988), 104.

[79] Ibid.

eventually the practice of theologians and laity was later vindicated in official Church teaching.[80] However, Dulles explains that the teaching of usury was the type of change that was possible because it was tied to the function of economics at the time. He notes some of the reasons for change: "The condemnations of usury in the Middle Ages were based upon valid moral principles, but were linked, more than was recognized at the time, to a precapitalist economy. Once the shift to capitalism had been made, the new moral teaching had to be modified."[81] Others have suggested that no change occurred in principle but only in the application of the principle due to changes in economics.[82] Ironically, Russell Shaw quotes Noonan stating, "This dogmatic teaching remains unchanged. What is a just title, what is technically to be treated as a loan, are matters of debate, positive law, and changing evaluation. The development on these points is great. But the pure and narrow dogma today is the same today as in 1200."[83] Therefore, the teaching on usury has not changed, but the application of that teaching has developed with changing socio-economic structures.

History provides more examples of changes, though. A typical list includes human rights, Church and state, slavery, torture, and religious freedom.[84] However, Ashley, Deblois, and O'Rourke explain: "In these matters the Church has come to see that it had too much conformed to the customs and opinions of secular society from which it has had to free itself to be true to the Gospel."[85] This is hardly supportive of what revisionists were trying to achieve. Therefore, contrary to being supportive of the revisionists' position, Ashley, Deblois, and O'Rourke argue, "The fact that the Church has

---

[80] John T. Noonan Jr., "The Amendment of Papal Teaching by Theologians," in *Contraception: Authority and Dissent*, ed. Charles E. Curran (New York: Herder and Herder, 1969), 41, 56, 75.

[81] Dulles, "Authority and Conscience," 104.

[82] Benedict M. Ashley, Jean Deblois, and Kevin D. O'Rourke, *Health Care Ethics: A Catholic Theological Analysis*, 5th ed. (Washington D.C.: Georgetown University Press, 2006), 28-29; Russell Shaw, "Contraception, Infallibility and the Ordinary Magisterium," in *Why Humanae Vitae Was Right: A Reader*, ed. Janet E. Smith (San Francisco: Ignatius Press, 1993), 357-358.

[83] Shaw, 357-358.

[84] Ashley, Deblois, and O'Rourke, 29.

[85] Ibid.

had to refine some of its moral teaching to support stricter standards of justice, far from showing that it is not to be relied on as a moral guide, demonstrates its growing fidelity to the Gospel and its increasing trustworthiness."[86] Thus, these examples may be more harmful to the revisionists' goal than helpful.

Traditionalists recognize change but argue that the reversal of the condemnation on contraception would not constitute legitimate development. Consequently, if the Church could be shown to have been mistaken about a moral issue taught through the ordinary Magisterium as important as this, what would prevent all moral teachings of the ordinary Magisterium from being called into question?[87] The problem that inevitably arose from the situation in the 1960s was that no matter what Bl. Paul VI did, the credibility of the Church would be called into question. Since, for all practical purposes, the revisionist position has become commonplace, and since HV a great number of teachings of the ordinary Magisterium have been called into question, we can conclude that this concern of the Minority Report was well-founded—what they predicted is noticeable throughout the Church, especially in so-called "cafeteria Catholics."

Third, the minority warned that opening the door for contraception would necessarily open the door to other sexual actions previously condemned by the Church. As traditionalists have been indicating throughout recent decades, ever more loudly, this warning is the most obviously evident in the decades following HV. Tentler explains, "The new mode of thinking was quickly applied to a wide range of issues, many having to do with sex. Was premarital intercourse licit, at least if the couple was in love? Almost 90 percent of twenty-something Catholics, polled in 1992, asserted that it was."[88] It has become historical fact that many revisionists who held the majority position on contraception came to the logical conclusion that other issues like masturbation, homosexuality, pre-marital sex, adultery, oral sex, and anal sex are also permissible. This change in moral position developed despite the fact that the majority was only

---

[86] Ibid.

[87] Janet E. Smith, *A Generation Later*, 17-18.

[88] Leslie Woodcock Tentler, "Catholics and Contraception: An American History" (Ithaca: Cornell UP, 2004), 275.

in favor of contraceptives being used in marriage on a limited basis and condemned all of these other actions. Revisionists who have made allowances for these other behaviors have made a decisive break with the bishops and theologians of the Majority Report. Lawler, Boyle, and May explain, "This argument was denied in the debates of the 1960s by those defending contraception, but the logic of the position they took has now become very clear. Recent history has shown that their original intention was mistaken: contraception could not be accepted while the other prohibitions of Christian sexual morality were maintained."[89] Even Charles Curran has admitted, "History has clearly shown that those who were afraid that a change in the teaching on contraception would lead to other changes [in the teaching on sexual morality] were quite accurate."[90] We can see the same developments outside of Catholicism as well— consider, for instance, the moral situation in Anglicanism that has gone so far as to permit the ordination of openly homosexual clergy.

Janet Smith explains the logic involved: "If the sex act need not be in any immediate way procreative, why must it be in any immediate way unitive? If the act can be seen as a part of a whole, why may not each separate act gain its moral specification from the ordination of the whole, in regard to both fertility and unity?"[91] Similarly, Atkinson and Moraczewski argue, "Those who justify the violation of the generative process by separating physically the unitive and procreative spheres can have no acceptable, principled basis for ruling out *a priori* any of these other practices;" to do so, one would need to "argue on a case-by-case basis and facing counterarguments which appeal to the very same values that have already been used to justify contraception and sterilization."[92] Without a doubt, the concern of the Minority Report that the moral reasoning employed by the Majority Report to justify contraceptive use for spouses would lead to all kinds of other moral abuses has been proven.

---

[89] Lawler, Boyle, and May, 156.

[90] Ibid., 65.

[91] Janet E. Smith, *A Generation Later*, 28.

[92] Gary Atkinson and Albert Moraczewski, *A Moral Evaluation of Contraception and Sterilization: A Dialogical Study* (St. Louis: Pope John XXIII Medical-Moral Research and Education Center, 1979), 67.

As recently as a September 2009 issue of the *New Oxford Review*, Howard P. Kainz discusses what he calls "contraception & logical consistency." He explains that the many Christian couples who use contraceptives yet maintain a position against either abortion and/or homosexuality are "logically inconsistent."[93] Contracepting couples intentionally suppress the procreative good of their sexual activity in order to emphasize the unitive dimension. Kainz argues, "Obviously, the characteristics of intense affection and commitment can also be present in relationships of non-married males and females—or to married persons who commit adultery and who experience an even greater commitment and affection to their adulterous partner than to their chosen spouse."[94] In terms of homosexuality Kainz states, "On what grounds could intentionally non-procreating heterosexual married couples oppose such homosexual unions?"[95] With procreation intentionally thwarted, little stands to differentiate contraception from other sexually deviant actions. Moreover, in terms of abortion Kainz notes, "For *if there is* then a universal right to enjoy sex without any obligation of openness to offspring, does this not imply a right to abort an unintended or unwanted pregnancy?"[96] As traditionalists have argued for decades, it is no less true today that the ethics of contraception open a moral "Pandora's box."

The effects of revisionist changes, and their wide acceptance in American Catholic culture and theology, have been immense. This single issue has revolutionized the Church. It has overturned, razed, and rebuilt moral theology and ecclesiology. Consequently, it is not difficult to conclude that the concerns of the minority members of the papal birth control commission were not only correct but also prophetic.

Magisterial Assessments

Since HV, revisionists have been the unfailing opposition of the Magisterium within the Church on moral issues. Some have

---

[93] Howard P. Kainz, "Contraception & Logical Consistency," *New Oxford Review* 76, no. 8 (September 2009): 39.

[94] Ibid., 40.

[95] Ibid.

[96] Howard P. Kainz, "Contraception & Logical Consistency," *New Oxford Review* 76, no. 8 (September 2009): 40.

suggested Bl. Paul VI backed off of the contraception issue following HV, perhaps because he never wrote another encyclical. However, his 1970 talk to the Teams of Our Lady, in which he continued to discuss the Church's teaching, suggests otherwise.[97] Nonetheless, revisionists had hope that a new pope might find reason to reconsider the issue, and the election of John Paul I in 1978 fueled such hope. From the revisionist perspective, Bernard Haring explains, "As Albino Luciani, [John Paul I] had suggested a change of doctrine; then when Paul VI in his encyclical *Humanae Vitae* reiterated the ban on contraception, he decided to keep silent. Soon after his election as pope, however, he left no doubt that he would propose a review of the teaching, with emphasis on a consultative approach."[98] Providence did not seem to favor the revisionists, though. Due to John Paul I's "long history of serious circulatory problems" and the newfound stress of taking the position as Supreme Pontiff, he died of a "massive heart attack" and was found in his bed "early on the morning of September 29, 1978," after only one month as pope.[99] St. John Paul II thereafter emerged as arguably the strongest defender of the Church's teaching on contraception. He was assisted by Joseph Cardinal Ratzinger, who became Prefect for the Congregation of the Doctrine of the Faith in 1981 and worked strongly in the teaching's defense—a legacy Ratzinger continued into his own pontificate as Pope Benedict XVI. Pope Francis too has shown no sign of wavering, despite revisionist hopes. For its part, therefore, the Magisterium has held incredibly strong against revisionist theology and prevailing cultural practices. Not only has the Magisterium resisted pressures to change, it has also worked consistently to counter the positions of revisionists and expose their positions as erroneous.

As the Church moved into the 1990's, the Magisterium was composing two very significant works that would have major ramifications for the topic of contraception, as well as the underlying

---

[97] Pope Paul VI, "To the Teams of Our Lady," in *Why Humanae Vitae Was Right: A Reader*, ed. Janet E. Smith (San Francisco: Ignatius Press, 1993), 85.

[98] Bernard Haring, "A Distrust that Wounds," in *Readings in Moral Theology No. 10: John Paul II and Moral Theology*, ed. Charles E. Curran and Richard A. McCormick (New York: Paulist Press, 1998), 43.

[99] Weigel, 246-247.

philosophies and theologies that were being used by traditionalists and revisionists. The first is St. John Paul II's Encyclical Letter of 1993, *Veritatis Splendor* (VS) or *The Splendor of Truth*. VS is primarily an encyclical on moral theology, and in that regard it discusses acceptable and unacceptable ways of approaching the contraception question, among other issues. The second is the *Catechism of the Catholic Church* (CCC). The CCC was the first new catechism for the Roman Catholic Church in over four centuries—since the Roman Catechism following the Council of Trent—whose purpose it was to make the Church's official teaching on all matters of faith and morality clearly accessible and identifiable.

At the beginning of VS, St. John Paul II reveals the occasion for its promulgation. He explains its purpose as, "To set forth, with regard to the problems being discussed, the principles of a moral teaching based upon Sacred Scripture and the living Apostolic Tradition, and at the same time to shed light on the presuppositions and consequences of the dissent which that teaching has met."[100] He describes the situation present in moral theology as a "genuine crisis," and maintains, "The Magisterium has the duty to state that some trends of theological thinking and certain philosophical affirmations are incompatible with revealed truth."[101] Citing canon 747, §2 of the 1983 *Code of Canon Law*, St. John Paul II asserts, "The Church has the right always and everywhere to proclaim moral principles, even in respect of the social order, and to make judgments about any human matter insofar as this is required by fundamental human rights or the salvation of souls."[102] In addressing his encyclical to all bishops of the Church, he works to rally them behind himself, as successors to the apostles behind the successor of Peter, to proclaim and uphold what he believes is the authentic teaching of the Church against "certain interpretations of Christian morality which are not consistent with 'sound teaching' (2 Tim 4:3)."[103] It is not

---

[100] Pope John Paul II, *Veritatis Splendor* (1993), Vatican Translation (Boston: Pauline), §5.

[101] Ibid., §5, 29.

[102] Ibid., §27.

[103] Ibid., §29.

difficult to see that this encyclical is directed heavily against revisionist principles.[104]

First, St. John Paul II recognizes the revisionist critique that traditional positions are too "physicalistic," which he answers by drawing attention to the fact that the revisionist position begins to take on a dualistic approach to human nature. He teaches, "A freedom which claims to be absolute ends up treating the human body as a raw datum, devoid of any meaning and moral values until freedom has shaped it in accordance with its design," and, "In this way of thinking, the tension between freedom and a nature conceived of in a reductive way is resolved by a division within man himself."[105] When revisionists emphasize the personal over the physical, they become guilty of separating them from one another and degrading the physical. It is not as if a person can say, "It was my *body* which killed the *body* of another person," as opposed to, "I (as an integral *person* of body and soul) killed another *person*." Consequently, St. John Paul II affirms, "A doctrine which dissociates the moral act from the bodily dimensions of its exercise is contrary to the teaching of Scripture and Tradition," and "Body and soul are inseparable: in the person, in the willing agent and in the deliberate act they stand or fall together."[106] Therefore, a person who recognizes the physical importance of the body in moral actions is not necessarily guilty of physicalism; on the contrary, this danger arises explicitly in pursuing a morality that separates body and soul, as revisionism tends to do.

Second, St. John Paul II recognizes that some of the foundational principles of morality have been called into question, and he takes up a defense of objective moral norms. He notes, "The great concern of our contemporaries for historicity and culture has led some to call into question *the immutability of the natural law* itself, and thus the existence of 'objective norms of morality.'"[107] To the contrary, revisionists have sought to expand the principle of totality to suggest that certain actions (pre-moral, ontic, or physical evils) may be permissible under certain circumstances if they contribute to an overall greater good. They hold that it may be permissible to negate

---

[104] Ibid., §47.
[105] Ibid., §48.
[106] Ibid., §49.
[107] Ibid., §53.

the good of procreation under certain circumstances in order to pursue another good, such as the unitive end. Accordingly, marriage *as a whole* would need to be open to the good/end of the transmission of life, as opposed to *every* act of intercourse in itself.

Third, St. John Paul II takes special note of what he calls "teleological" theories. He explains their approach: "The criteria for evaluating the moral rightness of an action are drawn from the *weighing of the non-moral or pre-moral goods* to be gained and the corresponding non-moral or pre-moral values to be respected. … Right conduct would be the one capable of 'maximizing' goods and 'minimizing' evils."[108] Two teleological theories are especially applicable to the contraception issue. First, consequentialism is understood by St. John Paul II as claiming "to draw the criteria of the rightness of a given way of acting solely from a calculation of foreseeable consequences deriving from a given choice."[109] Therefore, a consequentialist would make a moral decision on good and evil depending upon the results or end of an action. This position flies in the face of the Church's moral teaching—the end does not justify the means.

The other teleological theory is probably the most popular and is held by some of the most prominent revisionists—proportionalism. In judging a moral action, proportionalists agree with utilitarianism and consequentialism that there are no intrinsic evils; however, in morally evaluating an action, proportionalism considers all of the positives and negatives of the action, not simply its consequences.[110] In addition, it seeks to maximize the "greater good" or at least seek the "lesser evil" in a moral situation.[111] According to Twomey, this theory developed from "re-interpreting the principle of double effect on the assumption that no action or species of actions (more technically, the 'object' of the action) can be said to be intrinsically wrong," which is taken to a degree "subtly but radically different" than its usage in evaluating something based upon the principle of double effect.[112] In essence, proportionalism states, "Since all human

---

[108] VS, §74.
[109] Ibid., §75.
[110] Ashley, Deblois, and O'Rourke, 15-16.
[111] VS, §75.
[112] Twomey, 83.

actions…involve a mixture of good and evil, a good action is one where the proportion of good outweighs whatever inevitable evil may accompany the action."[113]

St. John Paul II rejects these theories saying, "Such theories however are not faithful to the Church's teaching when they believe they can justify, as morally good, deliberate choices or kinds of behavior contrary to the commandments of the divine and natural law. These theories cannot claim to be grounded in the Catholic moral tradition."[114] St. John Paul II seems to believe revisionists have rejected objective moral norms in favor of setting moral conditions based upon subjectively determined values.[115] Indeed, a critique of revisionist Richard McCormick's morality encapsulates the revisionist ethic:

> "In fear and trembling we commensurate"; "we *adopt* a hierarchy." This approach seems to concede that there is no rational way to determine the lesser evil. It proposes that one adopt, that one choose for oneself, a hierarchy of goods, as a way of rating the worth of the various goods. One cannot do it objectively; but one *decides* how one will weigh alternatives; then one chooses in the light of the subjective evaluation that one has given. What this means is that one does not discover what is morally good; one decides what one shall call good by arbitrary assessment.[116]

Lawler, Boyle, and May further comment, "Clearly, as St. John Paul II rightly insists, there can be no inalienable rights when there are no exceptionless duties."[117] Traditionalists rally behind objective morality against what they perceive to be revisionist subjective—or worse, relativistic—morality.

---

[113] Ibid.
[114] VS, §76.
[115] Ibid., §104.
[116] Lawler, Boyle, and May, 85.
[117] Ibid., 87.

The CCC describes how moral situations are to be evaluated, and it does so in ways that entirely reject teleological theories like utilitarianism, consequentialism, and proportionalism, as well as ideas like the principle of totality, fundamental option, and lesser evil proportionalism. The CCC lists the three "sources" of morality as the object, intention, and circumstances.[118] In order for any action to be considered morally good, all three must be morally good.[119] The object is what is done, the action.[120] Of the three sources, the object is most important, because if the object is evil, it spoils the entire moral situation.[121] This is where intrinsic evils step in; they make a moral situation evil no matter how good the intention and circumstances may be. A bad intention (or end) can spoil a good object, but the opposite is not true—"A good intention…does not make behavior that is intrinsically disordered, such as lying or calumny, good or just. The end does not justify the means."[122] St. John Paul II explains, "The reason why a good intention is not itself sufficient, but a correct choice of actions is also needed, is that the human act depends on the object, whether that object is *capable or not of being ordered* to God, to the One who 'alone is good,' and thus brings about the perfection of the person."[123] Committing objective evil is an offense against God, even when one's intentions may be honorable. Therefore, as the CCC reasserts, "One may not do evil so that good may result from it."[124] The intention must also be morally good, with the object, for an overall action to be morally good. Finally, "The *circumstances*, including consequences, are secondary elements of a moral act. They contribute to increasing or diminishing the moral goodness or evil of human acts (for example, the amount of a theft). They can also diminish or increase the agent's responsibility (such as acting out of a fear of death)."[125] Like a good

---

[118] CCC, §1750, 1757.
[119] Ibid., §1755.
[120] VS, §78l; CCC, §1751.
[121] CCC, §1755.
[122] Ibid., §1753.
[123] VS, §78.
[124] CCC, §1756.
[125] Ibid., §1754.

intention, good circumstances (including good consequences) cannot make an evil object good.[126]

Contrary to proportionalism, Church teaching maintains that the object determines the fundamental morality of an action. The intention and circumstances can reduce the gravity of an act, and/or the subject's culpability, but they cannot make an inherently evil action a good action as revisionists suggest. The two foundational formulas that shape this understanding are: (1) one may not do evil so that good may come from it, and (2) the end does not justify the means. St. John Paul II offers this closing remark on intrinsic evil:

> The primary and decisive element for moral judgment is the object of the human act, which establishes whether it is capable of being ordered to the good and to the ultimate end, which is God. ... Reason attests that there are objects of the human act which are by their nature "incapable of being ordered" to God, because they radically contradict the good of the person made in his image. These are the acts which, in the Church's moral tradition, have been termed "intrinsically evil."[127]

In this way, St. John Paul II keeps the Church's morality focused on its ultimate purpose—helping the faithful fulfill our calling and mission as adopted children of God and followers of Jesus Christ in this world so that we may enjoy eternal beatitude with God and others in heaven.

It should also be noted that revisionist arguments on the topic of contraception have undergone some reemphasis in recent years, perhaps largely due to Magisterial documents like *Veritatis Splendor* and the CCC. Writing in 2006, Ashley, Deblois, and O'Rourke explain that revisionists have moved away from many of the "theological arguments" used by the Majority Report and subsequent revisionists to denounce the Church's condemnation of contraceptives, possibly as a result of "the affirmation this teaching has received from Pope St. John Paul II and the *Catechism of the*

---

[126] Ibid.
[127] VS, §79, 80.

Catholic Church (CCC 2000, no. 2370) after consultation with the entire episcopate."[128] Constant and unequivocal Magisterial reaffirmation of the teaching on contraception and explicit rejection of revisionist theories in VS and the CCC, seem to have successfully integrated the physical and spiritual, moral and vocational elements at hand to better explain the Church's teaching. Revisionists have reverted to arguing that Bl. Paul VI was wrong to have rejected the advice of his own commission and a majority view by both theologians and bishops, or that the teaching of HV was only maintained due to Bl. Paul VI's fear that changing the teaching would diminish his authority.[129]

In addition, *Veritatis Splendor* and the CCC may have resuscitated some respect and appreciation for natural law. Romanus Cessario explains that natural law was practically ignored by most Catholic theologians before these documents were promulgated.[130] He suggests that since VS "devoted considerable time to repudiating the post-conciliar, large-scale dismissal of natural law," it could hardly continue to be ignored among Catholic moral theologians.[131]

---

[128] Ashley, Deblois, and O'Rourke, 76.

[129] Ibid.

[130] Romanus Cessario, *Introduction to Moral Theology* (Washington D.C.: Catholic University of America Press, 2001), 74.

[131] Ibid., 75.

Chapter 7
Authority, Assent, and Dissent

Intimately involved with the discussions about the morality of contraception are the topics of Church authority and how the faithful are to adhere to Church authority. One's understanding and approach to the entire moral life hinges upon one's understanding and appreciation for authority in the Church. Twomey has noted, "The crisis in the Church over the past forty years has been in many ways a crisis of authority, in particular with regard to the Church's moral teaching. Put simply, it is a crisis due to a lack of conviction that what the Church teaches, at least in the area of morals, is the truth which alone can make us free."[1] This is an additionally challenging topic for Americans who increasingly value personal freedom, self-sufficiency, and independence.

Furthermore, this issue was all the more complicated by the socio-cultural milieu of the 1960s and early 1970s within which the issue of contraception was essentially defined and battle-lines were drawn. The moral theology environment of the time was in the process of a necessary development from a pre-Conciliar moral theology described by Twomey as "legalistic," "rigorous," "overly concerned with sin," and "badly in need of reform."[2] The question was what kind of development was most appropriate. These shifts in moral theology collided with a political situation in which authoritative institutions were suspect, thus producing an authority crisis. Twomey illustrates: "A century of political ideologies that caused over one hundred million deaths and wrought havoc on numerous peoples throughout the world has brought about a general skepticism vis-à-vis all closed systems of thought and values, especially when they make absolute claims."[3] In addition, some have suggested the "anti-authoritarianism" and "anti-traditionalism" of the Enlightenment came to their apex in the 1960s at the same time as

---

[1] D. Vincent Twomey, *Moral Theology after Humanae Vitae: Fundamental Issues in Moral Theory and Sexual Ethics* (Dublin: Four Courts Press, 2010), 66.

[2] Ibid.

[3] Ibid., 35.

the sexual revolution.[4] In this context Bl. Paul VI's assertions in HV were not going to be met with thunderous applause.

Since the pope had made an official pronouncement on the issue of family planning in HV, those who disagreed with the Church's position needed theological support for the legitimacy of their disagreement. They had already constructed the foundations of a moral theology at odds with the Magisterial position; however, they now also needed an ecclesiological approach to justify disobeying an official moral teaching of the Church. Consequently, while HV was not an encyclical about the Church's teaching authority, reaction to it caused such issues to be thrust into high priority.[5] Traditionalists were primarily concerned about dissent in the early years and then moved on to defending the teaching with moral theology, while revisionists worked in the opposite order.

Meaning of Dissent

It will be helpful to understand what revisionists and traditionalists mean by "dissent" and what they are seeking to accomplish, because not everyone means the same thing by the term. Sincere revisionists claim they are not interested in undermining or subverting the authoritative Magisterium or the Church herself, though some traditionalists may view them this way. Also true is the fact that some people masquerading as revisionists may actually attempt such subversion, which does not help the sincere revisionist cause. Twomey, for example, explains that a primary tactic of some revisionists was to argue for the existence of another magisterium (that of the theologians) alongside that of the pope and bishops, and equal to them in rank, by which the faithful were to form their consciences.[6] On the contrary, authentic revisionists are seeking to improve the Church as they understand it while recognizing the special position of the Magisterium. As a primary leader of the revisionists on the issue of dissent, Charles Curran is clear about what dissent is not intended to mean: "Such dissent does not merely

---

[4] Ibid., 71.
[5] Joseph A. Komonchak, "Ordinary Papal Magisterium and Religious Assent," in
    Contraception: Authority and Dissent, ed. Charles E. Curran (New York: Herder
    and Herder, 1969), 101.
[6] Twomey, 71.

reduce the role of the papal teaching office to that of another theologian in the Church. Such dissent does not involve disrespect for the papal teaching office. No Catholic faithful or theologian can lightly dismiss the authoritative teaching of the papal or hierarchical teaching office of the Church."[7] Nonetheless, Curran is clear that he believes the Church is capable of being wrong, especially on a non-infallible issue. On this topic, Curran believes the Church teaching is in error.

Traditionalist William E. May recognizes that people may have good reason to withhold assent, as he notes, "Withholding assent, while continuing to study the matter with a willingness to accept the magisterial teaching in question, is quite different from actively dissenting."[8] What Curran calls dissent is likely equivalent to what May calls "withholding assent." What many traditionalists call dissent is likely equivalent to a stubborn or arrogant, outright rejection of Church teaching. Consequently, it is important to discern from individual authors what they mean when they speak of dissent. This may help to explain why revisionists are more tolerant of "dissent" than traditionalists.

Hierarchy of Teachings

To further our discussion of authority and appropriate adherence to Church authority, it is essential for us to have an understanding of the Church's hierarchy of teachings. Some of the faithful may tend to easily accept the authority of the Church (e.g. if the pope says it, it must be held as an absolute truth). Conversely, others may tend to take all Church teaching with a "grain of salt," as if official teachings were merely recommendations. The fallacy in either extreme is to see all Church teachings at the same level, which typically becomes apparent when something changes in the Church. For example, when the Eucharistic fast prior to receiving communion shifted from several hours to one hour, people of the former practice may have been scandalized. "How could the Church

---

[7] Charles E. Curran, introduction to *Contraception: Authority and Dissent*, ed. Charles E. Curran (New York: Herder and Herder, 1969), 9-10.

[8] William E. May, "Conscience Formation and the Teaching of the Church," in *Why Humanae Vitae Was Right: A Reader*, ed. Janet E. Smith (San Francisco: Ignatius Press, 1993), 379.

change such a thing?," they might ask themselves. "We were taught it was a mortal sin not to keep the (long) fast and subsequently receive communion," they may remark. Imagine how this group would react if in the future the Church began to allow priests to be married, under similar conditions as those currently set for permanent deacons, as is the practice of the Eastern Orthodox. On the other hand, when Pope Pius XII solemnly defined the dogma of the Assumption in 1950, people of the latter practice may have thought, "Well, it is fine that the Church wants to believe that about Mary, but I do not believe it, so I am just going to ignore it and believe what I currently believe." Imagine their reaction if the Church were to solemnly declare in dogmatic fashion that it is impossible to ordain women to the priesthood. In order to avoid each of these fallacious extremes, one must at least have some remote familiarity with the hierarchy of teachings, even if only in principle.

The Church has provided distinct categories or "levels" of teaching based upon the level of authority with which they have been taught, including levels of adherence required by members of the Church to particular levels of teaching. Richard R. Gaillardetz is an expert on the issue of Church authority, and his terminology for describing the different levels of teaching is useful. First, teachings of the highest level are called "definitive dogma", which require a "solemn declaration" of the teaching, assurance that it is part of God's revelation, and it must be on a matter of faith or morality.[9] Gaillardetz explains that definitive dogmas are "definitive, irreformable, permanent, or irreversible" and thus judged by the Church infallibly—meaning the Holy Spirit has prevented the Church from falling into "fundamental error" concerning one of these teachings.[10] Gaillardetz states, "A dogma faithfully communicates or mediates divine revelation," and a "hierarchy of truths" exists even among the dogmas of the Church.[11] This does not mean to suggest that even dogmas could not further develop—as we can never

---

[9] Benedict M. Ashley, Jean Deblois, and Kevin D. O'Rourke, *Health Care Ethics: A Catholic Theological Analysis*, 5th ed. (Washington D.C.: Georgetown University Press, 2006), 23-24;

[10] Richard R. Gaillardetz, *Teaching with Authority: A Theology of the Magisterium in the Church* (Collegeville: Liturgical Press, 1997), 102, 104.

[11] Ibid., 108, 115.

articulate the fullness of divine truths in human terms—yet it does affirm, "No dogma could so change or develop as to lead us away from the path to salvation," writes Gaillardetz.[12] Consequently, these teachings require "assent of faith," and believers are to make "an act of faith, trusting that this teaching is revealed by God."[13]

The CCC explains three ways in which a teaching may be judged infallible. First, the pope alone may make such a declaration by himself when he speaks *ex cathedra* (i.e. "from the chair" of Peter); as the "head of the college of bishops," also as "supreme pastor and teacher of all the faithful;" and on a matter of faith or morals.[14] *Ex cathedra* teachings are quite rare, and it has been suggested that the only examples are two dogmas on Mary, the Immaculate Conception (1854) and the Assumption (1950). Second, the bishops in union with the pope may make an infallible judgment when "they exercise the supreme Magisterium," which occurs "above all in an Ecumenical Council."[15] This does not mean everything spoken by a council is dogmatic, but it is certainly a place from which dogmatic teachings may be formulated and given to the faithful as such. Examples include the Church's belief in the divine revelation of the Bible, transubstantiation, and the Trinity. Gaillardetz includes two others: the divine and human natures of Christ as determined at the Council of Chalcedon (451) and the resurrection of Jesus.[16] Such teachings are guaranteed to be true by the Church and require the assent of faith. The third way of teaching infallibly relates to the second hierarchical level of teaching and is discussed below.

The second hierarchical level of Church teachings are not proposed solemnly but "in a definitive way." They are not divinely revealed but are "strictly and intimately connected with revelation," and involve matters of faith and/or morality.[17] Gaillardetz calls these teachings "definitive doctrine" and recognizes that while they are

---

[12] Ibid., 108.

[13] Ibid., 271; Richard R. Gaillardetz, *By What Authority?: A Primer on Scripture, the Magisterium, and the Sense of the Faithful* (Collegeville: Liturgical Press, 2003), 126.

[14] *Catechism of the Catholic Church: Modifications from the Editio Typica*, 2nd ed. (Washington, DC: United States Catholic Conference, Inc.—Libreria Editrice Vaticana, 1997), §891.

[15] Ibid.

[16] Gaillardetz, *Teaching with Authority*, 103.

[17] Ashley, Deblois, and O'Rourke, 23-24.

"nonrevealed truths," they are still "irreformable or irreversible" and "protected from the possibility of fundamental error by the infallible assistance of the Holy Spirit," like definitive dogma.[18] This second level of Church teaching can be a bit more difficult to determine, partly because their "scope has not yet been precisely defined by the magisterium," and, "The category itself is somewhat controversial."[19] Ashley, Deblois, and O'Rourke explain that while these teachings are not part of divine revelation, they "are so intimately connected with revealed truths that to deny them is equivalent to denying what is revealed."[20] An example of this level of teaching is the canon of the Bible, because while the canon itself was not revealed, "were such a determination to be false, divine revelation itself might be compromised," writes Gaillardetz.[21]

Here is where the third possibility of infallible judgments regarding a teaching by the Magisterium fits—the bishops in union with the pope may teach infallibly through the ordinary Magisterium, even if they do not state it definitively. The CCC explains this is possible when, "without arriving at an infallible definition and without pronouncing in a 'definitive manner,' they propose in the exercise of the ordinary Magisterium a teaching that leads to better understanding of Revelation in matters of faith and morals."[22] This level of teaching, though, does not require the same response from the faithful as one stated more definitively, "To this ordinary teaching the faithful 'are to adhere to it with religious assent' which, though distinct from the assent of faith, is nonetheless an extension of it," explains the CCC.[23]

When dealing with levels of teaching, examples are often helpful, so let us consider one that helps to illustrate the differences between the levels. Hotly contested, definitive doctrine is the level at which the Church affirms that only men may be ordained as priests. In 1994 St. John Paul II and the Congregation for the Doctrine of the Faith (CDF) reaffirmed this teaching. In his Apostolic Letter, *Ordinatio*

---

[18] Gaillardetz, *Teaching with Authority*, 117.
[19] Ibid.; Ashley, Deblois, and O'Rourke, 24; Gaillardetz.
[20] Ashley, Deblois, and O'Rourke, 24.
[21] Gaillardetz, *Teaching with Authority*, 119.
[22] CCC, §892.
[23] Ibid.

Sacerdotalis, St. John Paul II explains that Bl. Paul VI reminded the Anglicans—who were considering the ordination of women—of the Catholic Church's position that the priesthood is reserved to men only for three reasons: (1) divine revelation indicates Christ only chose men as spiritual leaders to follow him, (2) history admits no alternative practices than the one consistently held, and (3) the Church has always and everywhere taught this discipline to be true.[24] The reader will note similarities between the latter two reasons and those used against contraception. In 1976, Bl. Paul VI had the CDF compose *Inter Insigniores* to address the issue of the ordination of women and elaborate on its reasoning.[25] The CDF did so and also addressed various counterarguments, while pastorally addressing the concerns of those women who may have an attraction to the priesthood. Among them is the affirmation that, "The Church is a differentiated body, in which each individual has his or her role. The roles are distinct, and must not be confused; they do not favor the superiority of some vis-à-vis the others, nor do they provide an excuse for jealousy… The greatest in the Kingdom of Heaven are not the ministers but the saints."[26] Based upon this history, in 1994 St. John Paul II intended to lay this issue to rest and concluded:

> Wherefore, in order that all doubt may be removed regarding a matter of great importance, a matter which pertains to the Church's divine constitution itself, in virtue of my ministry of confirming the brethren (cf. Lk 22:32) I declare that the Church has no authority whatsoever to confer priestly ordination on women and that this judgment is to be definitively held by all the Church's faithful.[27]

---

[24] Pope John Paul II, *Ordinatio Sacerdotalis* (1994), http://www.vatican.va/holy_father/john_paul_ii/apost_letters/documents/hf_jp-ii/apl_22051994_ordinatio-sacerdotalis_en.html (accessed December 8, 2009), §1.

[25] Ibid., 2.

[26] Congregation for the Doctrine of the Faith, *Inter Insigniores* (1976), http://www.papalencyclicals.net/Paul06/p6interi.htm (accessed December 8, 2009), nearly last paragraph.

[27] Pope John Paul II, *Ordinatio Sacerdotalis*, §4.

Considering the words chosen by St. John Paul II, this statement was clearly definitive.

One year later, as Prefect for the CDF, Joseph Cardinal Ratzinger addressed St. John Paul II's Apostolic Letter, because it "was followed by a number of problematic and negative statements by certain theologians, organizations of priests and religious, as well as some associations of lay people."[28] In order to "dispel the doubts and reservations that have arisen," Ratzinger produced a clarification from the office of the Congregation for the Doctrine of the Faith, approved by St. John Paul II, which declared:

> This teaching requires definitive assent, since, founded on the written Word of God, and from the beginning constantly preserved and applied in the Tradition of the Church, it has been set forth infallibly by the ordinary and universal Magisterium (cf. Second Vatican Council, Dogmatic Constitution on the Church *Lumen Gentium* 25, 2). Thus, in the present circumstances, the Roman Pontiff, exercising his proper office of confirming the brethren (cf. Lk 22:32), has handed on this same teaching by a formal declaration, explicitly stating what is to be held always, everywhere, and by all, as belonging to the deposit of faith.[29]

St. John Paul II's treatment of the subject, clarified and affirmed by Ratzinger, clearly indicates that the matter is settled definitively and is not open for discussion. Quite predictably, though, revisionists would reject this teaching on the same grounds as the Church's teaching on contraception. Like dissent on contraception, dissent on the exclusively male priesthood has far-reaching implications for ecclesiology, authority, morality, and the relationships between members of the church at all levels.

---

[28] Joseph Ratzinger, "Concerning the Teaching Contained in *Ordinatio Sacerdotalis, Responsum Ad Dubium*" (1995), http://www.ewtn.com/library/curia/cdfrespo.htm (accessed December 8, 2009).

[29] Ibid.

The third level of teaching includes issues that are part of the ordinary Magisterium that have not been taught definitively, but which have been taught "with such consistency and universality that it is clear they must somehow involve principles that are true."[30] Gaillardetz refers to this level as "nondefinitive, authoritative doctrine"—they have not been definitively declared, and "the possibility of a substantive reversal cannot in principle be excluded."[31] Teachings at this level are meant to assist the faithful in understanding a point of divine revelation, or to protect the deposit of faith from errors.[32] An example of a teaching at this level was the Immaculate Conception of Mary, which caused disputes for centuries, because scholars were not sure how to reconcile it with the Biblical truth that all people need Christ as savior.[33] Since this has been resolved, the teaching of Immaculate Conception has moved up the hierarchy of teachings to the level of definitive dogma, by *ex cathedra* declaration.

The level of adherence required for this level of teaching is more flexible yet still firm. Ashley, Deblois, and O'Rourke explain that this level of teaching requires "religious submission of will and intellect," which "cannot be simply exterior or disciplinary but must be understood within the logic of faith and under the impulse of obedience to faith."[34] Similarly, Gaillardetz calls the adherence required, "A Religious Docility (or *Obsequium*) of Will and Intellect" by which, "The believer strives to assimilate a teaching of the Church into their religious stance, while recognizing the remote possibility of Church error."[35] Gaillardetz draws this from *Lumen Gentium*, which further states:

> This loyal submission of the will and intellect must be given, in a special way, to the authentic teaching authority of the Roman pontiff, even when he does not speak *ex cathedra*, in such wise, indeed,

---

[30] Ashley, Deblois, and O'Rourke, 24.
[31] Gaillardetz, *Teaching with Authority*, 121.
[32] Ashley, Deblois, and O'Rourke, 23-24.
[33] Ibid.
[34] Ibid.
[35] Gaillardetz, *Teaching with Authority*, 271; Gaillardetz, *By what Authority?*, 126.

that his supreme teaching authority be acknowledged with respect, and sincere assent be given to decisions made by him, conformably with his manifest mind and intention, which is made known principally either by the character of the documents in question, or by the frequency with which a certain doctrine is proposed or by the manner in which the doctrine is formulated.[36]

Gaillardetz recognizes that most people will not have trouble giving most of the Church's teachings at this level the "'obedience,' 'submission,' 'docility,' 'due respect,' or 'assent,'" they are due; however it is possible that some of the faithful may genuinely struggle with teachings at this level.[37] While such teachings are not definitive and have the slight possibility of being erroneous, they are nonetheless authoritative, and Gaillardetz affirms, "These teachings continue to provide the norm for Catholic belief and may not be simply dismissed."[38] For those who sincerely struggle with a teaching at this level and believe the Church's position may be in error, Gaillardetz offers the following helpful instruction of what is required of a believer:

> First, if I possess a religiously "docile" attitude to a problematic teaching I will be willing to engage in further study of the issue. ... Second, if the teaching in question regards matters of morality (e.g., cohabitation before marriage or recourse to artificial contraception), I ought to engage in an examination of conscience. This means asking myself some difficult questions regarding the nature of the difficulties I am having with a given teaching. Am I struggling with this teaching because I cannot discover in it the will of God, or is it because this teaching, if true, would demand some real

---

[36] *Lumen Gentium*, in *Vatican Council II*, ed. Austin Flannery (Northport: Costello Publishing Company, 1996), §25.
[37] Gaillardetz, *By what Authority?*, 124.
[38] Gaillardetz, *Teaching with Authority*, 121.

conversion? Perhaps some basic aspect of my present lifestyle would have to change. Third, I must consider whether my difficulties lie not with a particular teaching but with the very idea of a church teaching office. To be a faithful Catholic is to accept the basic legitimacy of the Church's teaching office, even if one may have some objections about how that office is structured and exercised in practice.

This is a fairly demanding regimen, as it ought to be if I am to take issue with accepted church teaching. However, if I have had difficulties with a particular teaching and I have fulfilled these three steps and still cannot give an internal assent to that teaching I have done all the Church can ask of me and my inability to give an internal assent to this teaching does not in any way separate me from the Roman Catholic communion.[39]

In this way Gaillardetz offers his professional theological opinion of what is required of a Catholic who encounters a teaching at this level to which he or she has difficulty adhering or assenting. He also seems to suggest that the Church's teaching on contraception exists at this level. We will consider this further after exploring the fourth level of teaching.

The fourth level involves, "the ordinary teaching of the Church [that] contains guidance concerning matters that require prudential judgment on how revealed principles apply to complex and changing situations."[40] Gaillardetz calls this level "prudential admonitions and provisional applications of church doctrine/discipline."[41] It is at this level that teachings may really change, because teachings at this level may be tied to certain situations, times, or places. As a result, teachings at this level must be respected, but "its authority for the most part is based on the reasons given for the particular statement, and Catholics may have an opinion at odds with the Church on such

---

[39] Gaillardetz, *By what Authority?*, 124-125.
[40] Ashley, Deblois, and O'Rourke, 23-24.
[41] Gaillardetz, *Teaching with Authority*, 271; Gaillardetz, *By what Authority?*, 126.

a teaching."[42] Gaillardetz explains the necessary response to this level of teaching to be, "The believer obeys (the spirit of) any church law or disciplinary action which does not lead to sin, even when questioning the ultimate value or wisdom of the law or action."[43] This is the level of Church teaching that we find the discipline of the Church having a celibate clergy, for example. Such discipline certainly has support in Scripture (e.g. Jesus' precedent and St. Paul's opinion noted in 1 Cor 7:32-35); however, it has not always been part of the Church's practice. The requirement of celibacy only took strong hold over Church discipline in the West in the second half of the Church's history. Scripture also speaks of Peter's mother-in-law whom Jesus healed (Luke 4:38), so the prime apostle and first bishop of Rome was married. The current practice is not even absolute, as occasionally the Church will ordain married men who have converted from a Christian ecclesial community where they served as a minister. Therefore, the likelihood of the Catholic Church having married priests is much higher than any possibility of women being ordained as priests, for example. Many Catholics hold the Church's teaching on contraception equivalent to this level, at least in terms of how they understand the Church's authority to have an impact on their decisions and on what they feel morally obliged to do. For those Catholics known disparagingly as "cafeteria Catholics" (picking and choosing the teachings of the Church to which they will subscribe) all teachings exist on this level—all are negotiable. For these Catholics, dogmas are stodgy formalities and ordinary teachings are purely optional. From top to bottom, the hierarchy of truth is negotiable.

Considered within this system, the teaching on contraception is more difficult to categorize than most. Due to the way it was proclaimed in HV and the lack of solemn declaration, it does not meet the requirements necessary for it to be declared dogma, at the highest level of teaching, and requiring the assent of faith. Nonetheless, it has been proposed "in a definitive way" and has been taught always and everywhere by the ordinary magisterium prior to the twentieth century. Consequently, some have argued that it must be "firmly accepted and held" at the second level—definitive doctrine. We must remember that this is a truth of natural law,

---

[42] Ashley, Deblois, and O'Rourke, 23-25.
[43] Gaillardetz, *Teaching with Authority*, 271; Gaillardetz, *By what Authority?*, 126.

holding its own weight regardless of ecclesiastical pronouncement, and has only become an issue of authority due to widespread dissent. Most revisionists would likely recognize that it is at least nondefinitive, authoritative doctrine and thus requiring *obsequium*. Yet, they maintain because the teaching has not been judged infallibly, it may be (Curran argues it *is*) in error, thus opening it to the possibility of legitimate dissent. This issue of whether the teaching has been infallibly declared has been an important point of contention for contraception, and dissent from (or at least nonconformity to) the Church's teaching. This, of course, is simply an "end run" around the historical reality of the teaching of the Church "always and everywhere" for almost 2,000 years.

Infallibility

The most significant point to which revisionists continually directed attention in terms of the authority of the teaching on contraception is the fact that it was not proclaimed infallibly and is not considered by them to be irreformable. Charles Curran explains that the Church's teaching against contraception stems from the ordinary magisterium and thereby deserves obedience; however, he also maintains that it is therefore not an infallible teaching and remains "open to development."[44] Revisionists point to the fact that it was made clear that HV was not meant to be an infallible teaching of the Supreme Pontiff. Haring explains, "Monsignor Lambruschini, the Curia official appointed by the Vatican to explain the encyclical to the press, emphasized that it was not an infallible statement, and that the possibility of a revised statement, if new data appeared, could not be excluded."[45] Traditionalists counter by explaining the context of Lambruschini's comments. As a member of the papal birth control commission, Lambruschini had reason to downplay the weight of the encyclical, and one of the authors of HV, Ermenegildo Lio, stated that Lambruschini's comments had not been authorized and were his

---

[44] Charles E. Curran, "Personal Reflections on Birth Control," In *The Catholic Case for Contraception*, ed. Daniel Callahan (London: Macmillan, 1969), 24-25.

[45] Bernard Haring, "The Encyclical Crisis," in *The Catholic Case for Contraception*, ed. Daniel Callahan (London: Macmillan, 1969), 78

own interpretation.[46] While Lambruschini was never "publicly corrected" concerning his comments, the Vatican newspaper, *L'Osservatore Romano*, did not include Lambruschini's comments in its coverage of the release of HV.[47] Eventually, Lio wrote against Lambruschini's statement, suggesting that the "language in *Humanae Vitae* meant to indicate that [Paul VI] was making a solemn definition of Church doctrine and that infallibility extends to such definitions"—Lio's writing remains only in Italian and has not generated responses.[48] Even Bernard Haring notes that the "tone" of HV did not seem to allow much possibility of an official adjustment to the teaching.[49] Regardless of these circumstances, revisionists who could not accept the teaching were encouraged in their doubt by the possibility that the pope may have erred, believing HV was not infallibly declared. Most traditionalists concede this point and make their arguments in objection to dissent from the teaching in other ways. However, two Americans have taken up the issue of infallibility from another angle, and their work has provoked more discussion than Lio's.

In 1978 John Ford and Germain Grisez argued that the Church's ban on contraception is infallible, having been confirmed consistently by the Church's ordinary Magisterium.[50] They look to *Lumen Gentium* §25 and work to suggest that the history of the Church's teaching on the issue and HV conform to the requirements laid down by Vatican II to make it infallible—if the teaching had been taught as true by all bishops throughout history, it would make it infallible.[51] They further state, "No teaching which the Church proposes as a serious doctrine of faith or morals, necessarily to be followed in order to attain eternal salvation, and proposed universally through even one century, can be substantially in error."[52] A primary response to this position was formulated by Garth Hallett, who "is one of the few who contest that

---

[46] Janet E. Smith, *Humanae Vitae: A Generation Later* (Washington D.C.: Catholic University of America Press, 1991), 155-156.

[47] Janet E. Smith, *A Generation Later*, 155-156.

[48] Ibid., 156.

[49] Haring, "The Encyclical Crisis," 78-79.

[50] John C. Ford and Germain Grisez, "Contraception and the Infallibility of the Ordinary Magisterium," *Theological Studies* 39, no. 2 (Je 1978): 259.

[51] Ibid., 273.

[52] Ibid., 303, 304.

the Church has had a constant teaching against contraception," according to Janet Smith.[53] Hallett recognizes that the Church has never taught that contraception is good, consistently opposing it throughout history; however, he suggests that the Church has not always had the same reasons for opposing contraception, so the teaching fails to meet the requirements of *Lumen Gentium* §25, and thus may be open to the possibility of error.[54] After further discussion between Grisez and Hallett, the disagreement has remained unresolved. These theologians represent two rare points of view from their sides, because Grisez is one of the few traditionalists to hold that the teaching was infallibly determined by the ordinary magisterium, and Hallett is perhaps the only revisionist who does not believe the Church's teaching against contraception has been constant. From a more centrist perspective, Gaillardetz has noted Canon 749 §3, which states, "No doctrine is understood to be infallibly defined unless it is clearly established as such," which he interprets to mean that in cases where there is debate as to whether an infallible judgment has been made concerning a teaching of the Church, it ought not be considered infallibly defined, as "the burden of proof is on the magisterium to demonstrate that it is [infallibly defining a teaching] in accord with the accepted conditions established in church tradition."[55]

Assent and Dissent

If the teaching of HV has not been infallibly declared, but rather is an authoritative non-infallible teaching, how must a faithful Catholic understand and subscribe to what it teaches? Revisionists maintain that since the Church's condemnation is not based upon divine revelation, it cannot be infallible, and it could therefore be in error. However, revisionists also recognize that no one is to approach a non-infallible teaching such as HV lightly, *assuming* that it is in error.[56] Komonchak explains that the level of assent owed a teaching

---

[53] Janet E. Smith, *A Generation Later*, 158.
[54] Garth L. Hallett, "Contraception and Prescriptive Infallibility," *Theological Studies* 43, no. 4 (D 1982): 650.
[55] Gaillardetz, *By what Authority?*, 85-86.
[56] Komonchak, 107.

of the ordinary Magisterium is "internal, religious assent."[57] While different from "assent of divine faith," which must necessarily be given to matters of dogma like transubstantiation, Komonchak continues, "The assent must be internal and sincere; external conformity or respectful silence are not sufficient. Finally the assent is termed 'religious,' because its motive lies in the fact that the pope has been given authority to teach by Christ," even though this specific teaching was not taught by Christ.[58] Avery Dulles provides the official terminology of what is required as *"obsequium animi religiosum*—a term that, depending on the context, can be suitably translated by 'religious submission of the mind,' 'respectful readiness to accept,' or some such phrase."[59] Granted the teaching of the Church regarding contraception requires a level of obedience to the Church, is dissent on this issue impossible? Josef Fuchs argues "no" as he suggests, "If all dissent in the Church were excluded, nothing could ever be corrected."[60]

We may now inquire how a person might dissent from an authoritative non-infallible teaching in an acceptable manner. Following the release of HV, one of the first groups of bishops to respond were the Belgians, and their response included an answer to this question. They explained that the type of Catholic who is "competent in the matter under consideration and capable of forming a personal and well-founded judgment—which necessarily presupposes a sufficient amount of knowledge—may, after a serious examination before God, come to other conclusions on certain points."[61] However, they also are careful to include a statement affirming, "In such a case [this type of Catholic] has the right to

---

[57] Ibid.

[58] Ibid.

[59] Avery Dulles, "Authority and Conscience," In *Readings in Moral Theology No. 6: Dissent in the Church*, ed. Charles E. Curran and Richard A. McCormick (New York: Paulist Press, 1988), 105.

[60] Joseph Fuchs, "Teaching Morality: The Tension Between Bishops and Theologians Within the Church," In *Readings in Moral Theology No. 6: Dissent in the Church*, ed. Charles E. Curran and Richard A. McCormick (New York: Paulist Press, 1988), 339.

[61] Richard A. McCormick, "'Humanae Vitae' 25 Years Later," *America* (July 17, 1993), http://www. americamagazine.org/content/article.cfm? article_id=10960 (accessed October 14, 2009): 1 of 7.

follow his conviction provided that he remains sincerely disposed to continue his inquiry."[62] Therefore, while opening up the possibility for a well-educated Catholic who has carefully considered the issue to act differently than what HV teaches, they require such a person to continue to keep his or her mind open and continue to reevaluate the issue. This final statement requires any dissenter to continue to keep his or her mind open on the matter, continuing to give the Magisterium the benefit of the doubt, and perpetually seeking to understand the teaching as the Church has proposed it.

The Belgians, however, were not the only bishops to comment on the issue. The United States bishops also released a statement that began, "There exists in the Church a lawful freedom of inquiry and of thought and also general norms of licit dissent."[63] Nonetheless, the US bishops affirmed, "When there is question of theological dissent from non-infallible doctrine, we must recall that there is always a presumption in favor of the magisterium."[64] Similar to the Belgians, the U.S. bishops recognize a legitimacy of dissent in terms of non-infallible teachings, yet they too put limitations on such a stance. Furthermore, they affirm, "The expression of theological dissent from the Magisterium is in order only if the reasons are serious and well-founded, if the manner of the dissent does not question or impugn the teaching authority of the Church and is such as not to give scandal."[65] The conditions continue as the bishops note, "Even responsible dissent does not excuse one from faithful presentation of the authentic doctrine of the Church when one is performing a pastoral ministry in Her name."[66] Thus, pastors, teachers, theologians, etc. may not allow their personal opinions to cloud or distort their duties related to their positions in terms of educating and shepherding others.

From these statements we may deduce that there may be times when dissent may be licit; however, benefit of the doubt is given to the Magisterium so that the dissenter must possess a continually open

---

[62] Ibid.

[63] National Conference of Catholic Bishops, "Norms of Licit Theological Dissent," in *Readings in Moral Theology No. 6: Dissent in the Church*, ed. Charles E. Curran and Richard A. McCormick (New York: Paulist Press, 1988), 127.

[64] Ibid., 127-128.

[65] Ibid.

[66] Ibid., 128.

mind on the issue should he or she be in error, it must not create scandal or undermine the Magisterium, and the dissenter must have serious and sufficient reason for his or her position. The burden of proof rests on the dissenter, as they would need to believe that there is an error in the teaching, which calls into question whether the Church or the individual dissenter is being guided by the Holy Spirit. With all of these requirements, legitimate dissent is obviously a rare occurrence. Dulles concludes, "Dissent in the Church means that a member of the Church takes exception to the position that has become official. Dissent therefore cannot be absolute."[67] One of the greatest points to consider is the revisionist insistence upon an individual's need to seriously consider the topic, with solid information, an open mind, and an openness to continually reconsider the issue. Lamentably, this does not seem to have occurred in recent decades, and we may also infer that many who do not agree with the Church's teaching today are not truly "dissenting" appropriately. Authentic dissent has acquired a bad name over the past few decades, especially among traditionalists, likely due to the incredibly deficient effort and discernment of people who struggle (or refuse to engage in a struggle) with this teaching of the Church to understand and attempt to live it.

Some revisionists have gone so far as to assert an obligation to dissent from Church teaching, in some cases motivated by a fear of losing Catholics over the issue.[68] Reflecting back upon the aftermath of HV, Curran writes, "It was important for Roman Catholic spouses to know that they did not have to make a choice between using artificial contraception under some conditions and ceasing to be members of the Roman Catholic Church. The Catholic theologian, among others, had an obligation to tell this to the Catholic spouses."[69] It is evident that Curran, and likely many others, felt it

---

[67] Avery Dulles, "Doctrinal Authority for a Pilgrim Church." In *Readings in Moral Theology No. 3: The Magisterium and Morality*, edited by Charles E. Curran and Richard A. McCormick, 247-270. New York: Paulist Press, 1982), 262.

[68] Mary Perkins Ryan and John Julian Ryan, "Have You Thought It Out All the Way?," in *The Catholic Case for Contraception*, ed. Daniel Callahan (London: Macmillan, 1969), 105.

[69] Charles E. Curran, "Public Dissent in the Church," In *Readings in Moral Theology No. 6: Dissent in the Church*, ed. Charles E. Curran and Richard A. McCormick (New York: Paulist Press, 1988), 403.

was important for them as prominent members of the Church to inform the laity who were struggling with the teaching of HV that they were not alone and that it might be possible for them to use contraceptives and remain "good" Catholics. This reasoning seems to be shared by Daniel Callahan and comes up in the introduction of his 1969 book, *The Catholic Case for Contraception*, as its *raison d'etre*.[70] He collected all kinds of articles from scientists, married couples, and theologians to help Catholic couples feel at ease about using contraceptives.

Traditionalists, though, did not see things the same way. Avery Dulles has observed:

> Since Vatican II a certain number of Catholics in this country, having become thoroughly Americanized, resent any interference with their freedom to think as they see fit. When confronted by anything less than a solemn dogmatic pronouncement from Rome, they are inclined to respond: "This teaching is not infallible; I do not have to believe it." Such Catholics might do well to ask themselves whether it is really better to believe less rather than more, and to be defiant rather than trusting. Do their critical attitudes in fact correspond to the ideals of humility, concord, and submission that are so powerfully commended in the New Testament?[71]

Here Dulles touches upon a serious part of the issue involving Church teaching and dissent. Even the most notorious dissenter, Curran, explained, "The Catholic should gratefully receive the teaching of the hierarchical magisterium and only for serious reasons and after commensurate reflection make a conscientious decision in opposition to it."[72] The problem remains—how many average

---

[70] Daniel Callahan, introduction to *The Catholic Case for Contraception*, ed. Daniel Callahan (London: Macmillan, 1969), x.

[71] Dulles, "Authority and Conscience," 107.

[72] Charles E. Curran, "Pluralism in Catholic Moral Theology," in *Readings in Moral Theology No. 3: The Magisterium and Morality*, ed. Charles E. Curran and Richard A. McCormick (New York: Paulist Press, 1982), 386.

Catholics have seriously considered this issue? This is a point all the more pertinent for today's young adult Catholics who have likely not even been taught the official position or been exposed to a reasonable explanation of the teaching.

Overall, traditionalists are much less likely to allow for the possibility of legitimate dissent. Going back to Pius XII's encyclical *Humani Generis*, John Ford and Gerald Kelly discuss the relationship between theologians and the Magisterium, noting that even if an encyclical does not speak dogmatically or infallibly, an intention to "settle points hitherto disputed...demand of themselves a positive assent on the part of the faithful, theologians included."[73] This is fully supported by *Lumen Gentium* §25 as cited above. In this way they suggest dissent in this case, at least to the degree it has taken place, is not legitimate.

Archbishop William Levada, Ratzinger's successor as Prefect of the CDF, took up the traditionalist defense of assent back in 1986: "Dissent is a decision not to grow any further in the direction of the God who reveals himself in and through Christ and his church. For dissent would seem to say, 'Not what the church says, but what I say.'"[74] Interestingly, Germain Grisez identifies widespread dissent as an impetus for the 1985 bishops' synod that commissioned the CCC, perhaps to contest such an attitude as Levada identifies.[75] Rejecting a teaching of the Church, Levada continues, carries with it a certain rejection of the Church, the Magisterium, and the idea that the Holy Spirit has assisted her in her teaching.[76] Levada claimed that moral dissent puts self above Church: "I would say that Catholic theology does not recognize the right to dissent, if by that we mean adopting conclusions which are contrary to the clear teachings of the

---

[73] John C. Ford and Gerald Kelly, "Doctrinal Value and Interpretation of Papal Teaching," in *Readings in Moral Theology No. 3: The Magisterium and Morality*, ed. Charles E. Curran and Richard A. McCormick (New York: Paulist Press, 1982), 4-5.

[74] William Levada, "Dissent and the Catholic Religion Teacher," in *Readings in Moral Theology No. 6: Dissent in the Church*, ed. Charles E. Curran and Richard A. McCormick (New York: Paulist Press, 1988), 139-140.

[75] Germain Grisez, "How to Deal with Theological Dissent," in *Readings in Moral Theology No. 6: Dissent in the Church*, ed. Charles E. Curran and Richard A. McCormick (New York: Paulist Press, 1988), 444.

[76] Levada, 144.

authoritative, non-infallible magisterium and are presented to the public in such a way as to constitute equivalently an alternative, personal magisterium."[77]

Levada is in good company, as Pope St. John Paul II took similar positions. In a Los Angeles speech, the Holy Father said, "It is sometimes claimed that dissent from the magisterium is totally compatible with being a 'good Catholic' and poses no obstacle to the reception of the sacraments. This is a grave error that challenges the teaching office of the bishops of the United States and elsewhere."[78] Clearly, St. John Paul II approaches the issue in no less serious terms than Levada. In VS he further states, "*Dissent, in the form of carefully orchestrated protests and polemics carried on in the media, is opposed to ecclesial communion and to a correct understanding of the hierarchical constitution of the People of God.*"[79] In this statement, St. John Paul II practically targets Curran and others who protested HV with their public statement within days of the encyclical's promulgation.

Finally, it must be noted how the issue of dissent relates to an ecclesiological point-of-view. A master of ecclesiology, Dulles offers an explanation of how the Church must necessarily operate differently than secular institutions in the following:

> The church…exists only to the extent that it continues to adhere to a very specific vision of the world—one centered on Jesus Christ as Lord and Savior. Unlike any secular organization, the church has a deposit of faith that must be maintained intact and transmitted to new members. Thus the church cannot accommodate the same kind of ideological pluralism that is acceptable in the secular state or university.
>
> A second difference flows from the origin of the church. Unlike the secular state, the university, or any other institution on the face of the earth, the church according to Christian belief, has been established by

---

[77] Ibid., 147.
[78] Janet E. Smith, *A Generation Later*, 264.
[79] Pope John Paul II, *Veritatis Splendor* (1993), Vatican Translation (Boston: Pauline), §113.

the action of God in Jesus Christ. The members of the church, including the highest officeholders, are not free to change in a substantive way the beliefs, structures, purposes, and forms of worship of the church. They are trustees, obliged to safeguard the trust committed to them.[80]

The very fact that one dissents seems to *de facto* betray these truths about the Church's role in the world, her authority, and how she exercises that authority over the Body of Christ.

In *Called to Communion*, Joseph Cardinal Ratzinger articulates the importance of obedience and faith in the Church: "Most people have trouble with the Church because she is an institution like many others, which as such restricts my freedom."[81] People may argue therefore that it is their duty to "make the Church" themselves.[82] This attitude is unacceptable according to Ratzinger, because, "A church based on human resolutions becomes a merely human church. It is reduced to the level of the makeable, of the obvious, of opinion. Opinion replaces faith."[83] He explains the danger of such an approach as well as its incompatibility with authentic Christianity:

> Like the Corinthians, we too run the risk of fragmenting the Church into a factional strife in which every contestant develops his own idea of Christianity. In this way the rightness of one's own position becomes more important than God's claim on us, than being right before him. Our own idea conceals from us the word of the living God, and the Church disappears behind the parties that grow out of our personal opinion....
>
> When I advocate a party, it thereby becomes *my* party, whereas the Church of Jesus Christ is never *my* Church but always *his* Church. Indeed, the essence of

---

[80] Dulles, "Authority and Dissent," 100.
[81] Joseph Ratzinger, *Called to Communion: Understanding the Church Today*, trans. Adrian Walker (San Francisco: Ignatius Press, 1996), 134.
[82] Ibid., 137.
[83] Ibid., 139.

conversion lies precisely in the fact that I cease to pursue a party of my own that safeguards my interests and conforms to my taste but that I put myself in his hands and become his, a member of his Body, the Church.[84]

Cardinal Ratzinger argues that adhering to Church authority promotes greater freedom:

> The more we ourselves do in the Church, the more uninhabitable she becomes, because everything human is limited and is in opposition to other human realities. The Church will be all the more the homeland for man's heart, the more we listen to God and the more what comes from him is of central importance in her: his Word and the sacraments he has given us. The obedience of all toward him is the guarantee of our freedom....
> Only the unity of the Church's faith and her authority, which is binding on each member, assures us that we are not following human opinions and adhering to self-made party groupings but that we belong to the Lord and are obeying him.[85]

Within the Church various offices and roles exist with different responsibilities and authority. The bishops have the role of teaching, sanctifying, and governing in union with the pope and with the help of priests and deacons.[86] St. John Paul II explains that in cases of dissent, bishops have the duty to insist that *"the right of the faithful* to receive Catholic doctrine in its purity and integrity must always be respected."[87] To theologians, quoting from *Donum Veritatis*, he writes, "Never forgetting that he too is a member of the People of God, the theologian must be respectful of [the faithful], and be committed to offering them a teaching which in no way does harm to the doctrine

---

[84] Ibid., 157-158
[85] Ibid., 162, 163-164.
[86] CCC, §883, 939, 888-896.
[87] VS, §113.

271

of faith."[88] Theologians are an essential arrow in the quiver of a bishop in order to help him fulfill his duties, especially as teacher. In a theologian's role there must be a healthy tension between affirming the Church's current teachings and a scholarly freedom necessary in order to work for legitimate developments, as has been argued by revisionists like Fuchs and McBrien as well as traditionalists like Grisez.[89] Grisez explains that the Magisterium plays a special role in Catholicism, one that theologians cannot replicate. He explains that only the bishops make "official" actions within the Church,[90] although all members of the Church as Body of Christ contribute to her. A mutual respect between Church authorities and scholars must be found and maintained, while appropriate roles are respected.

Conscience

A frequently affirmed point made by revisionists revolves around the idea of conscience. The idea is, after carefully and respectfully considering the Church's moral position on the issue, some people may still come to a conclusion different from that of the Church and are obligated by their conscience to do what they believe is the true good. As revisionists maintain, for some this may mean using contraceptives. Traditionalists contend that such a conclusion is invincibly ignorant, at best, and produced by an erroneous conscience. Working the details of conscience out in the post-HV milieu of American Catholicism has created a veritable nightmare. Tentler explains the challenges of the situation in the following:

> There are risks inherent in this new mode of moral decision making, to which women are arguably more vulnerable than men, since it is they who get pregnant. Many decisions about sex are made by the young. Nearly all are informed by short-term notions of self-interest. How to ensure, in such circumstances,

---

[88] Ibid.

[89] Fuchs, "Teaching Morality," 337; Richard P. McBrien, "Theologians Under Fire." in *Readings in Moral Theology No. 6: Dissent in the Church*, ed. Charles E. Curran and Richard A. McCormick (New York: Paulist Press, 1988), 489; Grisez, "How to Deal," 456-457.

[90] Grisez, "How to Deal," 458.

that the decision maker is in possession of the relevant moral data and knows how to weigh it correctly? It does not help that many Catholics, especially the young, attend church infrequently. Weekly Mass attendance nationwide declined from 71 percent in 1961, on the eve of the Second Vatican Council, to 37 percent in 1999. Nor does it help that younger Catholics are by nearly all measures less theologically literate than their elders. They are no less intelligent and presumably no less committed to the moral life. But many are wholly detached from the assumptions, language, and logic that once defined the interior lives of Catholics and guided their moral choices. On what basis, then, do they form the conscience that now looms so large as an arbiter of morality?[91]

It is a person's obligation to form his or her conscience in light of official Church teaching, yet exactly how a person may dissent from what has been proposed as an objective moral teaching while avoiding moral subjectivity is a bit unclear. Soon after HV, revisionist Bernard Haring offered four ideas of how Catholics ought to operate in terms of their consciences on this issue:

My answer along these lines is this: (1) those who can accept the encyclical with an honest conscience must do so, with all the consequences; (2) those who doubt whether they can, must study it thoroughly and also make use of further information in order to form a clear conscience; (3) those who, with an honest conscience, cannot accept the teaching and requirements of *Humanae Vitae*, must follow their honest conscience. When married couples, then, for good reasons and with a good conscience use birth regulation which in their minds are the most suitable—abortion is obviously excluded—they need

---

[91] Leslie Woodcock Tentler, "Catholics and Contraception: An American History" (Ithaca: Cornell UP, 2004), 276.

not mention it in confession; (4) Priests must instruct the faithful clearly about the Pope's teaching. However, I do not see how they can be denied the right to speak out their own opinion with equal honesty.[92]

An outright rejection of the teaching is not allowable, even according to Haring. While his suggestions do allow for the use of contraceptives, in good conscience, he seems to suggest that any such legitimate dissent would be difficult and seemingly much rarer than it has become. Due to the understanding revisionists had of authority, assent due to non-infallible authoritative teachings, and conscience, they were able to suggest that people may justify the moral use of contraceptives. In this way they were able to help calm the concerns of many Catholics.[93] It seems that the laity were fairly open to accept and implement the arguments of the revisionists—such positions were, after all, certainly supportive of the change in family planning already effected by many Catholic couples prior to HV.

The revisionist argument for the possibility of using contraceptives, made by both theologians and bishops, was often from the motivation to soften the Church's teaching for couples in an attempt to be pastorally sensitive. One example is the statement made by the Canadian bishops immediately following HV called the Winnipeg Statement. Recognizing those families that may have trouble with the reaffirmed teaching on contraception, they stated, "If these persons have tried sincerely but without success to pursue a line of conduct in keeping with the given directives, they may be safely assured that whoever honestly chooses that course which seems right to him does so in good conscience."[94] However, the course of time yielded some changes in position on conscience. For example, already in 1974 the Canadians issued a revised position, in which they proposed: "A Catholic would have a very difficult—if not impossible—time rejecting the Church's teaching in good

---

[92] Haring, "The Encyclical Crisis," 90.

[93] Sidney Callahan, "Procreation and Control," in *The Catholic Case for Contraception*, ed. Daniel Callahan (London: Macmillan, 1969), 63.

[94] Janet E. Smith, *A Generation Later*, 149.

conscience."[95] Within a decade of HV, the ecclesial tides began to change, and they have continued on the same path. The Canadian bishops would make further amendments in 1989, 2003, and in 2008 which constituted what Patrick Coffin refers to as "a *de facto* repudiation of their Winnipeg Statement."[96] Twenty years after HV the Austrian bishops firmed up their statement on the issue and noted, "There is freedom of conscience but no freedom from building a correct conscience."[97] Likewise, in 2010 Twomey wrote, "The Church's authoritative moral teaching, in a word, binds the conscience of all Catholics. It is impossible knowingly to act in contradiction to that teaching and yet claim to act 'with a good conscience' as a Catholic."[98]

The contemporary discussion of conscience among Catholics in large part centers on the treatment of conscience by the Second Vatican Council:

> Deep within their consciences men and women discover a law which they have not laid upon themselves and which they must obey. Its voice, ever calling them to love and to do what is good and to avoid evil, tells them inwardly at the right moment: do this, shun that. For they have in their hearts a law inscribed by God. Their dignity rests in observing this law, and by it they will be judged. Their conscience is people's most secret core, and their sanctuary. There they are alone with God whose voice echoes in their depths. … The more a correct conscience prevails, the more do persons and groups turn aside from blind choice and endeavor to conform to the objective standards of moral conduct.[99]

The council provides a comprehensive description that emphasizes right conscience.

---

[95] Ibid., 150.
[96] Patrick Coffin, *Sex au Naturel* (Steubenville, OH: Emmaus Road, 2010), 15-16.
[97] Janet E. Smith, *A Generation Later*, 150.
[98] Twomey, 61.
[99] GS, §16.

First, the ability to determine what is good and evil, and the moral laws we must follow, comes from God, not us.[100] We do not determine morality, rather we are to use our conscience "as a faculty of discernment" to lead us to understand what is already good or evil, and act accordingly.[101] The revisionist position takes the truth that we must follow our conscience out of context and makes it an absolute over all other conditions. Therefore, revisionists argue, if people do not agree with the Church's teaching, and for serious reasons believe they need to use contraceptives, they are obligated to abide by their judgment. The Church does teach that we must obey our consciences, even if they are wrong; however, she also notes that this obligation to follow our conscience only applies when we are sure of the judgment of our conscience.[102] A person with a doubtful conscience ought not to act unless absolutely necessary. In the case of invincible ignorance, there is no sin; however, those acting on an erroneous conscience are still committing evil, though they may not be culpable for it.

Therefore, when our consciences are in doubt, we are obliged to continue forming them and remain open to constantly reconsidering and studying an issue to which we struggle to give full assent. The issue here is that our consciences can fail to bring us to know God's will; they can fail to be that place where God speaks to us in the silence of our hearts; they can be silenced or quieted through our sinfulness and concupiscence. We must form our consciences correctly, and an integral part of this is considering (and reconsidering, if need be) the Church's position. If Catholics believe the Church to be what she claims to be, this is not much to ask, for as May explains, we believe "the Catholic Church is the living body of Christ; we regard the Church as the *Lumen Gentium*, God's light to the people of the world."[103]

Ultimately, we are responsible for our formation of conscience.[104] There are many sources that help us form and inform our consciences. The Catholic must look to the Scriptures, the

---

[100] VS, §35.
[101] Levada, 148; Janet E. Smith, *A Generation Later*, 153.
[102] CCC, §1778, 1790; VS, §59, 60.
[103] May, 372.
[104] CCC, §1790-1793; Dulles "Authority and Conscience," 97-98.

Church, and utilize prayer and discernment for proper conscience formation.[105] With a properly formed and informed conscience, the Catholic will be able to *correctly* discern God's will in a particular, concrete circumstance and act in accordance with it. Dulles suggests, "Conscience therefore bids one to recognize authority, and authority, in turn, educates one's conscience."[106] In short, as St. John Paul II states, "Conscience has rights because it has duties."[107]

Dulles further discusses the relation of conscience and dissent: "Only through a perversion of speech does conscience come to be coupled with dissent and authority with abuse. Conscience and authority normally concur because both are given by the same God as helps for knowing what is to be believed and done."[108] The CCC is more direct: "Personal conscience and reason should not be set in opposition to the moral law or the Magisterium of the Church."[109] Similarly, Levada argues, "It is not correct to think that one can oppose one's own conscience to the teaching of the church."[110] In light of this, Janet Smith provides a quote from a speech St. John Paul II gave in which he refers to the relationship between the Church, conscience, and the believer: "Since the Magisterium of the Church was created by Christ the Lord to enlighten the conscience, then to appeal to that conscience precisely to contest the truth of what is taught by the Magisterium implies rejection of the Catholic concept both of the Magisterium and moral conscience."[111] Twomey argues that our self-fulfillment is wrapped up in a well-formed conscience: "To live by one's conscience is to live by certain moral principles and norms that are non-negotiable, which will be counter-cultural to the extent that culture is dominated by relativism, by a consumerism that panders to our every comfort, and by an interpretation of self-fulfillment which transforms one's felt needs

---

[105] CCC, §1784, 1785; Ronald Lawler, Joseph Boyle Jr., and William E. May, *Catholic Sexual Ethics: A Summary, Explanation, & Defense*, 2nd ed. (Huntington, Indiana: Our Sunday Visitor, 1998), 107; *Dignitatis Humanae*, In *Vatican Council II*, ed. Austin Flannery (Northport: Costello Publishing Company, 1996), §14.
[106] Dulles, "Authority and Conscience," 107.
[107] VS, §34.
[108] Dulles, "Authority and Conscience," 107.
[109] CCC, §2039.
[110] Levada, 149.
[111] Janet E. Smith, *A Generation Later*, 264.

into 'rights' understood as entitlements."[112] In closing, May also provides a helpful thought:

> In our struggle to come to know what we are to do if we are to be the beings God wills us to be we need help. God is our best and greatest friend and he has come to our help. For he has, through his Son, given to us the Church in which the Spirit dwells. It is the house of truth, the light to the nations, the guide for our consciences.[113]

The Church and her official moral teachings are essential guides for Catholics to form and inform their consciences and live moral lives in conformity with God's will. Conscience bears witness to the law by the indwelling of the Law-Giver himself. It can never be reduced to a loophole to justify evil.

Sensus Fidelium

Another approach used by revisionists to support dissent revolves around the idea of the *sensus fidelium*, or "sense of the faithful."[114] Some revisionists have argued that Vatican II recognized the possibility that if a pope would ever err in an authoritative non-infallible teaching, the Holy Spirit may illuminate the truth through the reaction of bishops, theologians, and the faithful.[115] The immediate reaction to the encyclical seemed to suggest that many were not reacting to the Church's teaching well, which has bolstered this argument. Ashley notes, "Since certain theologians have successfully refuted the various arguments first made against *Humanae Vitae*, many Catholic theologians who dissent from it have come to rely on the specious argument that since so many Catholics ignore its teaching it has not been 'received' by the *sensus fidelium*."[116] However, Ashley, Deblois, and O'Rourke explain that history presents several

---

[112] Twomey, 62.

[113] May, 380.

[114] Benedict Ashley, "Contraception: Did *Humanae Vitae* Contradict Itself?," in *Medicine, Health Care, & Ethics*, ed. John F. Morris (Washington D.C.: Catholic University Press, 2007), 103; Ashley, Deblois, and O'Rourke, 27-28.

[115] Komonchak, 121, 112.

[116] Ashley, 103.

cases in which large masses of people "dissented" from official Church teaching in order to uphold "their rights to be slave owners, racists, sexists, militarists, and anti-Semites!"[117] Another example stems from the early Church in which monumental numbers of Catholics, including large numbers of bishops and theologians, held an opinion that is undoubtedly false. Around the fourth century, the Arian heresy had grown and reached a point in which the majority of laypeople, theologians, and bishops rejected the full divinity of Christ.[118] Is it possible that mass numbers of Christians may be deceived today? Finally, Gaillardetz is of the perspective that it is inappropriate to talk of any type of *sensus fidelium* (clergy as well as laity) unless all are in agreement. He writes, "When the faithful are united in their belief, manifesting a true consensus, we can speak of a *consensus fidelium*. It is this situation that the council had in mind when it affirmed the infallibility of the whole people of God."[119] Thus, laity cannot be pitted against the hierarchy.

Ashley, Deblois, and O'Rourke further argue that human moral error is the reason why the Church was founded by Christ and exists "to discriminate between the *sensus fidelium*, or human opinions within the church, and the *sensus fidei*, or 'sense of the faith.'"[120] This latter term refers more closely to the truth of the Church's teaching. For example, some may suggest we might arrive at the *sensus fidelium* simply by taking a poll of Catholics on their opinion. However, Ashley et al. explain that to arrive at an authentic gauge of the *sensus fidei*, we must ask a question like, "What has been transmitted to you through the Christian community of all time as God's Word revealed in Jesus Christ about contraception?"[121] Such a question may generate a very different answer than merely taking a vote of all self-declared "good Catholics" on their personal opinion. Accordingly, St. John Paul II once stated, "Truth cannot be measured by majority opinion."[122] Gaillardetz offers a helpful consideration concerning the *sensus fidelium* in the following:

---

[117] Ashley, Deblois, and O'Rourke, 27-28
[118] Lawler, Boyle, and May, 150-151.
[119] Gaillardetz, *By what Authority?*, 109.
[120] Ashley, Deblois, and O'Rourke, 28.
[121] Ibid., 77.
[122] Janet E. Smith, *A Generation Later*, 263.

This vision of the Church as a community of dialogue will reject the tendency to play the hierarchy off of the laity or to appeal to the sense of the faithful as a mere counter-position to official church teaching. Those who embrace this vision of the Church will insist that the "sense of the faithful" includes the whole faithful, cleric and lay. Consequently, they will reject any idea that the sense of the faithful represents some opposition party gathering in protest outside the walls of church leadership.[123]

Thus, the idea of *sensus fidelium* cannot be used as some revisionists have suggested.

As with other issues of history, like the widespread subscription to Arianism and rejection of Christ's divinity, the possibility of great numbers of laity, theologians, and even bishops adopting an error in opposition to Magisterial teaching is significant. Certainly, revisionists may argue that the traditionalists and the Magisterium are in error in this case. However is it more likely that the Church, "the pillar and foundation of truth" (1 Tim 3:15) has erred, or that great numbers of people in an age of individualism, relativism, and hedonism have been deceived? We must recall Jesus' rebuke of Peter in Mt 16:23, "Get behind me, Satan! You are an obstacle to me. You are thinking not as God does, but as human beings do." Sometimes human "wisdom" is entirely contrary to heavenly wisdom and the truth.

---

[123] Gaillardetz, *By what Authority?*, 118.

Conclusion

We live in an age in which the Church's teaching on family planning is largely ignored and is hardly even considered an issue worthy of discussion. On the contrary, this issue is of inestimable importance, and it cannot be allowed to slip into obscurity. It influences fundamental elements of moral theology, and its implications are felt throughout the Church, within marriages and families, and pour out into the world. D. Vincent Twomey comments on its significance:

> What has become obvious over the past forty years is that the issues raised by *Humanae Vitae* have their origin in, or at least reflect, that radical cultural shift—a truly paradigmatic shift—in human sensibilities and behaviour which has transformed Western civilization. The publication of *Humanae Vitae* could be seen as a protest against that cultural shift and its values or disvalues. It caused a crisis within the Church that has yet to be resolved.[1]

The issue affects ecclesiology, morality, and indeed all of society. The faithful at every level need to discover and unpack the Church's vision in seeking to live the truth and follow God's will. Then Archbishop of Denver, Charles J. Chaput, has suggested,

> We have a problem, and it's killing us as a people. … In seeking to become whole again as persons and as people of faith, we would do well to revisit *Humanae Vitae* with open hearts. *Humanae Vitae* is filled with truth about our sexuality, our purpose as human beings, and the nature of married love. Lived

---

[1] D. Vincent Twomey, *Moral Theology after Humanae Vitae: Fundamental Issues in Moral Theory and Sexual Ethics* (Dublin: Four Courts Press, 2010), 13.

selflessly, it is a source of real joy. We impoverish ourselves and those we love by ignoring it.[2]

The corrosive effects of our dissent and sexual licentiousness urge us on to repentance. It takes great courage to reconsider a route we have already chosen and to admit when we have gone astray. Failure to do so only leads to greater problems and takes us further from our destination. Janet Smith shares a reflection worth noting: "G.K. Chesterton's remark that Christianity has not been tried and found wanting, it has been found difficult and not tried, could be applied to *Humanae Vitae*: it has not been studied and taught and been rejected, it has not been studied and taught."[3] This statement has become ever truer for young couples today. This issue cries out to be addressed and considered in the lives of believers both young and old.

Additionally, we must carefully and prayerfully discern God's will and tirelessly strive to live that will in our lives. We must seek to grow in virtue, live lives of holiness, and become saints—Christian faith calls for nothing less of us. Christ did not call his people to pursue disordered pleasure, but to find joy in the true goods of life. When this involves delayed gratification and self-mastery, we are encouraged to pick up our cross and follow Christ. He has promised, "My yoke is easy and my burden is light" (Mt 11:30).

We must also keep in mind that God's help is not far off. He knows our weaknesses and does not allow us to be tried beyond what we can handle. Ultimately we must rely on his grace to live the virtuous life we are called as Christians to live. Fr. Rhonheimer encourages:

> The Church always has taught that—in the given situation of fallen mankind—all the exigencies of natural law cannot be fulfilled except by the help of redeeming grace, which, as far as human weakness is

---

[2] "Contraception: A Symposium." *First Things* 88 (December 1998), http://www.firstthings.com/article/2007/01contraception-a-symposium-28 (accessed December 21, 2009).

[3] Janet E. Smith, "*Humanae Vitae* at Twenty," in *Why Humanae Vitae Was Right: A Reader*, ed. Janet E. Smith (San Francisco: Ignatius Press, 1993), 517.

concerned, has a healing power. Thus, the truth may be hard, but the means offered by the Church to overcome this hardship are most efficient. They permit man not only to strive for sanctity, but thereby to fully develop his very humanity. This striving always has been the seal of authentic Christian life, which is also called to defend worldly goods—such as sexuality, human love, and marriage—against their deprivation by a world marked by both sin and the human weakness springing from it.[4]

As Christians we have an obligation to imitate and follow our Lord. A passage occasionally alluded to in discussion of contraception is Jesus' presentation in the Temple. Simeon prophesied about Jesus saying, "This child is destined for the fall and rise of many in Israel, and to be a sign that will be contradicted" (Lk 2:34). To follow Jesus means to go against the ways of the world, to swim against the current, to blaze new trails, to do what is right no matter the cost. To stand with Jesus is to be a sign of contradiction with him—it is to be contradicted by the world and the world's often false "wisdom." Pope Bl. Paul VI knew his teaching in HV would not be popular. In the encyclical he recognized, "It comes as no surprise to the Church that she, no less than her divine Founder, is destined to be a 'sign of contradiction.'"[5]

However, Bl. Paul VI did not likely realize just how poorly the teaching would be received, or the extent to which he and his encyclical would also become signs of contradiction. Still, the Church remains steadfast in the truth. Cardinal Karol Wojtyla (later Pope John Paul II) called attention to this as he led an annual Lenten Retreat for Pope Bl. Paul VI and his co-workers when he stated:

---

[4] Martin Rhonheimer, *Ethics of Procreation and the Defense of Human Life: Contraception, Artificial Fertilization, and Abortion*, ed. William F. Murphy Jr. (Washington D.C.: Catholic University of America Press, 2010), 131.

[5] Pope Paul VI, Humanae Vitae, http://www.vatican.va/holy_father/paul_vi/encyclicals/documents/hf_p-vi_enc_25071968_humanae-vitae_en.html (accessed July 14, 2009), §18.

Jesus sealed his witness with his own blood. And that is the inheritance he has bequeathed to the Church. The inheritance of salvific truth is an extremely demanding one, fraught with difficulties. Inevitably the Church's activities, and those of the Supreme Pontiff in particular, often become a "sign of contradiction". This too shows that her mission is that of Christ, who continues to be a sign of contradiction.[6]

As the Church perseveres in the truth with Christ Jesus, they invite us to join them. Over the last few decades, a larger and stronger community has been gathering behind this teaching. Preaching in San Francisco in 1987, Pope St. John Paul II stated, "The family that truly lives the truth of the Gospel in love is most certainly a sign of contradiction; and at the same time it is a source of great hope for those who are eager to do good."[7] May more and more families rally to meet this challenge and become what God wills them to be—signs of contradiction and signs to be contradicted, in imitation of Jesus Christ.

For those who have become convinced of the truth and wisdom of the Church's teaching on family planning, including its rejection of contraceptives and affirmation of NFP, a necessary question arises— what can be done to build upon and spread the NFP movement? The current situation has its pros and cons. Many young people and theologians are much more open to exploring the Church's teaching than earlier generations. Certainly, the rise of a subgroup of evangelical Catholics, who take the best from both sides of the polarization in the Church, indicates a strong resurgence of educated, faithful Catholics adamant about and convinced by the Church's teaching. We are seeing ecumenical concord on the Church's teaching as Protestants explore the Scriptures, reason, and the mind of the Church on issues of marital sexuality and the gift of fertility. Even scientists as opposed to religion as Lionel Tiger have submitted work

---

[6] Wojtyla, Karol. *Sign of Contradiction.* (New York: Seabury, 1979), 124.
[7] Anthony F. Chiffolo, ed., *Pope John Paul II: In My Own Words* (New York: Barnes & Noble, 1998), 61.

284

significantly supportive of the Church's moral theology. Lawler, Boyle, and May hold that we have learned from our mistakes:

> The astonishing growth of the Natural Family Planning (NFP) movement, with its joyful discovery of how valuable the Catholic teaching is, and how it is both livable and able to enrich married life, presages a happy return to a fuller acceptance of Catholic teaching everywhere. The terrible disadvantages of the contraceptive movement are becoming more visible, and it is evident that NFP provides in more human and nobler ways the goods that contraception was seeking to reach.[8]

The U.S. Bishops also have continued to support the Church's teaching and have made statements such as the following over two decades ago on HV's 25th anniversary, "We rededicate ourselves to increase our efforts to expand Christian education, pastoral programs for engaged and married couples, and natural family planning services."[9] Finally, the testimony of couples has become a factor in drawing attention back to the benefits of NFP: "Natural family planning is the best-kept secret right now. The only negative is that it needs more publicity and for society to see its credibility."[10]

Much must yet be done, though, to make NFP education and support more accessible to all couples. We may begin by confronting misconceptions and misinformation about NFP among Catholic health care professionals, clergy, religious, and laypeople so that at least Catholic parishes and health care facilities may be a source of support and encouragement in the midst of a world that has always

---

[8] Ronald Lawler, Joseph Boyle Jr., and William E. May, *Catholic Sexual Ethics: A Summary, Explanation, & Defense*, 2nd ed. (Huntington, Indiana: Our Sunday Visitor, 1998), 151.

[9] National Conference of Catholic Bishops' Committee for Pro-Life Activities, *Human Sexuality from God's Perspective: Humanae Vitae 25 Years Later* (1993), http://www.usccb.org/prolife/issues/nfp/humanae25.shtml (accessed October 14, 2009).

[10] Leona VandeVusse et al., "Couples' Views of the Effects of Natural Family Planning on Marital Dynamics," *Journal of Nursing Scholarship* 35, no. 2 (2nd Quarter 2003): 176.

opposed God's kingdom. This is a very necessary and achievable ambition for the Church to accomplish in the next few decades. As recent decades have proven, failure to do so will be perilous, as continued widespread use of contraception will exacerbate the already tragic erosion of respect for women and the mutual self-gift of spouses.

The elements necessary for change seem to be prepared and ready to catch fire. It is as if the current NFP movement is a small but hot, smoldering pile of kindling in the midst of a dry and dying forest. All it needs is a bit more fuel, some care, and more time to renew the whole scene. Consider what Jesus exclaims in Luke 12:49, "I have come to set the earth on fire, and how I wish it were already blazing!" Our landscape is in need of renewal. Sometimes only the pain of fire is capable of reducing things to their essence, reinvigorating the soils out of which life springs, and inviting dormant seeds to germinate and bring forth a flourishing renewal of life. If we believe this to be God's will for the Church and the world, we must work to make his kingdom manifest as much as possible on earth as we pray in the Our Father, as Christ taught us. At the end of each day, however, we must leave it in the hands of God, and entrust it to our Blessed Mother Mary, for without the graces of the Holy Spirit the NFP movement can do nothing. We must also be patient. It has taken many years to get from Vatican II and HV to where we are today, and it is likely to take another long while for the Church— perhaps if we are blessed, society as well—to recover and mature from the sexual revolution and sort out what it means to be authentic post-Vatican II and post-*Humanae Vitae* Catholics as God wills.

Many things must come together to make progress, and they all must grow together, supporting and nourishing one another, for the NFP movement to ignite the world and the Church's teaching on family planning to be appreciated and implemented. Certainly, the Church needs to rebuild a foundation encouraging and accommodating NFP. It cannot merely be either a top-down or grassroots approach, it must be both. It cannot merely be either a new revolution by the young or reconsideration by the old, it must be both. It cannot merely be either a work of the bishops, clergy, and religious or laypeople, doctors, and teachers, it must include all. Perhaps this is what God intends anyway—for his kingdom to be

286

realized, it cannot be completed by any minority—it takes all of his people in cooperation with him and his grace to achieve his plans. Only when bishops mobilize behind the teaching; seminaries form clergy in the truth of the teaching; universities educate theologians, teachers, and laypeople in the teaching; schools and parishes faithfully promote the teaching; pastors courageously preach and teach the truth; laypeople learn about, share, and live the teaching; physicians discover, promote, and support the teaching; and families witness to the teaching through their marriages and lives, will we *begin* to make the fullness of the Church's teaching on marriage, family, and sexuality—contrary to all forms of contraception—a reality. It will take whole families, parishes, dioceses, nations, verily the whole Church to uphold, teach, and share the wisdom and magnificence of the Church's teaching—God's teaching—on marriage, sexuality, and family life.

There is never a better time to begin something great than the present. The longest and most profound journeys all begin with one step. Let us accomplish God's work and will in the world together, as has been our Christian calling from the beginning and will be until the end of time, so that God's kingdom may be all the more present here and now, as a foretaste of the eternal beatitude we hope to share with him in heaven. Adapting the ancient blessing prayer of Numbers 6:24-26, we pray for the Church and the whole world: May the LORD bless us and keep us! May the LORD let his face shine upon us, and be gracious to us! May the LORD look upon us kindly and give us peace! Amen.

Bibliography

Ananthaswamy, Anil. "Sing Out Sister." *New Scientist* 173, no. 2336 (March 30, 2002): 8.

Anscombe, G. E. M. "Contraception and Chastity." In *Why Humanae Vitae Was Right: A Reader*, edited by Janet E. Smith, 119-150. San Francisco: Ignatius Press, 1993.

Arraj, James. *Is there a Solution to the Catholic Debate on Contraception?* Chiloquin, OR: Inner Growth Books, 1989.

Ashley, Benedict. "Contraception: Did *Humanae Vitae* Contradict Itself?" In *Medicine, Health Care, & Ethics*, edited by John F. Morris, 89-106. Washington D.C.: Catholic University Press, 2007.

Ashley, Benedict M., Jean Deblois, and Kevin D. O'Rourke. *Health Care Ethics: A Catholic Theological Analysis*. 5th ed. Washington D.C.: Georgetown University Press, 2006.

Atkinson, Gary, and Albert Moraczewski. *A Moral Evaluation of Contraception and Sterilization: A Dialogical Study*. St. Louis: Pope John XXIII Medical-Moral Research and Education Center, 1979.

Baggot, Paddy "Jim". "Mea Culpa, Mea Culpa, Mea Maxima Culpa." In *Physicians Healed: Personal, Inspiring, and Compelling Stories of Fifteen Courageous Physicians Who Do Not Prescribe Contraception*, edited by Cleta Hartman, 11-14. Dayton: One More Soul, 1998.

Benedict XVI, Pope. *Anglicanorum Coetibus.* 2009.
    http://www.vatican.va/holy_father/benedict
    _xvi/apost_constitutions/documents/hf_ben-
    xvi_apc_20091104_anglicanorum-coetibus_en.html (accessed
    December 21, 2009).

---------. *Caritas In Veritate.* 2009.
    http://www.vatican.va/holy_father/benedict_xvi/encyclicals
    /documents/hf_ben-xvi_enc_20090629_caritas-in-
    veritate_en.html (accessed August 15, 2009).

---------. *Light of the World: The Pope, the Church, and the Signs of the
    Times – A Conversation with Peter Seewald.* Translated by
    Michael J. Miller and Adrian J. Walker. San Francisco:
    Ignatius Press, 2010.

"Birth Control Pills (Oral Contraceptives)." *CRS – Pediatric Advisor*
    (January 1, 2009).

Bitto, Adenike, Ronald H. Gray, Joe L. Simpson, John T.
    Queenan, Robert T. Kambic, Alfredo Perez, Patricio
    Mena, Michele Barbarto, Chuanjun Li, and Victoria
    Jennings. "Adverse Outcomes of Planned and Unplanned
    Pregnancies among Users of Natural Family Planning: A
    Prospective Study." *American Journal of Public Health* 87, no. 3
    (March 1997): 338-343.

Boyle, Joseph M. "Contraception and Natural Family Planning." In
    Why Humanae Vitae Was Right: A Reader, edited by Janet E.
    Smith, 407-418. San Francisco: Ignatius Press, 1993.

Brown, Raymond E. "The Magisterium vs. the Theologians:
    Debunking Some Fictions." In *Readings in Moral Theology No.
    3: The Magisterium and Morality*, edited by Charles E. Curran
    and Richard A. McCormick, 277-296. New York: Paulist
    Press, 1982.

Brown, Robert McAfee. "*Humanae Vitae* a Protestant Reaction." In *Contraception: Authority and Dissent*, edited by Charles E. Curran, 193-215. New York: Herder and Herder, 1969.

Bryner, Jeanna. "The Pill Makes Women Pick Bad Mates." *Live Science* (August 12, 2008) http://www.livescience.com/culture/080812-contraceptive-smell.html (accessed October 15, 2008).

Buechlein, Daniel M. "Integrating Faith and Science through Natural Family Planning." In *Integrating Faith and Science through Natural Family Planning*, edited by Richard J. Fehring and Theresa Notare, 15-27. Milwaukee: Marquette UP, 2004.

Callahan, Daniel. Introduction to *The Catholic Case for Contraception*, edited by Daniel Callahan, vii-xvi. London: Macmillan, 1969.

Callahan, Sidney. "Procreation and Control." In *The Catholic Case for Contraception*, edited by Daniel Callahan, 41-64. London: Macmillan, 1969.

Cannon, Robert R., "Except in Theory, Dioceses Offer Little Support for Natural Family Planning." *National Catholic Reporter* 29, no. 39 (September 10, 1993): 24.

Carroll, Colleen. *The New Faithful: Why Young Adults are Embracing Christian Orthodoxy*. Chicago: Loyola Press, 2002.

Catechism of the Catholic Church. Modifications from the Editio Typica 2nd ed. Washington D.C.: United States Catholic Conference, Inc.—Libreria Editrice Vaticana, 1997.

Cessario, Romanus. *Introduction to Moral Theology*. Washington D.C.: Catholic University of America Press, 2001.

Chiffolo, Anthony F., ed. *Pope John Paul II: In My Own Words*. New York: Barnes & Noble, 1998.

Claussen, Janet. "My Argument with Natural Family Planning." *America* 172, no. 4 (Feb 1995): 20-22.

Clifford, Richard J. and Roland E. Murphy. "Genesis." In *The New Jerome Biblical Commentary*, edited by Raymond E. Brown, Joseph A Fitzmyer, and Roland E. Murphy, 8-43. Englewood Cliffs NJ: Prentice Hall, 1990.

Code of Canon Law. 1983. http://www.vatican.va/archive/ENG1104/_INDEX.HTM (accessed October 2, 2009).

Coffin, Patrick. *Sex au Naturel.* Steubenville, OH: Emmaus Road, 2010.

Congregation for the Doctrine of the Faith. *Inter Insigniores.* 1976. http://www.papal encyclicals.net/Paul06/p6interi.htm (accessed December 8, 2009).

---------. *Persona Humana: Declaration on Certain Questions Concerning Sexual Ethics.* 1975. http://www.vatican.va/roman_curia/congregations/cfaith/d ocuments/rc_con_cfaith_doc_ 19751229_persona-humana_en.html (accessed October 2, 2009).

Coulson, John. "Living with Authority—The Nineteenth Century." In *Contraception: Authority and Dissent*, edited by Charles E. Curran, 19-40. New York: Herder and Herder, 1969.

Couple to Couple League. *The Art of Natural Family Planning: Student Guide.* Cincinnati: The Couple to Couple League International, Inc., 2007.

Crosby, John F. "The Personalism of John Paul II as the Basis of His Approach to the Teaching of *Humanae Vitae*." In *Why Humanae Vitae Was Right: A Reader*, edited by Janet E. Smith, 193-228. San Francisco: Ignatius Press, 1993.

Curran, Charles E. Introduction to *Contraception: Authority and Dissent*, edited by Charles E. Curran, 9-16. New York: Herder and Herder, 1969.

---------. "Humanae Vitae: Still Controversial at 30." *National Catholic Reporter* 34, no. 35 (June 1998): 12-13.

---------. *The Moral Theology of Pope John Paul II*. Washington D.C.: Georgetown University Press, 2005.

---------. "Natural Law and Contemporary Moral Theology." In *Contraception: Authority and Dissent*, edited by Charles E. Curran, 151-175. New York: Herder and Herder, 1969.

---------. "Personal Reflections on Birth Control." In *The Catholic Case for Contraception*, edited by Daniel Callahan, 77-91. London: Macmillan, 1969.

---------. "Pluralism in Catholic Moral Theology." In *Readings in Moral Theology No. 3: The Magisterium and Morality*, edited by Charles E. Curran and Richard A. McCormick, 364-387. New York: Paulist Press, 1982.

---------. "Public Dissent in the Church." In *Readings in Moral Theology No. 6: Dissent in the Church*, edited by Charles E. Curran and Richard A. McCormick, 387-407. New York: Paulist Press, 1988.

---------. ed. *Readings in Moral Theology No. 13: Change in Official Catholic Moral Teachings*. New York: Paulist Press, 2003.

‒‒‒‒‒‒‒‒. Forward to *The Sexual Person: Toward a Renewed Catholic Anthropology*, by Todd A. Salzman and Michael G. Lawler, xi-xvi. Washington D.C.: Georgetown University Press, 2008.

Davenport, Mary. "Never Too Late." In *Physicians Healed: Personal, Inspiring, and Compelling Stories of Fifteen Courageous Physicians Who Do Not Prescribe Contraception*, edited by Cleta Hartman, 15-26. Dayton: One More Soul, 1998.

Dei Verbum. In *Vatican Council II*. Edited by Austin Flannery. Northport: Costello Publishing Company, 1996.

Dignitatis Humanae. In *Vatican Council II*. Edited by Austin Flannery. Northport: Costello Publishing Company, 1996.

Draper, Thomas F. "A Catholic Pediatrician on Family Planning." In *The Catholic Case for Contraception*, edited by Daniel Callahan, 128-135. London: Macmillan, 1969.

Dulles, Avery. "Authority and Conscience." In *Readings in Moral Theology No. 6: Dissent in the Church*, edited by Charles E. Curran and Richard A. McCormick, 97-111. New York: Paulist Press, 1988.

‒‒‒‒‒‒‒‒. "Doctrinal Authority for a Pilgrim Church." In *Readings in Moral Theology No. 3: The Magisterium and Morality*, edited by Charles E. Curran and Richard A. McCormick, 247-270. New York: Paulist Press, 1982.

Dworkin, Norine. "What You May Not Know About Natural Birth Control." *Vegetarian Times*, no. 251 (July 1998): 82-89.

Dwyer, Devin. "Obama Rejects Contraception Exemption for Catholic Hospitals, Schools." *ABC News* (January 20, 2012). http://abcnews.go.com/blogs/politics/2012/01/obama-rejects-contraception-exemption-for-catholic-hospitals-schools/ (accessed April 5, 2012).

Eberstadt, Mary. "The Vindication of Humanae Vitae." *First Things*, no. 185 (Aug/Sep 2008): 35-42.

Evert, Jason. *If You Really Loved Me: 100 Questions on Dating, Relationships, and Sexual Purity*. Denver: Totus Tuus Press, 2013.

Evert, Jason, Crystalina Evert, and Brian Butler. *Theology of the Body for Teens: Discovering God's Plan for Love and Life*. West Chester, PA: Ascension Press, 2006.

Finnis, John M. "Personal Integrity, Sexual Morality and Responsible Parenthood." In *Why Humanae Vitae Was Right: A Reader*, edited by Janet E. Smith, 171-192. San Francisco: Ignatius Press, 1993.

Ford, John Cuthbert and Germain Gabriel Grisez. "Contraception and the Infallibility of the Ordinary Magisterium." *Theological Studies* 39, no. 2 (Je 1978): 258-312.

Ford, John C. and Gerald Kelly. "Doctrinal Value and Interpretation of Papal Teaching." In *Readings in Moral Theology No. 3: The Magisterium and Morality*, edited by Charles E. Curran and Richard A. McCormick, 1-13. New York: Paulist Press, 1982.

Fuchs, Joseph. "The Absoluteness of Moral Terms." In *Readings in Moral Theology No. 1: Moral Norms and Catholic Tradition*, edited by Charles E. Curran and Richard A. McCormick, 94-137. New York: Paulist Press, 1979.

---------. "Teaching Morality: The Tension Between Bishops and Theologians Within the Church." In *Readings in Moral Theology No. 6: Dissent in the Church*, edited by Charles E. Curran and Richard A. McCormick, 330-356. New York: Paulist Press, 1988.

Fukuyama, Francis. *The Great Disruption: Human Nature and the Reconstitution of Social Order*. New York: Touchstone, 1999.

Gaillardetz, Richard R. *By What Authority?: A Primer on Scripture, the Magisterium, and the Sense of the Faithful.* Collegeville: Liturgical Press, 2003.

---------. *Teaching with Authority: A Theology of the Magisterium in the Church.* Collegeville: Liturgical Press, 1997.

Gallagher, John. "Magisterial Teaching from 1918 to the Present." In *Readings in Moral Theology No. 8: Dialogue about Catholic Sexual Teaching,* edited by Charles E. Curran and Richard A. McCormick, 71-92. New York: Paulist Press, 1993.

Gaudium et Spes. In *Vatican Council II.* Edited by Austin Flannery. Northport: Costello Publishing Company, 1996.

Gilbert, Kathleen. "Co-Creator of the Pill Laments Results." *LifeSiteNews* (January 9, 2009). http://www.catholic.org/international/international_story.php?id=31473 (accessed December 30, 2011).

Grabowski, John S. "Natural Family Planning and Marital Spirituality." In *Integrating Faith and Science Through Natural Family Planning,* edited by Richard J. Fehring and Theresa Notare, 29-45. Milwaukee: Marquette UP, 2004.

Graham, Mark. *Josef Fuchs on Natural Law.* Washington D.C.: Georgetown University Press, 2002.

Green, Ann. "Not Your Mother's Rhythm Method." *U.S. Catholic* 74, no. 5 (May 2009): 23-25.

Green, Edward C. "Condoms, HIV-AIDS and Africa – The Pope Was Right." *Washington Post* (March 29, 2009). http://www.washingtonpost.com/wp-dyn/content/article/2009/03/27/ AR20090327.2825.html (accessed April 3, 2012).

Green, Edward C. and Allison Herling Ruark. "AIDS and the Churches: Getting the Story Right." *First Things* (April 2008). http://www.firstthings.com/article/2008/03/002-aids-and-the-churces-getting-the-story-right-27 (accessed April 3, 2012).

Grisez, Germain. "How to Deal with Theological Dissent." In *Readings in Moral Theology No. 6: Dissent in the Church*, edited by Charles E. Curran and Richard A. McCormick, 442-472. New York: Paulist Press, 1988.

---------. "Infallibility and Contraception: A Reply to Garth Hallett." *Theological Studies* 47, no. 1 (Mr 1986): 134-145.

---------. "The Ordinary Magisterium's Infallibility: A Reply to Some New Arguments." *Theological Studies* 55, no. 4 (D 1994): 720-738.

Grisez, Germain, Joseph Boyle, John Finnis, and William E. May. "NFP: Not Contralife." In *Readings in Moral Theology No. 8: Dialogue about Catholic Sexual Teaching*, edited by Charles E. Curran and Richard A. McCormick, 126-134. New York: Paulist Press, 1993.

Hagen, John D. Jr. "Humanae Vitae's Legacy." *Commonweal* 131, no. 11 (June 4th, 2004): 8-9.

Hahn, Kimberly. *Life-Giving Love: Embracing God's Beautiful Design for Marriage*. Ann Arbor: Servant, 2001.

Hahn, Scott, and Kimberly Hahn. *Rome Sweet Home: Our Journey to Catholicism*. San Francisco: Ignatius Press, 1993.

Hallett, Garth L. "Contraception and Prescriptive Infallibility." *Theological Studies* 43, no. 4 (D 1982): 629-650.

---------. "Infallibility and Contraception: The Debate Continues." *Theological Studies* 49, no. 3 (S 1988): 517-528.

Haring, Bernard. "A Distrust that Wounds." In *Readings in Moral Theology No. 10: John Paul II and Moral Theology*, edited by Charles E. Curran and Richard A. McCormick, 42-46. New York: Paulist Press, 1998.

---------. "The Encyclical Crisis." In *The Catholic Case for Contraception*, edited by Daniel Callahan, 77-91. London: Macmillan, 1969.

---------. "The Inseparability of the Unitive-Procreative Functions of the Marital Act." In *Readings in Moral Theology No. 8: Dialogue about Catholic Sexual Teaching*, edited by Charles E. Curran and Richard A. McCormick, 153-167. New York: Paulist Press, 1993.

Hartman, John. "The Stone Which the Builders Rejected." In *Physicians Healed: Personal, Inspiring, and Compelling Stories of Fifteen Courageous Physicians Who Do Not Prescribe Contraception*, edited by Cleta Hartman, 41-54. Dayton: One More Soul, 1998.

Hellegers, Andre E. "A Scientist's Analysis." In *Contraception: Authority and Dissent*, edited by Charles E. Curran, 216-237. New York: Herder and Herder, 1969.

Hilgers, Thomas W. *Creighton Model FertilityCare System: An Authentic Language of a Woman's Health and Fertility*. 5th ed. Omaha: Pope Paul VI Institute Press, 2003.

---------. "Infertility." In *In Their Own Words: Women Healed*, edited by Jean Blair Packard, 59-60. Omaha: Pope Paul VI Institute Press, 2004.

Hogan, Richard M. and John M. LeVoir. "The Family and Sexuality." In *Readings in Moral Theology No. 10: John Paul II and Moral Theology*, edited by Charles E. Curran and Richard A. McCormick, 157-183. New York: Paulist Press, 1998.

Homan, R. Patrick "Marital Chastity: A Blessing for Marriage, Family and Spiritual Life." In *Trust the Truth: A symposium on the Twentieth Anniversary of the Encyclical Humanae Vitae*, edited by Russell E. Smith, 133-144. Braintree, MA: The Pope John XXIII Medical-Moral Research and Education Center, 1991.

Janssens, Louis. "Ontic Evil and Moral Evil." In *Readings in Moral Theology No. 1: Moral Norms and Catholic Tradition*, edited by Charles E. Curran and Richard A. McCormick, 40-93. New York: Paulist Press, 1979.

Jay, George. "Thank You, Jesus, for Healing Me." In *Physicians Healed: Personal, Inspiring, and Compelling Stories of Fifteen Courageous Physicians Who Do Not Prescribe Contraception*, edited by Cleta Hartman, 55-68. Dayton: One More Soul, 1998.

John Paul II, Pope. *Familiaris Consortio*. 1981. http://www.vatican.va/holy_father/ john_paul_ii/apost_exhortations/documents/hf_jp-ii_exh_19811122_familiaris-consortio_en.html (accessed July 14, 2009).

---------. *Gratissimam Sane*. 1994. http://www.vatican.va/holy_father/john_paul_ii/letters/ Documents/hf_jp-ii/let_02021994_families_en.html (accessed November 19, 2009).

---------. *Ordinatio Sacerdotalis*. 1994. http://www.vatican.va/holy_father/john_paul_ii/apost_ letters/documents/hf_jp-ii/apl_22051994_ordinatio-sacerdotalis_en.html (accessed December 8, 2009).

---------. *The Theology of the Body: Human Love in the Divine Plan*. Boston: Pauline, 1997.

---------. *Veritatis Splendor*. 1993. Vatican Translation. Boston: Pauline.

Johnson, Luke Timothy. "A Disembodied 'Theology of the Body'." *Commonweal* 128, no. 2 (Jan 2001): 11-17.

Jones-Nosacek, Cynthia. "Response to Teresa Wagner, Esq." In *Integrating Faith and Science Through Natural Family Planning*, edited by Richard J. Fehring and Theresa Notare, 62-69. Milwaukee: Marquette UP, 2004.

Joyce, Mary Rosera. "The Meaning of Contraception." In *Why Humanae Vitae Was Right: A Reader*, edited by Janet E. Smith, 105-118. San Francisco: Ignatius Press, 1993.

Kahlenborn, Chris. *Breast Cancer: Its Link to Abortion and the Birth Control Pill*. New Hope, KY: One More Soul, 2000.

Kahlenborn, Chris, Francesmary Modugno, Douglas M. Potter, and Walter B. Severs. "Oral Contraceptive Use as a Risk Factor for Premenopausal Breast Cancer: A Meta-analysis." *Mayo Clinic Proceedings* 81, no. 10 (October 2006): 1290-1302.

Kainz, Howard P. "Contraception & Logical Consistency." *New Oxford Review* 76, no. 8 (September 2009): 39-40.

---------. *Natural Law: An Introduction and Re-examination*. Chicago: Open Court, 2004.

---------. "Sexual Mores, Ethical Theories, and the Overpopulation Myth." *Heythrop Journal* 49, no. 3 (May 2008): 361-369.

Kane, Emily A., "Natural Birth Control." *Better Nutrition* (December 2010).

Keane, Philip S. *Sexual Morality: A Catholic Perspective*. New York: Paulist Press, 1977.

Kelly, Matthew. *Rediscovering Catholicism: Journeying Toward Our Spiritual North Star*. Cincinnati: Beacon, 2002.

Kingsbury, Kathleen. "Sex and the Eco-City." *Time* 174, no. 16 (October 26, 2009): 51-52.

Kippley, John F. *Sex and the Marriage Covenant: A Basis for Morality.* 2nd ed. San Francisco: Ignatius Press, 2005.

---------. "The Sexual Revolution: How to Counter It." *Catholic Social Science Review* 13 (2008) 373-386.

Kippley, John F. and Sheila K. *The Art of Natural Family Planning.* 4th ed. Cincinnati: Couple to Couple League International Inc., 1996.

---------. *Natural Family Planning: The Complete Approach.* Cincinnati: NFP International, 2009. http://www.nfpandmore.org/nfphowto.shtml (accessed January 15, 2010).

Kippley, Sheila. *Breastfeeding and Catholic Motherhood: God's Plan for You & Your Baby.* Manchester, NH: Sophia Institute Press, 2005.

Klaus, Hanna. "Natural Family Planning: A Review." *Obstetrical & Gynecological Survey* 37, no. 2 (1982): 128-150.

Komonchak, Joseph A. "Ordinary Papal Magisterium and Religious Assent." In *Contraception: Authority and Dissent*, edited by Charles E. Curran, 101-126. New York: Herder and Herder, 1969.

Kosnik, Anthony, William Carroll, Agnes Cunningham, Ronald Modras, and James Schulte. *Human Sexuality: New Directions in American Catholic Thought.* New York: Paulist Press, 1977.

Larsen, Matthew C. "Statement of Dr. Matthew C. Larsen, Associate Director for Water, U.S. Geological Survey, U.S. Department of the Interior Before the Committee on Transportation and Infrastructure Subcommittee on Water Resources and Environment." (September 18, 2008). http://www.usgs.gov/congressional/hearings/docs/Larsen_ 18sept08.doc (accessed December 18, 2009).

Lasseter, Ruth D. "Sensible Sex." In *Why Humanae Vitae Was Right: A Reader*, edited by Janet E. Smith, 473-498. San Francisco: Ignatius Press, 1993.

Lawler, Ronald, Joseph Boyle Jr., and William E. May. *Catholic Sexual Ethics: A Summary, Explanation, & Defense*. 2nd ed. Huntington, Indiana: Our Sunday Visitor, 1998.

Levada, William. "Dissent and the Catholic Religion Teacher." In *Readings in Moral Theology No. 6: Dissent in the Church*, edited by Charles E. Curran and Richard A. McCormick, 133-151. New York: Paulist Press, 1988.

Lonergan, Bernard J. F. "The Transition from a Classicist World-View to Historical-Mindedness." In *A Second Collection*, edited by William F. J. Ryan and Bernard J. Tyrrell, 1-10. Philadelphia: Westminster Press, 1974.

Lumen Gentium. In *Vatican Council II*. Edited by Austin Flannery. Northport: Costello Publishing Company, 1996.

MacIntyre, Alasdair. *After Virtue*. 2nd ed. Notre Dame: University of Notre Dame Press, 1984.

"Majority Papal Commission Report." In *The Catholic Case for Contraception*, edited by Daniel Callahan, 149-173. London: Macmillan, 1969.

Masek, Lawrence. "Improving the Analogies in Contralife Arguments: The Consistency of Catholic Teachings about Regulating Births." *Heythrop Journal* 49, no. 3 (May 2008): 442-452.

May, William E. "Conscience Formation and the Teaching of the Church." In *Why Humanae Vitae Was Right: A Reader*, edited by Janet E. Smith, 363-382. San Francisco: Ignatius Press, 1993.

McBrien, Richard P. "Theologians Under Fire." In *Readings in Moral Theology No. 6: Dissent in the Church*, edited by Charles E. Curran and Richard A. McCormick, 484-490. New York: Paulist Press, 1988.

McCarthy, David M. "Procreation, the Development of Peoples, and the Final Destiny of Humanity." *Communio* 26 (Winter 1999): 698-721.

---------. "Shifting Settings from Subculture to Pluralism; Catholic Moral Theology in an Evangelical Key." *Communio* 31 (Spring 2004): 85-111.

McCormick, Richard A. "'Humanae Vitae' 25 Years Later." *America* (July 17, 1993). http://www.america magazine.org/content/article.cfm?article_id=10960 (accessed October 14, 2009).

---------. "Notes on Moral Theology: January-June, 1968: Magisterium and Contraception before Humanae Vitae." *Theological Studies* 29, no. 4 (December 1968): 718-725.

"Minority Papal Commission Report." In *The Catholic Case for Contraception*, edited by Daniel Callahan, 174-211. London: Macmillan, 1969.

Moore, Gareth. *The Body in Context: Sex and Catholicism*. New York: Continuum, 1992.

Myers, John J. "The Rejection and Rediscovery by Christians of the Truths of *Humanae Vitae*." In *Trust the Truth: A symposium on the Twentieth Anniversary of the Encyclical Humanae Vitae*, edited by Russell E. Smith, 65-78. Braintree, MA: The Pope John XXIII Medical-Moral Research and Education Center, 1991.

National Conference of Catholic Bishops. "Norms of Licit Theological Dissent." In *Readings in Moral Theology No. 6: Dissent in the Church*, edited by Charles E. Curran and Richard A. McCormick, 127-128. New York: Paulist Press, 1988.

National Conference of Catholic Bishops' Committee for Pro-Life Activities. *Human Sexuality from God's Perspective: Humanae Vitae 25 Years Later*. 1993. http://www.usccb.org/prolife/issues/nfp/humanae25.shtml (accessed October 14, 2009).

"Natural Family Planning." *CRS—Adult Health Advisor* (January 1, 2009).

Noonan, John T. Jr. "The Amendment of Papal Teaching by Theologians." In *Contraception: Authority and Dissent*, edited by Charles E. Curran, 41-75. New York: Herder and Herder, 1969.

---------. *The Church & Contraception: The Issues at Stake*. New York: Paulist Press, 1967.

---------. *Contraception: A History of Its Treatment by the Catholic Theologians and Canonists*. Cambridge: Harvard University Press, 1965.

---------. "Contraception and the Council." In *The Catholic Case for Contraception*, edited by Daniel Callahan, 3-18. London: Macmillan, 1969.

Norton, John. "Ethicist: Pope Intended Condom Use/AIDS Reflection." *OSV Newsweekly* (December 19, 2010).

Novak, Michael. "Frequent, Even Daily, Communion." In *The Catholic Case for Contraception*, edited by Daniel Callahan, 92-102. London: Macmillan, 1969.

O'Brien, Nancy Frazier. "Catholics of All Ages See U.S. Moral Values on Decline, Survey Says." *Catholic News Service* (February 15, 2010). http://www.catholicnews.com/data/Stories/cns/1000653.htm (accessed February 22, 2010).

O'Donovan, Cat. "Birth Control Pills Can Make You Pick the Wrong Lover." *Cosmos Magazine* (August 13, 2008). http://www.cosmosmagazine.com/news/2136/birth-control-pills-make-you-pick-wrong-lover (accessed October 15, 2008).

O'Hare, Patrick F. *The Facts About Luther*. Rockford: TAN, 1987.

Pallone, Stephen R. and George R. Bergus. "Fertility Awareness-Based Methods: Another Option for Family Planning." *Journal of the American Board of Family Medicine*. 22 (2009): 147-157. http://www.jabfm.org/content/22/2/147.long (accessed October 24, 2013).

Patton, Jessica Rae. "Make Love, Not Waste." *E – The Environmental Magazine* 19, no. 5 (Sep/Oct 2008): 40-41.

Paul VI, Pope. *Humane Vitae*. 1968. http://www.vatican.va/holy_father/paul_vi/encyclicals/documents/hf_p-vi_enc_25071968_humanae-vitae_en.html (accessed July 14, 2009).

---------. "To the Teams of Our Lady." In *Why Humanae Vitae Was Right: A Reader*, edited by Janet E. Smith, 85-104. San Francisco: Ignatius Press, 1993.

"Paul VI Vindicated, Denver Bishops Says." *National Catholic Reporter* 34, no. 35 (July 31, 1998): 12-13.

Pius XI, Pope. Casti Connubii. 1930.
http://www.vatican.va/holy_father/pius_xi/encyclicals/
documents/hf_p-xi_enc_31121930_casti-connubii_en.html
(accessed July 14, 2009).

Pius XII, Pope. *Address to Midwives on the Nature of Their Profession.*
1951. http://www.papal
encyclicals.net/Pius12/p12midwives.htm (accessed October
2, 2009).

Planned Parenthood. "Breastfeeding as Birth Control."
http://www.plannedparenthood.org/health-info/birth-
control/breastfeeding (accessed December 15, 2014).

---------. "Comparing Effectiveness of Birth Control Methods" Chart.
http://www.
plannedparenthood.org/health-topics/birth-control/birth-
control-effectiveness-chart-22710.htm (accessed December
21, 2009).

---------. "Fertility Awareness-Based Methods (FAMs)."
http://www.plannedparent
hood.org/heath-topics/birth-control/fertility-awareness-
4217.htm (accessed December 21, 2009).

Pollard, Andrew C. and Mercedes Arzu-Wilson. "Correlates of
Marital Satisfaction in a Sample of NFP Women." In
Integrating Faith and Science Through Natural Family Planning,"
edited by Richard J. Fehring and Theresa Notare, 139-165.
Milwaukee: Marquette UP, 2004.

Popcak, Gregory K. "A Natural Argument for NFP." *Family
Foundations* vol. 38 no. 2 (September/October 2011), 30-31.

Popiel, Jennifer J. "Necessary Connections? Catholicism, Feminism
and Contraception." *America* (November 27, 1999): 22-26.

Portier, William L. "Here Come the Evangelical Catholics." *Communio* 31 (Spring 2004): 35-66.

Povich, Mark. "Truth and Consequences." In *Physicians Healed: Personal, Inspiring, and Compelling Stories of Fifteen Courageous Physicians Who Do Not Prescribe Contraception*, edited by Cleta Hartman, 103-104. Dayton: One More Soul, 1998.

Provan, Charles D. *The Bible and Birth Control*. Monongahela, PA: Zimmer Printing, 1989.

Quay, Paul M. "Contraception and Conjugal Love." In *Why Humanae Vitae Was Right: A Reader*, edited by Janet E. Smith, 17-46. San Francisco: Ignatius Press, 1993.

Ratzinger, Joseph. *Called to Communion: Understanding the Church Today*. Translated by Adrian Walker. San Francisco: Ignatius Press, 1996.

---------. "Concerning the Teaching Contained in *Ordinatio Sacerdotalis, Responsum Ad Dubium*." 1995. http://www.ewtn.com/library/curia/cdfrespo.htm (accessed December 8, 2009).

---------. "The Drama of Morality." In *Readings in Moral Theology No. 6: Dissent in the Church*, edited by Charles E. Curran and Richard A. McCormick, 307-314. New York: Paulist Press, 1988.

Raviele, Kathleen. "A Gynecologist's Journey from Contraception to NFP." In *Physicians Healed: Personal, Inspiring, and Compelling Stories of Fifteen Courageous Physicians Who Do Not Prescribe Contraception*, edited by Cleta Hartman, 105-108. Dayton: One More Soul, 1998.

Regas, Jennine and Philip Regas. "Preliminary Comparison of Algorithm-Interpreted Fertility Monitor Readings with Established Natural Family Planning Methods." In *Integrating Faith and Science Through Natural Family Planning*, edited by Richard J. Fehring and Theresa Notare, 169-177. Milwaukee: Marquette UP, 2004.

Religion News Service. "Poll: Catholic Doctors Don't Always Follow Church Teaching." *National Catholic Reporter* 41, no. 27 (May 6, 2005), 11.

Rhonheimer, Martin. *Ethics of Procreation and the Defense of Human Life: Contraception, Artificial Fertilization, and Abortion*, edited by William F. Murphy Jr. Washington D.C.: Catholic University of America Press, 2010.

Rocca, Francis X. "Pope Condemns Abortion as Product of 'Throwaway Culture.'" *Catholic News Service* (September 20, 2013). http://www.catholicnews.com/data/stories/cns/1303991.htm (accessed September 30, 2013).

Rubio, Julie Hanlon. "Beyond the Liberal/Conservative Divide on Contraception: The Wisdom of Practitioners of Natural Family Planning and Artificial Birth Control." *Horizons* 32, no. 2 (Fall 2005): 270-294.

Ruddy, Christopher. "Young Theologians—Between a Rock & a Hard Place." *Commonweal* April 21, 2000. http://findarticles.com/p/articles/mi_m1252/is_8_127/ai_61795234/ (accessed December 17, 2009).

Ruether, Rosemary Radford. "Birth Control and the Ideals of Marital Sexuality." In *Readings in Moral Theology No. 8: Dialogue about Catholic Sexual Teaching*, edited by Charles E. Curran and Richard A. McCormick, 138-152. New York: Paulist Press, 1993.

Ryan, Mary Perkins and John Julian Ryan. "Have You Thought It Out All the Way?" In *The Catholic Case for Contraception*, edited by Daniel Callahan, 103-127. London: Macmillan, 1969.

Ryder, R. E. J. "'Natural Family Planning': Effective Birth Control Supported by the Catholic Church." *British Medical Journal* 307 (September 1993): 723-726.

Sadowski, Dennis. "On 40th Anniversary, 'Humanae Vitae' Starts to Gain More Attention." *Catholic News Service* (July 18, 2008). http://www.catholicnews.com/data/stories/cns/0803746.htm (accessed October 14, 2009).

Salzman, Todd A. and Michael G. Lawler. *The Sexual Person: Toward a Renewed Catholic Anthropology*. Washington D.C.: Georgetown University Press, 2008.

Savinetti-Rose, Barbara. "Response to 'Preliminary Comparison of Algorithm—Interpreted Fertility Monitor Readings with Established NFP Methods." In *Integrating Faith and Science Through Natural Family Planning*, edited by Richard J. Fehring and Theresa Notare, 178-182. Milwaukee: Marquette UP, 2004.

Scarnecchia, D. Brian. *Bioethics, Law, and Human Life Issues: A Catholic Perspective on Marriage, Family, Contraception, Abortion, Reproductive Technology, and Death and Dying*. Lanham: Scarecrow Press, 2010.

Selling, J.A. "Magisterial Teaching on Marriage 1880-1986: Historical Constancy or Radical Development?" In *Readings in Moral Theology No. 8: Dialogue about Catholic Sexual Teaching*, edited by Charles E. Curran and Richard A. McCormick, 93-97. New York: Paulist Press, 1993.

Shannon, James Patrick. *Reluctant Dissenter: A Catholic Bishop's Journey of Faith*. New York: Crossroad, 1998.

Shannon, Marilyn M. *Fertility, Cycles & Nutrition.* 4th ed. Cincinnati: Couple to Couple League, 2009.

Shaw, Russell. "Contraception, Infallibility and the Ordinary Magisterium." In *Why Humanae Vitae Was Right: A Reader*, edited by Janet E. Smith, 343-362. San Francisco: Ignatius Press, 1993.

Sheehan, Kevin and Gary Buiso. "Dolan Blasts White House Contraception Plan as 'Freedom of Religion Battle'." *New York Post* (March 3, 2012). http://www.nypost.com/p/news/local/ dolan_blasts_white_house_contraception_tlOdFvb1saw2qld wedIUpL?utm_medium=rss&utm_content=Local (accessed April 5, 2012).

Shorto, Russell. "Contra-Contraception." *New York Times* (May 7, 2006). http://www.nytimes. com/2006/05/07/magazine/07contraception.html (accessed December 21, 2009).

Simpson, Victor L. "Pope Says Condoms Worsen HIV Problem." *Washington Post* (March 18, 2009). http://www.washingtonpost.com/wp- dyn/content/article/2009/03/17/AR20090 31703369.html (accessed April 3, 2012).

Sinai, Irit, Rebecka Lundgren, Marcos Arevalo and Victoria Jennings. "Fertility Awareness-Based Methods of Family Planning: Predictors of Correct Use." *International Family Planning Perspectives* 32, no. 2 (June 2006): 94-100.

Smith, Christian, and Melinda Lundquist Denton. *Soul Searching: The Religious and Spiritual Lives of American Teenagers.* New York: Oxford, 2005.

Smith, Herbert F. "The Proliferation of Population Problems." In *Why Humanae Vitae Was Right: A Reader*, edited by Janet E. Smith, 383-406. San Francisco: Ignatius Press, 1993.

Smith, Janet E. *Humanae Vitae: A Generation Later*. Washington D.C.: Catholic University of America Press, 1991.

---------. *"Humanae Vitae* at Twenty." In *Why Humanae Vitae Was Right: A Reader*, edited by Janet E. Smith, 499-518. San Francisco: Ignatius Press, 1993.

---------. "The Moral Use of Natural Family Planning." In *Why Humanae Vitae Was Right: A Reader*, edited by Janet E. Smith, 445-472. San Francisco: Ignatius Press, 1993.

---------. "Paul VI as Prophet." In *Why Humanae Vitae Was Right: A Reader*, edited by Janet E. Smith, 519-532. San Francisco: Ignatius Press, 1993.

---------. "Pope John Paul II and *Humanae Vitae*." In *Why Humanae Vitae Was Right: A Reader*, edited by Janet E. Smith, 229-252. San Francisco: Ignatius Press, 1993.

---------. Introduction to *Why Humanae Vitae Was Right: A Reader*, edited by Janet E. Smith, 11-13. San Francisco: Ignatius Press, 1993.

Sommer, Joseph. *Catholic Thought on Contraception through the Centuries*. Liguori, MO: Liguorian, 1970.

Spadaro, Antonio. "A Big Heart Open to God." *America*. Vol. 209 No. 8 (September 2013): http://www.americamagazine.org/pope-interview (accessed 9-30-2013).

Stanford, Joseph. "My Personal and Professional Journey with Regard to Moral Issues in Human Procreation." In *Physicians Healed: Personal, Inspiring, and Compelling Stories of Fifteen Courageous Physicians Who Do Not Prescribe Contraception*, edited by Cleta Hartman, 109-124. Dayton: One More Soul, 1998.

"Statement by Catholic Theologians, Washington, D.C., July 30, 1968." In *Readings in Moral Theology No. 8: Dialogue about Catholic Sexual Teaching*, edited by Charles E. Curran and Richard A. McCormick, 135-137. New York: Paulist Press, 1993.

St. Francis de Sales. *Philothea, or An Introduction to the Devout Life.* Rockford: TAN, 1994.

St. Ignatius of Loyola. *The Spiritual Exercises of St. Ignatius.* Translated by Louis J. Puhl. Chicago: Loyola Press, 1951.

Stormon, E. J., ed. and trans. *Towards the Healing of Schism: The sees of Rome and Constantinople, Public statements and correspondence between the Holy See and the Ecumenical Patriarchate 1958-1984.* Manwah, NJ: Paulist Press, 1987.

Sullivan, Francis A. "The Authority of the Magisterium on Questions of Natural Moral Law." In *Readings in Moral Theology No. 6: Dissent in the Church*, edited by Charles E. Curran and Richard A. McCormick, 42-57. New York: Paulist Press, 1988.

T., A. "Not Quite Worry-Free." *Environment* 45, no. 1 (Jan/Feb 2003): 6-7.

Tapper, Jake. "Policy and Politics of Contraception Rule Fiercely Debated Within White House." *ABC News* (Februrary 9, 2012), http://abcnews.go.com/blogs/politics/2012/02/policy-and-politics-of-contraception-rule-fiercely-debated-within-white-house/ (accessed April 5, 2012).

Tennant, Agnieszka. "A Hard Pill to Swallow." *Christianity Today* 49, no. 11 (November 2005): 70-73.

Tentler, Leslie Woodcock. "Catholics and Contraception: An American History." Ithaca: Cornell UP, 2004.

Teresa of Calcutta, Mother. "Nobel Lecture." (1979). http://nobelprize.org/nobel_prizes/peace/ laureates/1979/teresa-lecture.html (accessed December 15, 2009).

----------. "Whatever You Did Unto One of the Least, You Did Unto Me" (February 3, 1994). http://www.columbia.edu/cu/augustine/arch/teresa94.html (accessed December 15, 2009).

Ternier, Jim and Marie-Louise Ternier-Gommers. "Speaking up for Natural Family Planning." *National Catholic Reporter* 40, no. 15 (February 13, 2004): 19.

Thompson, Damian. "Traditional Anglicans 'to be Offered Personal Prelature by Pope.'" *The Telegraph* (January 29, 2009). http://www.challengeonline.org/modules/news/article. php?storyid=228 (accessed December 21, 2009).

Tiger, Lionel. *The Decline of Males: The First Look at an Unexpected New World for Men and Women.* New York: St. Martin's Griffin, 1999.

Torode, Sam and Bethany Torode. "Make Love and Babies." *Christianity Today* 45, no. 14 (November 12, 2001): 48-52.

----------. *Open Embrace: A Protestant Couple Rethinks Contraception.* Grand Rapids: Wm. B. Eerdmans Publishing Co., 2002.

Twomey, D. Vincent. *Moral Theology after Humanae Vitae: Fundamental Issues in Moral Theory and Sexual Ethics.* Dublin: Four Courts Press, 2010.

United States Conference of Catholic Bishops. "Ethical and Religious Directives for Catholic Heath Care Services." 4th ed. http://www.usccb.org/bishops/directives.shtml (accessed December 11, 2009).

United States Conference of Catholic Bishops. "Marriage: Love and Life in the Divine Plan" (November 17, 2009). http://www.usccb.org/laity/LoveandLife/MarriageFINAL.pdf (accessed November 19, 2009).

United States Conference of Catholic Bishops. "Married Love and the Gift of Life" (November, 14, 2006). http://www.usccb.org/laity/marriage/MarriedLove.pdf (accessed December 17, 2009).

VandeVusse, Leona, Lisa Hanson, Richard J. Fehring, Amy Newman, and Jamie Fox. "Couples' Views of the Effects of Natural Family Planning on Marital Dynamics." *Journal of Nursing Scholarship* 35, no. 2 (2nd Quarter 2003): 171-176.

"Vatican Welcomes Anglicans into Catholic Church." *CNN* (October 21, 2009). http://edition.cnn.com/2009/WORLD/Europe/10/20/vatican.anglican.church/index.html (accessed December 21, 2009).

Vaughan, Austin B. "*Humanae Vitae* and Respect for the Dignity of the Human Person." In *Trust the Truth: A symposium on the Twentieth Anniversary of the Encyclical Humanae Vitae*, edited by Russell E. Smith, 15-36. Braintree, MA: The Pope John XXIII Medical-Moral Research and Education Center, 1991.

Von Geusau, Leo Alting. "International Reaction to the Encyclical Humanae Vitae." *Studies in Family Planning* 1, no. 50 (Feb. 1970): 8-12.

Von Hildebrand, Dietrich. "The Encyclical *Humanae Vitae*: A Sign of Contradiction." In *Why Humanae Vitae Was Right: A Reader*, edited by Janet E. Smith, 47-84. San Francisco: Ignatius Press, 1993.

Wagner, Teresa. "Contraception, Natural Family Planning, and Women." In *Integrating Faith and Science Through Natural Family Planning*, edited by Richard J. Fehring and Theresa Notare, 49-61. Milwaukee: Marquette UP, 2004.

Weigel, George. *Witness to Hope: The Biography of Pope John Paul II*. New York: Harper Collins, 2001.

West, Christopher. *Good News about Sex & Marriage: Answers to Your Honest Questions about Catholic Teaching*. Ann Arbor: Servant, 2000.

---------. *Theology of the Body Explained: A Commentary on John Paul II's "Gospel of the Body"*. Boston: Pauline, 2003.

---------. *Theology of the Body for Beginners: A Basic Introduction to Pope John Paul II's Sexual Revolution*. West Chester, Pennsylvania: Ascension Press, 2004.

Williams, Thomas D. "Theology of the Body and *Humanae Vitae*." *Alpha Omega* 11, no. 3 (2008): 365-386.

Wojcik, Elzbieta. "Natural Regulation of Conception and Contraception." In *Why Humanae Vitae Was Right: A Reader*, edited by Janet E. Smith, 419-444. San Francisco: Ignatius Press, 1993.

Wojtyla, Karol (Pope John Paul II). *Love and Responsibility*. Translated by H. T. Willetts. San Francisco: Ignatius Press, 1993.

---------. *Sign of Contradiction*. New York: Seabury, 1979.

World Health Organization. "IARC Monographs Programme Finds Combined Estrogen-Progestogen Contraceptives and Menopausal Therapy are Carcinogenic to Humans." *International Agency for Research on Cancer.* Press Release 167 (29 July 2005).

Zaphiris, Chrysostom. "The Morality of Contraception: An Eastern Orthodox Opinion." *Journal of Ecumenical Studies* 11, no. 4 (Fall 1974): 677-690.

Zinaman, Michael J. "Using Cervical Mucus and Other Easily Observed Biomarkers to Identify Ovulation in Prospective Pregnancy Trials." *Paediatric & Perinatal Epidemiology* 20 supplement (November 2006): 26-29.

INDEX

317

Joyce, Mary R. 51, 52, 300

K

Kahlenborn, Chris, 63, 64, 65, 66, 117, 300
Kainz, Howard P., 1, 58, 99, 101, 103, 231, 240, 300
Keane, Philip S., 211, 212, 214, 215, 300
Kelly, 32, 138, 268, 295, 300
Kippley, John 7, 44, 222
Kippley, Sheila 11, 18, 58, 59, 60
Kippleys, 18, 20, 23, 36, 41
Klaus, Hanna, 16, 17, 18, 20, 40, 43, 301
Komonchak, Joseph A., 250, 263, 278, 301
Kosnik, Anthony, 11, 212, 213, 215, 301

L

Lactational Amenorrhea, xi, 58
Lambeth, 149, 173, 180
Lambruschini, 261
Larsen, Matthew C., 108, 302
Lasseter, Ruth D., 35, 88, 96, 302
Lawler, 1, 16, 31, 50, 52, 118, 119, 121, 165, 170, 171, 177, 181, 184, 186, 207, 208, 212, 225, 234, 235, 239, 245, 277, 279, 285, 293, 302, 309
Levada, William, 268, 269, 276, 277, 302
Lio, Ermenegildo, 261
liver cancer, 65
Locht, Pierre de, 183, 184
Lonergan, Bernard, 205, 302

M

MacIntyre, Alasdair, 137, 302
Magisterium, 1, 114, 115, 121, 124, 126, 143, 172, 182, 186, 188, 189, 190, 212, 231, 234, 236, 237, 238, 240, 241, 242, 250, 252, 253, 254, 256, 257, 262, 264, 265, 266, 267, 268, 272, 277, 280, 290, 293, 294, 295, 296, 297, 301, 303, 310, 312
Majority Report, 67, 186, 187, 188, 192, 193, 214, 237, 239, 247
Malthus, Thomas, 99, 103, 171
Marthaler, Berard, 196
Masek, Lawrence, 57, 58, 303

May, William E., 16, 31, 40, 50, 52, 57, 72, 99, 118, 119, 152, 177, 225, 231, 234, 235, 239, 245, 251, 276, 277, 278, 279, 285, 294, 296, 297, 300, 302, 303, 308, 310
McBrien, Richard P., 272, 303
McCarthy, David M., 91, 92, 97, 102, 130, 131, 132, 133, 134, 135, 143, 144, 145, 146, 147, 303
McClintock, Martha, 85
McCormick, Richard A., 13, 30, 50, 121, 124, 143, 175, 190, 197, 203, 205, 209, 210, 215, 223, 225, 235, 236, 241, 245, 264, 265, 266, 267, 268, 272, 290, 293, 294, 295, 296, 297, 298, 299, 302, 303, 304, 307, 308, 309, 312
MHC (Major Histocompatibility Complex), ix, 87
minipill, 65, 68
Minority Report, v, 186, 187, 188, 193, 194, 212, 214, 234, 235, 238, 239
Mohler, R. Albert, 151, 152
Moore, Gareth, 55, 56, 303
Moraczewski, Albert, 196, 239, 289
Myers, John J., 128, 304

N

NaProTECHNOLOGY, 39
Natural Family Planning, (see NFP) iii, ix, xi, 5, 11, 12, 13, 14, 17, 18, 20, 22, 25, 34, 38, 46, 49, 50, 61, 90, 94, 95, 124, 134, 159, 215, 285, 290, 291, 292, 296, 300, 301, 304, 306, 308, 309, 311, 313, 314, 315
natural law, 151, 156, 167, 185, 201, 205, 206, 207, 213, 218, 221, 230, 231, 232, 233, 236, 243, 245, 248, 260, 282
Nevins, Joseph, 172
New Natural Law Theory, v, 50, 230, 234
NFP, (see Natural Family Planning) iii, iv, ix, xi, 8, 11, 13, 14, 15, 16, 18, 19, 20, 21, 22, 23, 24, 25, 26, 27, 28, 29, 30, 31, 32, 33, 34, 35, 36, 37, 38, 39, 40, 41, 42, 43, 44, 45, 46, 47, 48, 49, 50, 51, 52, 53, 54, 55, 56, 57, 58, 61, 66, 72, 74, 75, 76, 81, 89, 90, 94, 95, 96, 102, 104, 105, 106, 107, 117, 136, 137, 140, 145, 150, 154, 155, 158,

320

202, 203, 204, 214, 215, 284, 285, 286, 297, 301, 306, 307, 309
Noonan, John T. Jr., 67, 165, 166, 167, 168, 169, 170, 171, 174, 175, 176, 177, 178, 179, 180, 181, 190, 214, 236, 237, 304
Norplant, (see contraception), 62, 68
Novak, Michael, 5, 13, 30, 34, 305

O

O'Brien, Nancy F., 77, 128, 305
O'Rourke, Kevin D., 54, 119, 184, 185, 237, 244, 247, 248, 252, 253, 254, 257, 259, 260, 278, 279, 289
OCP (Oral Contraceptive Pill), ix, xii, 21, 23, 33, 53, 61, 62, 63, 64, 65, 66, 67, 68, 69, 72, 73, 74, 79, 80, 82, 84, 86, 87, 92, 101, 109, 117, 118, 152, 177, 178, 182, 183, 193, 194, 198, 202, 204, 205, 210, 214, 215
overpopulation, 20, 98, 99, 101, 102, 103, 171, 179, 183, 201
ovulation method, 19, 20, 23, 24, 26, 27

P

Pacholczyk, Tadeusz, 125
Pallone, Stephen R., 26, 33, 36, 48, 305
Paul VI, Pope, 1, 2, 14, 19, 27, 33, 35, 39, 40, 75, 76, 77, 88, 89, 91, 92, 98, 102, 117, 118, 125, 129, 131, 143, 144, 145, 146, 147, 152, 182, 183, 184, 189, 190, 191, 192, 193, 194, 195, 197, 198, 218, 233, 241, 248, 255, 262, 283, 298, 305, 311
Pawley, 99
Pediatric Advisor, 62, 290
personalism, 126, 157, 207, 217, 221, 229, 232, 233
personalist, 52, 132, 207, 212, 218, 221, 224, 229
personalistic, 174, 192, 218, 221, 222, 225, 226, 234
pheromones, 83, 84, 85
physicalist, 206, 213, 231, 232
Popcak, Gregory K., 34, 39, 41, 61, 63, 109, 306
Popiel, Jennifer J., 88, 93, 95, 306
Populorum Progressio, 143, 146

Portier, William L., 128, 129, 130, 131, 132, 307
principle of totality, 187, 188, 193, 210, 214, 228, 243, 246
probabilism, 190
procreation, xi, xii, 3, 14, 50, 56, 70, 71, 97, 119, 143, 147, 151, 154, 166, 167, 169, 170, 173, 174, 175, 176, 177, 181, 186, 188, 192, 193, 194, 207, 211, 224, 227, 235, 240, 244
procreative, 6, 7, 20, 50, 51, 52, 70, 71, 119, 141, 146, 157, 158, 160, 175, 187, 193, 198, 206, 207, 208, 210, 211, 213, 216, 218, 220, 224, 227, 228, 233, 234, 236, 239, 240
proportionalism, 134, 185, 244, 246, 247
Provan, Charles D., 154, 168, 173, 307

Q

Quay, Paul M., 218, 219, 220, 223, 307

R

replacement level, 100
revisionist, 1, 11, 12, 13, 29, 34, 42, 55, 67, 78, 121, 125, 132, 134, 149, 152, 165, 166, 201, 202, 203, 204, 205, 206, 207, 208, 210, 211, 212, 213, 214, 215, 217, 219, 220, 225, 229, 230, 231, 232, 234, 235, 236, 237, 238, 239, 240, 242, 243, 244, 245, 247, 248, 250, 251, 256, 261, 263, 266, 272, 273, 274, 276, 278, 280
Rhonheimer, Martin, 51, 71, 113, 114, 139, 140, 141, 227, 228, 232, 282, 283, 308
rhythm, xi, 11, 12, 14, 16, 20, 26, 27, 28, 30, 33, 40, 105, 179, 185, 201, 202, 203, 204, 205, 215
Roberts, Craig, 86, 87
Ruark, Allison H., 110, 111, 112, 113, 297
Rubio, Julie H., 124, 133, 134, 135, 136, 137, 308
Ruddy, Christopher, 135, 136, 308
Ryder, R. E. J., 20, 21, 43, 309

S

Sadowski, Dennis, 125, 309
Salzman, Todd, 1, 121, 165, 170, 171, 181, 184, 186, 207, 208, 212, 293, 309
Sebelius, Kathleen, 61, 160
Second Vatican Council, iv, 6, 180, 256, 273, 275
self-mastery, 223, 224, 282
sensus fidelium, 278, 279, 280
Shannon, James P., 204
Shannon, Marylin 41, 118
sign of contradiction, 1, 2, 32, 150, 195, 283, 284
Smith and Denton, 122, 123
Smith, Christian 122
Smith, Herbert F., 99, 100, 103, 104
Smith, Janet E., 14, 27, 35, 53, 54, 77, 80, 125, 129, 144, 169, 232, 233, 239, 263, 277, 282
Sommer, Joseph, 169, 170, 171, 173, 174, 175, 177, 178, 181, 187, 196, 311
Stanford, Joseph, 44, 45, 154, 155, 312
STD, 27
sterilization, xii, 23, 24, 144, 158, 176, 178, 188, 193, 196, 239
sympto-thermal, xi, 18, 22, 23, 24, 26, 37, 53

T

Tentler, Leslie W., 12, 13, 172, 173, 174, 179, 180, 189, 196, 199, 200, 238, 272, 273, 313
Ternier, Jim and Marie-Louise Ternier-Gommers, 46, 94, 95, 96, 97, 104, 313
the pill, xii, 33, 42, 61, 63, 66, 69, 80, 81, 83, 84, 86, 101, 105, 152, 177, 178, 291, 296
Theology of the Body, iv, v, ix, 62, 126, 127, 157, 221, 222, 223, 225, 228, 229, 295, 299, 300, 315
Tiger, Lionel, 69, 80, 81, 82, 83, 84, 85, 87, 88, 284, 313
traditionalists, 1, 50, 53, 55, 121, 132, 165, 166, 201, 206, 212, 217, 221, 226, 227, 229, 233, 234, 238, 240, 242, 250, 251, 262, 263, 266, 268, 272, 280

twenty-first century, iii, 4, 7, 8, 9, 16, 33, 43, 70, 121, 136, 153, 207, 221
Twomey, D. Vincent, 76, 88, 94, 137, 138, 139, 145, 222, 230, 233, 244, 249, 250, 275, 277, 278, 281, 313

U

unitive, 6, 7, 51, 52, 70, 71, 119, 135, 154, 157, 158, 160, 175, 193, 198, 202, 207, 208, 210, 211, 213, 216, 218, 227, 234, 235, 239, 240, 244

V

VandeVusse, Leona, 13, 27, 34, 35, 37, 47, 285, 314
Vaughan, Austin B., 44, 89, 90, 91, 144, 314
virtue, 32, 35, 53, 56, 96, 114, 137, 138, 139, 140, 141, 255, 282
von Hildebrand, Dietrich, 52, 174, 175, 181, 207, 219, 220, 222, 234

W

Wagner, Teresa 61, 89, 90, 159, 300, 315
Wedekind, Claus, 86
Weigel, George, 104, 191, 192, 217, 221, 241, 315
West, Christopher, 126, 127, 260, 295, 315
WHO (World Health Organization), ix, 13, 20, 21, 65, 66, 183
Wojcik, Elzbieta, 16, 68, 315
Wojtyla, Karol, (see also John Paul II), 2, 191, 217, 218, 221, 233, 283, 284, 315
Wolf, Naomi, 94

Z

Zalba, Marcellinus, 184

About the Author:

Anthony J. Digmann is a husband and father who serves the Church as a Catholic speaker, author, and educator. He holds a MA degree in Theology as well as a double major BA degree in Religious Studies and Communications: Electronic Media with a minor in Ethics. Anthony is a member of the theology faculty at Beckman Catholic High School in Dyersville, Iowa. He is also the founder and Chief Executive Manager of Capture This Video Productions. Anthony is available to speak on numerous topics related to Catholic faith and theology. Visit his webpage at:

anthonydigmann.com.